# Letters from Berlin

Margarete J.G.
April 1945
Berlin

# Letters from Berlin

## A Story of War, Survival, and the
## Redeeming Power of Love and Friendship

Margarete Dos
and
Kerstin Lieff

LYONS PRESS
Guilford, Connecticut
An imprint of Globe Pequot Press

Copyright © 2013 by Kerstin Lieff

Lyons Press is an imprint of Globe Pequot Press.

All photos from the author's archives or family archives except where noted.
Maps created from materials supplied by Verlag Pharus-Plan and from Rand McNally maps.

Maps by Melissa Baker © Morris Book Publishing, LLC
Project editor: Meredith Dias
Text design: Sheryl P. Kober
Layout: Casey Shain

Library of Congress Cataloging-in-Publication Data
Dos, Margarete, 1924-2005.
    Letters from Berlin : a story of war, survival, and the redeeming
power of love and friendship / Margarete Dos and Kerstin Lieff.
      p. cm.
    Includes bibliographical references.
    ISBN 978-0-7627-7798-3
      1. Dos, Margarete, 1924-2005. 2. Dos, Margarete,
1924–2005—Correspondence. 3. World War, 1939–1945—Germany—Berlin. 4.
World War, 1939–1945—Personal narratives, German. 5.
Nurses—Germany—Berlin—Biography. 6. Deutsches Rotes
Kreuz—Biography. 7. Berlin (Germany)—Biography. 8. World War,
1939-1945—Medical care—Germany—Berlin. 9. Prisoners of war—Russia
(Federation)—Novomoskovsk—Biography. 10. World War,
1939–1945—Prisoners and prisons, Soviet. I. Lieff, Kerstin, 1952– II. Title.
D811.5.D637 2013
940.53'43155092—dc23
[B]
                                                                          2012006257
Printed in the United States of America
10 9 8 7 6 5 4 3 2 1

*For Dieter*

# Contents

## PART III: JOURNEY TO A NEW LIFE, 1945–1949

## CODA: SWEDEN, 1952

*So let me enter, and let all the storms of fate*
*That have been raging round me now be left behind.*

—JOHANN WOLFGANG VON GOETHE, *FAUST*

(3.1.8507–10)

≈

*I would like to step out of my heart*
*and go walking beneath the enormous sky.*
*I would like to pray.*
*And surely of all the stars that perished*
*long ago,*
*one still exists.*
*I think that I know which one it is—*
*which one, at the end of its beam in the sky,*
*stands like a white city . . .*

—RAINER MARIA RILKE, "LAMENT"

# Introduction

I don't know why I did it. Was it the butter?

The freezer in my home when I was growing up never had anything but butter in it. One-pound bricks, packed top to bottom, back to front.

There was the soap, too. Was it that? The twenty-plus bars stacked under each of our bathroom sinks?

Maybe it was this: that, whenever I said my mother had been in a prison camp in the 1940s, the response, nearly always, was "Wow. I didn't know you were Jewish!" We aren't Jewish, I'd say, but even I didn't fully understand why she had been in a prison camp.

Or maybe it was simply the nagging thought that would not let me be: *What if she dies and never tells her story?* I could not accept this. It was too precious, this life lived *während des Krieges*, during the war—a phrase I heard so often as a child. She had to tell someone! And why not me? The eldest daughter, the one in her womb before she even made her final escape to the United States.

It was on a day, then, in 1999 that I did it. I asked her to tell me about her life. The part she had kept secret for so long. I was in my late forties; I had two grown children already. My mother, Margarete, was in her late seventies.

"Your stories will go to your grave," I told her. "Think how tragic would that be." And to goad her, I added, "Don't you want your grand-children to know who you were?"

I asked, I say, but more accurately I begged. I knew most people had never heard this version of history. Most certainly I had not. I knew it had been a terrible time for her. So terrible, she only ever said, "*Ach.* We don't need to talk about those times." But because she was German, her experiences always seemed, in a sense, "wrong." She was from the enemy's side, and from the side of the war that lost, and so she was determined to suffer in silence.

As much as she never wanted to talk, her memories sometimes flickered to the surface anyway: "During the war, there was so little to eat . . . In Russia, we had no warm clothes . . ." When asked about the freezer packed with butter and the cabinets stuffed with Yardley soap, my mother would say, "Just leave me alone about this." Then she would turn away, not wanting to say any more. When pressed—Why can't we have pizzas in our freezer, or ice cream, the way our American friends do?—she would reply it was because she'd never again in her life live without something to put on her bread. And she would never again endure having to be dirty. And that was to explain everything.

But when I came home from school one day, announcing how I had learned about Germany and the Nazis, her face clouded over. "Don't ever say we were Nazis! My family would *never* have stooped so low!" I was confused. Weren't all Germans in the 1930s and 1940s Nazis? But she would not talk, and so I remained ignorant of this "other side" of German history until finally, as an adult, I begged her to tell me about those years.

It took her two weeks to answer my plea. Two silent weeks. No messages on my answering machine. Not even the ordinary "I've baked a plum cake. Come have a piece and a small glass of wine with me." There was not a word from her, and I should have found this unusual.

Then it came. Her phone call.

"I've thought very hard about your question. You know it's a difficult one for me." She always spoke German with me.

I was stunned. Had she really been thinking about this for two weeks? And still, I was fully anticipating her next sentence: *We don't need to talk about those terrible times.* But, to my surprise and my eternal gratitude, she said yes.

"I will tell you everything exactly as I remember it," she said, "but I will tell you only once. I think I can manage once, but I shall never again speak another word about any of it, so listen carefully."

I knew this would be a long, and difficult, journey into her past. What I didn't know is that I would spend three years listening to history being retold in a way I'd never heard it before. Told by a German— not a Nazi, but a German nonetheless. And a German who was only a girl when it all began. She was eight when Hitler came to power and a teenager during the six years of war. She was a girl who wanted to live a girl's life: full of good grades, sports, friends, and boys, all in a proper 1940s fashion.

When she consented to tell her story, we proceeded to spend our Sundays—nearly every one of them over the course of those three years—in her apartment having hours-long conversations while I kept a tape recorder running. These were cozy Sundays. She always had breakfast waiting, and it was always first class, in Mamma style. Her linen napkins, her cut-crystal schnapps glasses ("Of course we should have a little schnapps. It's Sunday!"), and her gold-rimmed white china. She would have plates of *Schinken*, German smoked ham, and liver-wurst—my favorite—and cheeses. Edamer, Tilsiter, Limburger. And, of course, coffee. Strong. Very black, actually, to which you'd have to add cream, and the color, even then, would never get any lighter than milk chocolate.

We traveled to Berlin together during this project. It was an idea I had come up with, and she gladly said yes. She had not been back to the city she grew up in since she left it in 1947, when it was still mostly in ruin. She was thrilled. She'd be able to see her old classmates, and I would be able to see where she had lived and spent her days during the war years. We visited the boys'-school-turned-hospital on the Heerstrasse, where she worked as a medical assistant during the war; the Windscheidstrasse, where her home was, now rebuilt to look as if it had never been damaged; to Jena, where she had attended university; and to visit with friends from school and even from the Gulag.

"It was an incredible snowstorm," she begins on the first cassette, "like one you only ever see in North Dakota, where a farmer can no longer find his barn. The snow fell and fell . . ." I find it surprising that her remembrances begin in 1946, nearly a year after the war was over, not with the oppression of Hitler's regime, nor the terror of the bombings in Berlin. She remembers the beauty of the Russian landscape, and she speaks of it all with fondness, even though the snowstorm occurs on the very day she first realizes she is on her way to a Russian prison camp, the Gulag. But, this was my mother. The woman knew how to tell a story.

She came from an era when storytelling was still an art form. In her family, her father and mother and she and her brother would sit around the dinner table—which, in her home, was also the parlor—and talk for hours. Her Papa would tell about his life growing up, how the family had lost even their house during the Great Inflation, and her Mutti would tell about her day at the equestrian club. Margarete and Dieter would listen attentively. Now, in her old age, as she told me about her life, this passion for storytelling was rekindled. I noticed how she took her time when she spoke. She set the scene. She'd describe a limp or a mustache as if that person were right in the room with us; or she'd stop in midsentence to sing a song or recite a poem that came to mind; often she'd speak in someone else's voice—her father's, or her brother's, for example—from remembered conversations.

But it was evident from the very beginning that she intended to tell her story plainly. She wanted no ambiguity. She said what she saw; she let me make the judgments, if there were to be any. She was an idealist in many ways. She wanted to believe in her fellow man and tried to see the good even when it lay deeply hidden. It showed when she spoke about the Russians, her captors, whom she described as sentimental people, even kind and fun-loving; while a "brown nurse," who by definition was a Nazi, was an "uneducated woman and poorly informed."

My mother also spoke of what she did not see—of what eluded her and confused her at the time. Most notably, she said she didn't learn about what happened to the Jews in Germany until after the war was over. At first I did not believe her. How could she not have known?

Didn't all Germans know? I spent hours questioning my mother about this very issue. In the massive stacks of cassette tapes that resulted from our conversations, there is not one that does not include interruptions from me, questioning her about the Jews.

I regret this now, because I can hear a growing anxiety in her voice as she tried, again and again, to tell it exactly as she remembered it, leaving nothing untold, even her own ignorance or "stupidity," as she called it. And I can hear my interjecting voice, doubting her. There's a tone—I am ashamed to say—of disrespect for her answers. I believed what so many of us from the side that won the war want to believe—that all, or at least most, of the German people knew what was going on regarding the Jews, and that they turned their heads and did nothing about it.

My mother answered with empathy and sometimes a sense of guilt for what happened in her country during her generation. At times she broke down and wept for the tragedy she only learned of after the war was over. To my constant questioning, though, she only ever responded, "I would tell you if I knew. I really did not." For her, the insult, the realization that her country—a modern and educated country that had laws against killing—could have perpetrated such atrocities on *any* human was simply inconceivable.

The remembering and retelling of the cruel events of that war weighed heavily on my mother's psyche. She became depressed during our three years and often asked if we could skip a Sunday. She was having trouble sleeping, she told me. And then, in the winter of 2003, she attempted suicide.

It was the only time she ever did, to my knowledge, although, when hearing some of her stories, I could have easily thought, *Why didn't she just take her life back then when things were so bad?*

Her attempt to kill herself came two years before her actual death caused by congestive heart failure. Our country had just declared war on Iraq—for the second time, and for an unprovoked reason, as she saw it. There were several weeks during which I often had to correct her, saying, "But no, Mamma. This is Boulder, not Berlin," and she would not respond. Instead, with blank eyes, she would point her finger to the sky and say, "Just wait till the bombs start to fall! You'll see!"

Then, on July 12, 2005, she died, two days after her eighty-first birthday.

It fell to me, as the eldest in the family, to clean out her apartment, making sure all three of her daughters received what she wanted each to have. As anyone knows who has lost a parent, this wasn't an easy job. I missed her terribly. Every corner of her very German apartment smelled like her perfume. Every cup and pencil still held her warmth.

I went to her bedroom first, which also served as her writing and reading room. The window along one wall let in a soft northern light. She lived on the top floor of an apartment building and had a full view of our mountains and our picturesque city, Boulder, and here she would sit for long hours and read. Here, too, was her desk where she sat often to write letters. Long, thoughtful letters, mostly to relatives and friends still living in Germany. This desk, then, is where I started my job. Her drawers were neatly organized, so it was not difficult to sort: "keep" versus "discard," and there was a third pile for what I thought, perhaps, her grandchildren would appreciate: a china pen tray painted in gold leaf—an antique, surely German; a leather blotter; her fountain pen.

When I had finished sorting, there was still one drawer left to clean out. It was the last one on the bottom with all her unanswered letters and Christmas cards in it. I knew it would take time to go through, so I had left it for last. But when I opened it, I found something lying right on top that I'd never seen before. A book of sorts, with my mother's handwriting on it. I carefully picked it up. It was old; it had yellowed with time and looked, from the faded line across it, as though it once had a ribbon tied around it. Inside, on the first page, was her cursive writing, in fountain pen: *Briefe an mein geliebtes Franzel während der Belagerung von Berlin*— "Letters to my beloved Franzel during the siege of Berlin." In the bottom right corner she had written the place and date: *Berlin, 15 April 1945.*

I turned the pages. I was incredulous. Who was Franzel? From the first paragraph, where she wrote, "Was it to be the last time?" to the end, I was riveted. Might she have put the book of letters there only a few days ago, knowing I'd find it? But why, then, did she keep this secret from me all those years? Evidently she'd been in love. But who was he? Had the relationship pained her so much that even in old age she could not bring herself to speak of him?

I could not help but be amazed at the passion and the courage that burned throughout the letters as I read, and this thought came to me: I should translate them. Someone should hear what she wrote during the most harrowing weeks in Berlin in 1945. I wanted to believe she trusted me to make of her stories what I would. And the idea for this book was born.

I pulled out the cassette tapes, the ones with her stories, and listened to them again, now much more closely, one by one. I took notes. I asked myself questions. I transcribed, and then I researched. I began to read every book on the subject of that era and that war I could find: William Shirer, Aleksandr Solzhenitsyn, Albert Speer, Anne Applebaum—anyone who could give me more information about that time in her life, and that time in history.

Then I remembered something: On one of our Sundays, a later one when we were winding down and there was little more that she could recall, she had handed me a box. "I thought you'd be interested in this," she had said. The box contained documents, old family papers such as baptism and immunization certificates from her childhood in East Prussia. At the time, I simply thanked her, but asked her to keep it in her home. Somehow it seemed too old and too valuable—at least to her—to have it living in my home with dogs and wild grandchildren running around. I did not know then how important this box would become.

As I made an outline of the history of Germany before and during the Second World War and organized her stories around it, questions regarding time lines arose. Oh, what a blessing it was, now, to have that box of documents I so cavalierly told her to keep! In it, I found answers to so much that I was missing: a bundle of letters that her brother, Dieter, had sent from the war front. I found school report cards, and marriage certificates, the British interzone pass that allowed her, finally, to stay in West Germany. I found the Russian papers that certified her release from prison. And, to my disbelieving eyes, there was her *Ahnenpass*, the Nazi passport that certified her genealogy for the previous ten generations.

Another invaluable gift she left me was a number of photo albums. How they were preserved I can only guess. But now that I needed to confirm her stories, the photos were there. All of them. There were photos of the farm where she worked, of her Jewish friend, Hilde, and of her beloved maid, Bertha.

Little by little, as I transcribed and translated and cobbled together her memoirs, the arc of her story came into focus. I was introduced to a new woman, not the mother I had always known. She became a teenager who sometimes clashed with her parents and got herself in trouble. I learned of her longings, her disappointments in life, and her dreams. And, when I read her letters, she became a young woman in love. Evidently, she grew up to believe she would be her own person, free to pursue her passions and to make decisions based on her own values—something new for women, and something that may have given her the spirit to survive all those years of war and imprisonment.

Over the decades since 1945, the stories from wartime Europe seem to have organized themselves neatly into accounts of the good guys versus the bad, and understandably so. It was, to be sure, an era of extreme evil and heroism and persecution. Yet our many bookshelves dedicated to that era have left little space for the stories of the millions of others who also suffered but whose voices were stifled because they came from the wrong side of the war.

In this regard, to have been given a chance to peer into Margarete's young soul has been a profound privilege. She has left us with an important piece of history that is rapidly dying away, as fewer and fewer survivors and witnesses to that era remain alive. Hers is a testimonial seldom heard, one that had been silenced for more than fifty years.

Margarete would be happy to know, I am sure, that her stories and her letters, and her many years of unspeakable suffering, were not in vain. I hope I have done them justice.

*—Kerstin Lieff*

# Note to the Reader

When I told my family and the few friends who knew her that I planned to write my mother's memoir, "ambitious" was a word that came up more than once. And then, "daunting." I didn't think so. After all, I had all my mother's stories on cassette tapes. Wouldn't I just need to transcribe them and then translate? The information was all there: her stories in her own voice and her diary containing the letters written to Franzel. But as I began to write, I began to see the magnitude of the project: a life lived in three countries, on two continents, in three languages, and over the course of two decades—and then the story was not even my own! What I thought would be no more than a few months of typing became two exhausting years of research, correspondence, travels . . . and countless questions. I was, to say the least, daunted, and after two years I still didn't know if I had all the facts right.

As I read, wrote, and reviewed my mother's stories, I began to realize that she could have made some mistakes—that, as vivid as her recollections were, her memory, after fifty years, may have blurred, that characters may have actually been other than the ones she said they were, and that some dates were actually different from the ones she gave. In fact, I did find some errors. For example, she remembered *clearly* that the first day of war was a Sunday. She remembered it because they were at the beach that day when she heard the announcer over the loudspeaker and her Mutti broke down in tears. And yet September 1, 1939, was a Friday. I took pains to figure out what possibly happened on that Sunday that left her with such a profound memory, and I believe I discovered the answer— food rationing was announced on the Sunday just five days before the actual start of war. But I left her story as it was, mistakes and all.

I hope you will bear with me—those errors I was able to catch I noted. I dread to think some others may have slipped by unnoticed.

When it came to descriptions of places I'd never visited, I had to rely on friends, films, histories, memoirs, and other personal accounts to verify what she had told me. I've never been to Russia, but Russia was a big part of her life once, so I was faithful to her descriptions yet filled in certain historical gaps from research. Historians may question the accuracy of her historical and political comments. However, I decided to leave her story as she told it, making notes wherever I saw fit to clarify what may have been errors on her part.

She used many names in her stories—some I find fascinating that she even remembered at all: Felicitas Jahn, for example, a woman who shows up only once in her later life in the Gulag. But she doesn't remember her beloved maid's full name. It was only ever Bertha. She spoke of Hilde, one of her best friends, but never mentioned her full name, either. Some of the people she talked about with such emotion, and often tears, that I felt I needed to keep the names exactly as they were given to me. At other times, it seemed, she offered names in order to keep a flow to the story—something she was so good at. Whether someone actually existed as "Klaus" rather than "Wolfgang" I'll never know.

And in this vein, in a true Mamma vein, bits of dialogue often appeared in her narrative, and even the occasional long monologue. Summoning those voices was her way of introducing me to the characters of her past. In most instances, I followed my mother's lead and let those individuals speak for themselves—but always, of course, as she remembered them.

I would be remiss if I did not include the possibility that *I* have made some mistakes. I am not a historian; I've been an artist most of my life, and creative writing has been my passion. Thus, this book is not meant to teach history, but to share a young woman's personal experiences through her eyes. I took my mother's stories, which were often told out of chronological order, and often even repeated with varying details over our three years of collaboration together, and worked to put them into a readable memoir. In my research, I found some stories could have been remembered out of sequence, and when I could I annotated such instances.

As this story was told to me in German, there are words that I have not found a match for in the English language. My mother used a number of temporal idioms, such as *Landser* and *Lazarett*. Rather than repeat the tedious and rough translation of "infantrymen" and "army hospital," I took the liberty of keeping them German. However, there are other words that I personally have wanted to keep German because of the meaning they hold for me. For example, an "apartment" has never been as grand as a *Wohnung*. Surely this is because my grandmother in Hamburg always, in my memory, had a majestic Wohnung! Even visiting as an adult, I remember high, high ceilings with crown molding and door handles so large it took two hands to pull them down.

There are other words in this book, especially acronyms, that I have never pronounced in English. Jena, my mother's beloved university town, would lose all its charm if not pronounced "YAY-nah." The BDM will always be the "bay-day-em" for me, and the NKWD, the dreaded Soviet police, will always be the "en-kah-veh-day." I have left many of the nouns, those that are particularly German, capitalized, as is normal in the German language. Margarete studied "the Maths," because it is only right that she did so, and her parents will always be "Mutti" and "Papa." And so, I hope to have passed a bit of her German-ness on to you, the reader.

# Part I

## PARADISE LOST
### 1933–1942

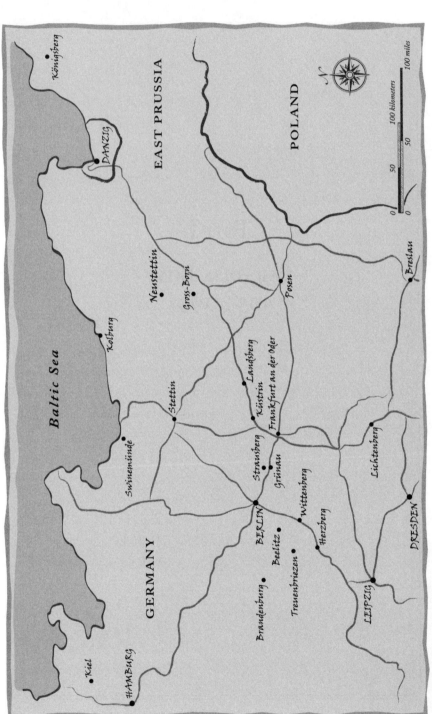

**CENTRAL GERMANY, 1940**

# 1

## PARADISE

### I.

The year I want to tell you about, the year everything changed forever, I was nine. Bertha cried, not because she was sad, but because she was happy. Papa fell off his horse. And my brother kept asking, "Am I still the way we used to be?"

### II.

My father, whom I called Papa and whose name was Werner, was a good rider. My mother always said this about him—and about herself too. He had turned thirty-nine in September, and he said that made him very old. He was a tall man, against other men, and had a clear forehead that reached all the way to where a thin line of dark hair wrapped around his head, and his eyes were brown and kind.

My mother's name was Helga, but I called her Mutti. She was beautiful, with green eyes and dark hair that she combed up into a bun, and she would tuck the stray hairs in at the back of her head with a comb made of ivory, from India. She was elegant, and her fingernails were painted red most of the time. Mutti was four years younger than my Papa. Her family had come from Sweden, which is where my grandmother and grandfather still lived and where we went to celebrate our Christmases most years. Mutti's dark hair, she told me, came from her mother, who was of French descent. I knew from my history class that many French people had been persecuted in France, and they had to flee that country, because they were Protestant. And I knew these people were called Huguenots. Her mother's family name had been deGobbin.

My brother, Dieter, was younger than me by twelve months and twenty-eight days. We were together, always. He was slight for a boy, and he had a serious face, delicate skin, and long fingers. He loved listening to Beethoven on the gramophone, and he was always singing songs he kept in his head. On indoor days, the days when the northern sky of Germany was heavy with rain, we recited poems to each other that we had learned by heart and I would play my violin. Dieter would sing along, but he only knew words to a few children's songs, so he would sing along to any melody I played: *Hola-hie, hola-ho, hola-hie, hola-ho,* which really meant nothing at all. And he knew the words to "Kling, Glöckchen, klinge-linge-ling"; it was a Christmas song, which didn't matter to him, because he loved to repeat the words that described the church bells ringing, *klinge-linge-ling, klinge-linge-ling.* This is what he would sing so many times I would finally have to tell him to stop. And then we would giggle. He was my little brother, after all, and I loved him.

Bertha was our maid, and I loved her too. She was a soft woman. Her voice was quiet, and her body was big and round. She had pale blue eyes and hair that curled around her ears on both sides, and she cut it herself. I know this because I used to watch her do it. Her body looked like a pillow that was divided in half by the apron she wore. It was a white starched apron, and it ran to the length of her skirt. Her hands, which were large and red, seemed always to be clasped in a sort of prayer just at her waist. It is what she did most of the time instead of talking.

Bertha helped my Mutti in the house, ironing our school uniforms and polishing our shoes. She dusted the furniture and peeled the potatoes in the kitchen. She cooked most of our meals, though Mutti always locked all the silver away in a drawer, and Bertha had to ask for the key to take it out each day before we ate. "Because," Mutti said, "one never wants to tempt the help in times like this, and silver, you know, is valuable."

Bertha swept the hallways and hung the washing out in the garden, and she lived with us most of the time, except when she went home to her family to visit for a weekend. Which rarely ever happened. Usually she stayed with us on these days to work, for which she would earn a few extra Marks.

Her room was a small one just off the kitchen, and it had its own door that she could lock with a key from the inside when she wanted to be alone. But she always allowed me to come in if I knocked. I sat on her bed and watched when she made herself ready for the day. Her bed had a fluffy duvet—we called it a *Steppdecke*—and several down pillows, large square ones, stuffed loosely into white linen pillowcases.

There was a tall window with long lace curtains at the far end of her narrow room, and on the windowsill below it was a photo of a boy inside a black frame. Bertha said it was her brother, and I think he was dead. Behind the window, just outside, was an apple tree. For me it was a magic tree. I was sure there were fairies living in it. In the spring it was fully pink—a perfect place for fairies to dance—and in the summer, when the red apples appeared, I thought elves had taken the fairies' place to sit among the leaves. In the winter there were only thin black branches on that tree and a few shriveled apples hanging here and there, and by that I knew the elves and fairies had left for the winter to live under a rock or somewhere else in the garden to stay warm. And then the spring and the pink would arrive again, and the dance would start all over.

Bertha always had large cups filled with coffee and warm milk waiting for Dieter and me when we awoke in the morning, and the breakfast table was heavy with cheeses and the smoked ham we called *Schinken*, and there was a basket with tiny pillows inside it that kept the soft-boiled eggs warm, each egg in its own pocket. Small bowls filled with jams of all colors—gooseberry, orange, and the large blackberries we called *Brombeeren*—were on the table too, and then, of course, there were *Brötchen*, warm bread rolls Bertha had just bought from the baker.

Next to my plate was Bertha's jar of dark honey with a small wooden spoon sticking out of it. She always placed it next to my plate so that I could be the first to have the honey for my Brötchen.

⁓

Swinemünde was the name of the small town where we lived.[1] It was on the Baltic Sea and had a white and sandy beach that ran along the northern shore, and there was a river that merged with the sea, called the Swine, just there where our house was. On the other side of the Swine there was a great lighthouse with a big and frightening head on it that lit up at night and peered at Dieter and me no matter where we were.

Swinemünde had broad streets and short houses, a cathedral and a town hall, and there were some very old houses that had been built so long ago—the Middle Ages, my Mutti told me—that they were built of handmade bricks, large, in the style called *Backstein*.

In 1934 there were not many people living in Swinemünde yet, mostly those employed by the sea—sea captains, sailors, shipping companies—and there were even a few people who came as tourists if they could afford it. They came to our town for a *Kur*—a visit to the sea, prescribed by a doctor, "in order to improve the health."

My Papa was not employed by the sea. He was the overseer for the mining operations in a coal mine somewhere else, and I didn't know where that was.[2] I knew he left home early each day, and he came home late each evening, and he often was tired.

My family owned two horses, which we boarded at a private riding club, where I took my riding lessons and where Mutti won championships. We had a real telephone and a car and a maid. My friends at school did not have these things. We were well off for a family in Swinemünde.

Margarete and Dieter, about ages six and five, on horseback.

Swinemünde was all I knew about the world, and the world, for me, was paradise. The sound of waves splashing against the yachts in the harbor and the ships that came in from far-off places like Hamburg or Stockholm, the caw of seagulls flying under a sky that hung low over the sea, sand between my toes when I came home at night, and the taste of salt in the air—this was my Swinemünde.

Winters were long in Swinemünde, but I knew there would always be spring, just as I knew the pink would come back, just as I knew my mittens would come off again when everything melted. Summers, on the other hand, were too short, but we filled them with adventures on the long beach and in the forest that went on forever.

We could see the lighthouse nearly everywhere we played, Dieter and I, and we told stories of who might live there. A witch, of course. And the purpose of the light she flooded over the iridescent sand at night was just to find us. We screamed out loud when we told each other these things. Each time the stories scared us more, and we would

7

run through the woods as fast as we could. Then at night—cold, out of breath, and dirty—we would run home, my hair in tangles (oh, would my Mutti scold!), my coat open to the wind, and often my knees and hands bloody.

## III.

The year I want to tell you about was 1933, the end of it, and 1934, the beginning. Life was difficult for many people, Mutti said often, and I didn't quite know what she meant. It didn't seem so for me, but my Papa told me his family had lost all their money during the Inflation, and that their house, where he grew up, had once had a real elevator in it, and that it had been sold for a bag of wheat to a rich lady. He said when he studied at university he wore white clothes and traveled in impressive circles and that he was a chosen student, a *Korps* student, and that even his father was a Korps student, someone from whom much would be expected, and that he used to put pomade into his hair. This all was because he thought he was important. And then the family became poor. And now Papa was who he was, and he also sang to me and played music for me on the piano, and at night he read to me from the book of Grimm's fairy tales.

One day Mutti told me that I needed to have compassion for Bertha because she was only a maid and she was one of those people for whom things were difficult; her family was very poor. If Bertha were not working for us, she would have nothing at all, and her family would have even less than they had now, so we needed to keep her working for us for as long as we could. The twenty Marks she received each month from Mutti and the few Pfennige her sister earned for mending clothes was all the money her family of ten had.

Bertha's father, like so many men in 1934, did not have work, and her family was "stamped." It meant that once a week her father stood in a long line at the Labor Office to get help. There he had to show his work certificate to a woman, and this certificate stated clearly that he was not working. The woman would put a stamp on his card, and with this he would receive cash for buying food. It would provide for the basics only, Mutti said: bread, mostly, perhaps some meat sometimes, but that was all.

Bertha had seven siblings. She was the oldest of the eight, and she had attended school only as far as the *Volksschule*. So, as I understood it, she had an education that was equal to the one I was to complete when I turned ten. This seemed odd to me because she was so smart.

Her family lived outside Swinemünde, somewhere in the countryside, about an hour from our home. Their house was small and shabby. It smelled bad whenever I visited, although I hardly ever did. Only when I went with Papa in the car to fetch her. Inside her house it was dark, and the odor that came to my nose was something like cooking, but it was putrid cooking that smelled like old sweat. Maybe it was her Papa's bathrobe that hadn't been laundered in a very long time.

꩜

One day I saw a dog skin hanging from the porch of Bertha's house, although I didn't know at the time that's what it was. I hopped out of my seat that day, expecting Meckie to run up to me to lick the back of my hand the way she always did. Meckie was a mutt, a skinny dog, mustard-colored, with a limp in her hind leg that she lifted as she ran, and I was always so excited to see her playing around in the dirt, just in front of the small barn where Bertha's family kept a pig and a goat. Oddly, on this day, though, Meckie didn't come, and the barn was still and no one was in the yard at all. I thought Meckie must be sick or sleeping under the porch somewhere. "Meckie! Meckie!" I called.

"*Ja.* Meckie," Bertha began to explain, as she lumbered down her front steps. "Meckie, our dear dog. I am sorry. She's not with us anymore." Bertha gently stroked my hair, and from the look on my

Papa's face, I knew that questions from me right now would be out of the question.

Papa later asked me if I had noticed what was hanging over the veranda railing. Well, yes, of course I saw it. It was a blanket of sorts, right? Fear gripped my stomach. I did notice it was the same mustard color I knew so well. And then Papa said it. "Yes, Gretel. It was a blanket of sorts."

Gretel. That was my name when I was a child.

"Was it a dog skin?" I mumbled. Papa always said nothing should be kept from a child, good or bad, a child should know what life is about, so I knew what he was about to tell me was something true.

"Yes, child. A dog skin. It's that way these days. People are hungry, Margarete."

He called me by my adult name now, and by that I knew this was something he wanted me to know. *People are hungry.* I repeated this over and over in my brain. But how could they? They ate *Meckie*? What would I know about it? What would I know about "that way"?

## IV.

The dining parlor was not a place for a maid to sit, but I saw it that morning—Bertha sitting there, resting her head in her red hands. Her elbows had made two smears Mutti would have made a fuss over on the mahogany table, right where she must have just finished polishing. I could see she'd been crying. *Was it another dog?* I went to her and placed my arm gently around her big waist. "Bertha?" I said quietly.

She looked up so suddenly she must not have known I was in the room. Indeed there were tears in her eyes, but her lips were soft and turned up in a gentle smile. "No, no, darling Gretel. These are not tears of sorrow. I am happy! Happy! I have learned the most wonderful news. I heard it on the radio today." She then opened her arms and lifted me onto her lap.

"The new Führer has declared that no one shall be out of work anymore! No one. That means my father will have work. The radio said,

Bertha. "She was a soft woman. Her voice was quiet, and her body was big and round."

within four years, this would happen. Everyone shall have work; no one shall be allowed to be without food again! This is what I heard. My Mutti, my Papa, things will be good again!"

With that she pressed my face into her bosom and stroked my hair and said, "Come. I have some warmed milk for you."

This about the new Führer was indeed news, and it was news my father should hear, I thought. He would be proud of me for knowing something so important, and that evening at dinner I walked over to his chair and said softly, "Papa? Excuse me."

"Yes, little one. What is it?"

"Do you know something? I heard it from Bertha today. A new time has come." I was so pleased with myself. "No one is allowed to be poor anymore! Everyone will have work! The new Führer has said this over the radio!" He would surely praise me, I thought, the way he did when I received good marks in school, and I stood by his side, eagerly waiting for his response.

But no! Papa was not happy at all. He seemed angry, in fact, something I rarely knew him to be. "You are *wrong!*" He turned and looked at me harshly; then he spoke louder than I'd ever heard him speak before, his finger pointed right at my nose. "Don't *ever* believe that!" He leaned down and looked very close into my face. "He who learns will have work. He who has earned it will have work. Work is not free!"

And I thought, *Oh my. How much I don't know.*

Later that evening, I overheard my parents speaking in hushed voices. Papa shook his head, and Mutti shook her head, and I knew it was about the new regime and Adolf Hitler, who only a few months earlier in January had been appointed Chancellor but called himself the Führer.

*Rechts-Bolschewiken,* Papa called them—those who joined the Nazi Party, professing to change the world, but who were in fact "stupid, stupid people, who say they are for freedom and equality, just like the Bolsheviks say their Communism stands for freedom and equality. But with them everyone will lose their freedom, they will lose everything. Just wait and see!" He called them fanatics, those who leaned to the right of right. Right Bolsheviks.

I didn't understand. None of this was important to me, but Papa was smart, this I knew.

My Mutti told me there was a time not long ago that had been very bad for many people. Women would run to the factories as soon as the night whistle blew so that they could get their husbands' pay. Every day they were paid, and in cash. The women then ran straight to the baker to buy bread as quickly as they could, because one never knew if the price of bread would double, even by the time they got there.

The new *Rentenmark* had recently been issued, its value based not on gold, but on Germany's land values and raw materials, and our money was fairly stable again. But many, many people were still out of work. People were hungry, and they wanted a change. More than twenty parties had been formed—all of them promising to help the situation—and a popular one was the Communist Party. Mutti and Papa told me that the Communists talked a lot to the people, approaching men like Bertha's Papa as they stood in those long lines. "Don't you want work? Communism will give you work! You have a right to feed your family. Communism will honor that right!"

But my Papa, who was much smarter than they, said it was a party to be feared. "No one in his right mind wants Communism," Papa said at the dinner table. "*That* party will be the downfall of this country!" And he would scowl. "It will be worse than anything we've ever seen." Then he would sit back and say, as if to himself, "And yet, we all want Communism's promises—work for everyone, food for everyone, and so what do we do?" Germany's new Führer and his party, the National Socialists—*Nazi* for short—promised what all the others promised: work and food for everyone. It was something we should be happy about. But he was not happy.

Many other things were whispered in the evening after the children left the dinner table, but I was too young to understand. What I heard: "Adolf Hitler will be the undoing of German industry." And, "You just wait and see." And then one evening I heard Papa shout: "This is impossible!" This time he was shouting about the Enabling Act, which had just been passed by the new regime.[3] Now Hitler would be in charge of the police and so much else I did not understand, and my Papa was furious.

## 2

# Am I Still the Way We Used to Be?

### I.

It was a day when the wind blew harshly off the sea and my brother and I ran along the shore calling to each other, though we could barely hear above the howl of the wind. That night, as on so many nights, we came home late with dirty knees and tangled hair. A strange darkness seemed to have enveloped the house when we skipped up the steps, and we found it all to be eerily quiet. Bertha was standing in the vestibule when we opened the door, not Mutti. This was already odd. Why was it Bertha, not Mutti? Not Papa? "*Kommt rein, Kinder.* I have your bread ready. And some cocoa. Come in where it's warm." All this was confusing. This was not how things went.

Papa had been out riding his horse earlier, Bertha said, as he and Mutti did often when the weather was fair, on days he did not work. Today was one of those days, a pleasant one, with the cool breezes of spring's new weather, the recently melted snow revealing crocuses here and there, and the trails of the forests black and muddy.

It was the large horse that Papa was on, Bertha told us, the black one, the one Mutti also loved to ride because he galloped so gallantly. "Your Papa was out riding." That part of the story we had heard already. Bertha kept saying it over and over.

But what happened then?

"He had a fall."

And what then?

Bertha fell silent for a while, and then replied, "Mutti is with him now."

Why? We both leaned into her. Where are they?

We tried to coax her to say more, but she wouldn't. She kept saying he was out riding and then he fell, and she kept pouring us more chocolate and fixing another piece of bread with jam.

What I understood was that the big black horse wouldn't jump over a log. The horse took a fright and reared up. Papa fell.

But he hadn't fallen completely off the horse, and this is the part Bertha left for later. Later, my Mutti explained it to us better. He had fallen so that one foot remained in the stirrup, Mutti said. The black horse then galloped all the way back to his stable, Papa banging his head against the stones in the pasture and the cobblestones of the city. He tried to protect his head with his hands, but he couldn't, and his head kept banging along the ground all the way home.

His hands would have been covered in blood, I imagined, as they held his head. Later I saw his fingernails had been ripped to the cuticle.

Perhaps, Mutti surmised, there was a new stream under that log, perhaps created by the snowmelt, that made the horse shy, even though he had made this jump so many times before.

Bertha reminded us that Papa had injured his head a few years earlier. That time it was in the winter and it was in Switzerland while our family was skiing in St. Moritz. Dieter and I attended a German school there that winter, and, with Papa's help, each morning we would strap on our wooden skis and our leather book packs, and with our big clumsy poles we would schuss off to school. One day Papa fell and hit his head against a tree, and what I remember seeing was a big boil on his forehead the size of an egg and a black circle under his eye. That eye remained as red as Christmas the rest of our stay in St. Moritz. I remember, too, that he joked about it then: "That's what I said. A fine-looking egg. On my head, I said!" He was funny about it, and he looked funny too, all swollen and red, with an egg on his head, and that's what I remember of that winter when I was six.

Margarete and Dieter with Papa Werner in St. Moritz, Switzerland.

Now Papa complained of pain all the time. He did not leave the house to go to work, and he spent his days sitting in the parlor in a chair in front of the window, holding his pained head in his hands and staring at the carpet between his shoes. I came to his lap one afternoon, just after school; I wanted him to talk to me the way he used to talk—"What did you learn today? Are you writing your letters well?" Instead, he only stared, distantly, a filmy glaze over his eyes. I then did what I often did—I reached into his vest pocket and pulled out the chain that had a gold watch hanging from it and asked him to say what time it was. Usually he would say, "Time for a story!" and he would tickle me, or muss my hair, but now he only smiled an awkward smile, his stiff mouth thinly bent up on one side. "Ja. Uhri." That's all he said, and then he closed his eyes and let his head fall back. "Uhri." It was said softly and in a funny voice like that of a child. He was trying to say *Uhr*, the German word for clock.

Margarete, Helga, Dieter, and Werner at the dinner table in Swinemünde. "It was a different man with a different voice."

Then he was no longer with us. Mutti had taken him to the hospital, where the doctors decided to cut open his brain. There were few anesthetics in 1934 for pain. What the surgeons used was ether. It was a temporary relief, from what I understood, and a numbing medication was injected into the scalp so that at least the skin just around the incision would feel no pain. But Papa said he felt every bit of it—he heard it even. This is what he told the family later: "*Grrrrhhh. Grrrrhhh.* The sound of the saw going through my bones, I heard it, the bones breaking. And I could hear them talking, the doctors. I knew they were cutting around in my brain. I could hear it!" When he told us this, though, it was no longer my Papa speaking. It was a different man, with a different voice.

Papa still had his face, the same face I knew, but now half his forehead was missing, and when he looked at me, he was lopsided. He walked lopsided, too. And then one day he stopped speaking. There were no more conversations at the dinner table, only silence and the sound of soupspoons clinking against our soup bowls. The stories he

17

told while I sat in his lap, the fairy tales, the tickles, even the late-night discussions between Mutti and Papa, the hushed voices speaking the name of Hitler—all that went away, and one month later he was dead.

## II.

My Papa was dead. No story had ever come to this, and no matter how I tried, I could not change it. Nothing had ever ended so abruptly. Mutti had found him in his study on the floor next to his desk that morning; his drawer was open as if he'd tried to take something from it, and then he must have fallen. It was early, maybe four o'clock.

There was a hubbub in our home in the days just after it happened. Bertha always seemed too busy, and Dieter and I were shuffled off to the back of the house to our bedrooms and told we were not to be seen. "This doesn't concern you," Mutti said, and we knew intuitively we were not to ask why: Questions were disrespectful at a time like this. But her face had a vague expression to it, as though she couldn't remember what she was supposed to be doing anymore.

Many visitors came to our home during those days after he died, with food, and the parlor was always full of people. The women were dressed all in black. Mutti was, as usual, fancy, but now in black too, with black stockings and black shoes with heels, and the seams of her stockings looked like an ink line had been drawn straight up the back of her legs.

It was all so confusing for me; I didn't know why I had to stay in my room. Dieter didn't know why either, and when I came to his room to talk to him, I would catch him pushing his tears away as he sat on his bed, and when he saw me, he'd fold his hands quietly into his lap, being an obedient child. He was seven, lonely in his grief, and I wanted to console him, but I didn't know how. We whispered to one another, and I held my arm around his shoulders, hoping to make him feel better. Dieter looked up then, with his tearful face, and asked, "Am I still the way we used to be?"

Dieter with his toy boat. "He was seven, lonely in his grief, and I wanted to console him."

On one of those afternoons, as women were chatting and teaspoons were clinking, I opened the door to his room and said to my little brother who was on the floor playing with his wooden boat, "I'm going in there, Dieter. I'm going to walk into that parlor." It wasn't bravery I felt at the time. It was objection. I couldn't let those women in there be in charge of my Papa any longer. Dieter only looked at me, startled.

I left his room and marched down the hallway, fast so that I wouldn't lose my confidence, and I opened the door to the parlor. I found them all sitting around the marble-topped table that had coffee and cake on it, and I saw the cups and plates were our best china.

I stopped in the doorway, wide-eyed and not sure about myself at all, but I opened my mouth all the same and blurted: "I'm here to announce something." I looked around and fear gripped my throat: Everyone was looking at me aghast. I then closed my eyes and the words came out all on their own: "My Papa is dead!" I opened my eyes, and my knees began to shake. Then I gave a curtsy as an obedient girl should.

Tears I had been fighting away burned my eyes and spilled onto my cheeks, while everyone in the room stared at me in horror. *What is this child thinking? Why is she not in her room?* My legs buckled just before I fell in a pile on the floor, and I could no longer control the sobbing. I buried my face inside my skirt that circled around me on the floor. No one came to comfort me. Instead, I was ushered quickly out the door by my Mutti, back to my room, and left there to be with Dieter—the two of us, once again, alone.

We were not invited to the funeral either. It all happened without us, the children, and that was the day I realized my world would never, ever return. I would never be the way we used to be.

# 3

# An Important Man Arrives

I.

This is us, when we were allowed, finally, to visit our Papa. The gravestone reads: WERNER DOS, 21 NOVEMBER 1894–13 MAY 1934. I could not help but notice the dash between the dates. Such an insignificant mark, and the thin sky and the drizzle, on this Sunday morning, made me shiver.

II.

Mutti was away from home more and more. Off, mostly, at the riding club or at the tennis club. We were alone now, most nights, left to eat our bread and cheese in a quiet parlor, and when we spoke, it was only with Bertha or with each other, but even that was rare. The lights seemed dim. There was no music in the house, no more stories; I never heard laughter. Dieter and I stayed indoors often now. We'd sit on his bed and play *Käsekasten*. Dieter had his notebook, and we drew lines on the paper and put Os and Xs between them, tic-tac-toe. And we played *Mensch ärgere dich nicht*, a board game that made us forget about things. Sometimes Dieter would hide his face and smear away the tears when he thought I wasn't looking, but mostly we both sat and were brave. Neither of us talked much about what our lives had become. Mostly we listened for more changes.

We heard something then, one evening when we weren't quite prepared. We had the feeling that something quite terrible was coming, there was such a flurry in the house, and still no one spoke. Mutti was home, but she kept to herself, and Bertha made a roast. Mutti came out of her room then, and she was wearing a new silk dress that was long and elegant and had bands that crisscrossed her back. It was dark blue like dusk. She had on her long string of pearls and her silk stockings. They were white with a small pattern woven into them, and they had seams up the back. She had made her lips dark red, and her hair was pinned up high, and she smelled beautiful. A man was coming for dinner. "He must be important," Dieter whispered to me, but I could see the fear in his little-boy eyes, eyes that were asking me *what now?* I had no answer; I did not know.

Bertha told us his name was Karl Spaeth, from Bavaria, and he was a naval officer with a high rank. And, she said, we should remember our manners. I should curtsy; Dieter should bow.

At five minutes before the hour of six, the bell rang like a shock. Dieter and I shot our eyes straight to the door. Bertha went to answer,

Karl Spaeth. "An important man arrives."

and I ran to stand just behind her. What I saw when she first opened the door was the man's frame, so large it filled the sky behind him. He was a blond man with a pencil line for a mustache, and he did not smile. This I recall. He did not look in my direction, either. He was a determined man, though; that was easy to see.

Karl Spaeth stood there in his naval uniform; in his right hand were roses he held properly upside down, then righted them up in order to hand them to Bertha. They were for my Mutti. Seeing the formality of this gesture, I knew it was time for my best manners, and I curtsied while I held the side of my skirt. Dieter promptly followed and bowed, giving the man his hand and his name, Dieter Dos.

We were not allowed to speak once dinner was served, and my stomach began to hurt. I suddenly missed my Papa, who would have said something just then to make me giggle. But now everything was strange, and when the conversation lapsed and Mutti sent a look in Bertha's direction, I knew she wanted to be left alone with this man. They were the adults, after all, and the conversation bored me anyway, so I asked, as soon as it was polite, if I might be excused, and Dieter followed right behind me. We disappeared into our rooms, and eight months later Karl Spaeth became my Papa.

Another event we were not invited to, and now Mutti's name would forever be different from mine: Frau Spaeth, no longer Dos.

❦

Karl Spaeth was the man I was supposed to call my Papa. But he was a stern man, a man who had never been married before, and it was clear that children, in particular Dieter and I, were not to make noise when he was at home. I decided to call him Papa Spaeth, separating him from the man I once loved.

Papa Spaeth was a great storyteller, and he would talk endlessly about adventures he'd had. His long stories in exotic settings fascinated me. I would try to imagine what he was telling us about by recalling pictures I had seen in my schoolbooks: Indians with great headdresses of feathers, birds in rainbow colors sitting high in a canopy of trees, and fruits and flowers the likes of which I'd never seen. He amazed me and impressed me and frightened me all at the same time.

It was on one of those evenings when my Papa Spaeth was giving one of his long speeches that he said he did not understand the meaning of *MAH-deh in Gher-MAH-nee*. "What is the meaning of this? Written on every article we buy!" And he thumped the table with his fist. I had to laugh and hide my grin behind my hands. I knew what the words meant! I had learned them in school: it was "Made in Germany"—not France, not England, and we should be proud of that. It was a law that had been written as a part of the Versailles Treaty just after the Great War and said all things manufactured had to be labeled, saying where they were made, and all those labels were to be written using English words, a language he did not know. Perhaps he was teasing us, but I quickly made my face serious to show my respect for him, this new Papa Spaeth who did not know what *Made in Germany* meant, but I would surely tell Dieter what I knew, later, when we had been sent to our rooms.

Over the months, Karl Spaeth told us about his past. He had been in the navy on a U-boat in the Great War when he was just eighteen, and he had opinions about that war, and after the war he studied chemical engineering. Mutti interjected that it was the Kali-Syndikat that employed him, Germany's largest fertilizer concern. They manufactured potash, and to this day I don't know what that is. Kali-Syndikat had ties in Algeria and countries in South America. Karl, at the age of twenty-four, traveled to all those exotic places in South America—Brazil, Argentina, Chile, Paraguay, and Uruguay, where he lived for nearly ten years.

One evening he told us how he had survived in the jungle. It was quite simple, he said. He ate what the Indians ate; he drank what the Indians drank; and he slept the way the Indians slept. He used their medicines. "I was determined never to become ill. Not even once. That was for the weak men, and so many of my compatriots were just that—weak men. They did not eat and drink like the Indians; they ate what they were used to—beef and boiled vegetables. They drank water, not tea, and many of them became sick. Many even died. They became infected with malaria, dysentery, typhoid, and diseases we did not even have names for. They got strange skin rashes and boils."

Papa Spaeth certainly made himself seem important. I thought he must be very smart, this man, and yet I feared him.

"Many of the men I was with, the Germans, began to drink, and I believe that was their undoing. I didn't do that. I watched the Indians who had been living in the jungle all their lives, and I saw that they didn't drink alcohol, not one drop. I paid attention to this."

Papa Spaeth's stories became grander and more heroic as our evenings progressed. He told us how he never spent his money while he was in South America. He saved it all, everything he'd made during the years he worked there. He took it to a German bank in Argentina, every penny of it, hoping to be rich when he got home. Then, in 1933, after ten years of service, when he was to return to Germany, the bank was gone. It had gone under during that time when so many of the banks went under, in America too, and his money was lost forever.

He said he had nowhere to go then, nothing to save him, so he went to the German embassy and asked for help. This is how he told the story: "I announced: I'm here. Take me. I have nothing left; everything is gone. Do with me what you like, but I have nothing and nowhere to go, not even the money for my fare home."

He was shipped back. It seemed the embassy did this. I'm not sure that's exactly what happened. He was a great spinner of stories, my Papa Spaeth, and this is the one he told. He landed, somehow, in

Germany, penniless, and contacted an old comrade from the Great War who suggested he reenlist. His comrade said he'd heard Hitler intended to reestablish the navy; it could be a grand opportunity for him. And with that advice, Papa Spaeth enlisted as a naval engineer. Not much later, he was promoted in rank to become a *Fregattenkapitän,* and then, only a few years after that, he became a *Kapitän zur See.*

Although my new Papa was a military man, his views did not differ much from those of my real Papa. For example, I heard him say once that the Great War, the one he participated in, in the waters of the North Sea, was "a war about nothing, a war started by old men who lied to us."

## III.

I was ten in 1935 when the man who had been our Führer now for more than two years held a rally for members of his Nazi Party in Nuremberg. Here he announced, for the first time publicly, his intention for the Jewish population of Germany: they were not to enlist in his army, and they were not to hold public office. They were told further what they could and could not do. Now many things would change for the Jews in Germany, and I didn't understand any of it, but my Mutti and my Papa Spaeth spoke of it quietly at home, and often at night.[4]

It was not noticeable at first. There were not many Jews living in Swinemünde, and I didn't know any. I didn't really even know the meaning of the word *Jude,* except that I heard it spoken only in hushed tones around the dinner table after the children were given permission to leave. Jude, as I understood it, was an important person; so important that my parents needed to wait until the children were gone to talk about him. But, I overheard this: "Das ist aber nicht möglich!" Impossible! Then there was the name Pastor Gottlieb. "Surely he'll be immune. He is not even Jewish; he's a pastor in a Protestant church, for God's sake." And another man whose name Papa Spaeth brought up time and again:

"But he won the Iron Cross in the Great War. Surely he'll be immune!" Things I didn't understand until many, many years later.

One thing about the new Nazi regime I did understand. It was early still, before that Nuremberg rally. I was perhaps nine years old when I found a pair of men's underpants. I thought of something funny to do, and I wanted to make my friends laugh, so I pulled on the rope of the flagpole in front of our school and lowered the new red flag with its black swastika on it—we called it the *Hakenkreuz*—all the way down. I suppose this alone was an act of treason, but I thought my idea was a humorous one, so I didn't stop. I decided to replace the flag with the underpants and pulled those old ragged things all the way to the top. All day those shorts flew around up there in the wind, and no one noticed, except me and the children I told, "Look up! Look up! Tell me what you see!" We all giggled behind our hands and then ran off. Perhaps I knew there would be consequences, but it was not until that evening, when the school director appeared at our home, that I understood I had done a very bad thing.

I was relieved that my parents would not punish me, but the school director made sure I understood how serious my offense had been: "You must understand, Herr Spaeth. This cannot happen!" I was to write an essay, he said, two essays in fact. One about the meaning of the Hakenkreuz, the other about the importance of the Nazi Party.

It was on an evening not long thereafter that Mutti piped up at the dinner table with something dreadful she wanted to share with us. It was something that had happened to her just that day and it frightened her very much. Her eyes went wide as she began her story. She said our telephone rang and she went to answer it. The person on the wire did not identify himself, which already was quite unusual. A caller always replied with "Spaeth hier," or "Meyer hier," or "Hier" whatever his name was. This caller, however, just started to speak and then kept speaking as if he knew her: "Frau Spaeth" this, and "Frau Spaeth" that, and he said things like "Hitler is the Devil, Hitler will undermine our country," and then the voice suddenly asked innocently, "Don't you agree?"

Mutti was confused and distrustful, thank God, and she didn't answer him. She didn't say a thing. He kept at it, though, and when she still did not respond, the phone just clicked off. He had hung up, and there was nothing but silence while she held the telephone receiver and stared at it, bewildered. It was a ploy, she surmised, someone wanting to trick her, and the thought of it terrified her. My parents had never joined the *Partei*—as the Nazi Party came to be known. And yet my Mutti's husband was a military man, so perhaps the Partei had their suspicions. Perhaps someone wanted to see where her allegiance stood.

~

Even before the Weimar Republic, there was a law on the books that said no officer was allowed to be affiliated with any party. Country loyalty, yes; party loyalty, no. That was how it was written. And even now, with the Nazis in power, it was still a law. No officer could join the Nazi Party or any party. So the idea that all German officers were Nazis is a false one. Even though the Nazis became the only legal party in Hitler's regime, an officer of any military branch was never allowed to join. Throughout the entire era of the Nazis, officers remained "party-neutral."[5]

So, Papa Spaeth was perhaps suspected or merely being tested for his loyalty to Hitler, because his beliefs and how he had once voted were never publicly discussed. Perhaps someone hoped my Mutti might speak. Maybe she would tell, give Papa Spaeth's ideas away. I don't know the reason behind this telephone incident. But it gave my Mutti a fright and she became determined not to speak out again, not ever in public, and even at home she became silent.

My Papa Spaeth said nothing.

## 4

# A City I Would Fall in Love With

### I.

Papa Spaeth had become important in the world. He had moved from the rank of Fregattenkapitän in the navy to Kapitän zur See, and this meant we had to leave Swinemünde. It was a sad parting. All I ever knew of life was what I learned in Swinemünde, but now with my new Papa at the helm of our family, everything was changing rapidly.

We moved first to Pillau, a city on the Baltic Sea three hundred miles east of where I had lived my entire childhood. I no longer saw Bertha in the kitchen; it was someone else now, and it was two of them. New maids, both of whom Mutti soon released, because she suspected them of stealing. But none of this mattered anyway, because a few months later Papa Spaeth was told his new post was to be at the *OKM Oberkommando,* the high command, the National Office for Military Planning, the German Department of Defense. You could, I suppose, compare it to the Pentagon.

And for this post, we would move to Berlin.

### II.

I was fourteen now, and old enough to recognize that first day Mutti and I walked all the way down and then all the way back up the avenue, Unter den Linden, right through the center of Berlin, that I would fall in love with this city. What I loved first was the fragrance. It was early summer, but a hot day, and what was so remarkable about that walk was the shade. Unter den Linden was canopied, from one side to the other, with blooming flowers hanging long from large, old linden trees.

The perfume in the air in Berlin on that day was a breath from heaven, something that will always stay with me.

My new life was one of awe and fascination. I lived in a city now, and I was becoming a woman. Shopping trips with Mutti on the Kurfürstendamm, the street of fancy shops, showed me things I suddenly wanted to buy, things I'd never thought of before, like hosiery and nail polish and silk.

Papa Spaeth and Mutti took us to the opera at the Staatsoper on Sundays. My favorite performance that year was Herbert von Karajan's *Die Zauberflöte* by Mozart, and my favorite orchestral music was written by my favorites, the "three Bs": Brahms, Beethoven, and Bach. The Staatsoper was a joy to visit. It was an old building with figures carved into the pediment and a frieze above the entry with the name of our Kaiser from the time of its opening, Friedrich der Grosse. Majestic Corinthian columns decorated the front, and I always felt so glamorous coming here for an evening.

Berlin introduced me to other things, too, that I had never seen before. Bad things, things that astounded me. For the first time in my life, I saw—often—men without a leg or missing an arm. These men hobbled along using a crutch or simply waving a stump. The pant leg or the empty sleeve was folded under, pressed and neatly pinned in place. Many of them wore a black band around the upper arm as well. Mutti said it was to signify a lost comrade from the Great War. I also saw men wearing a patch over one eye. Another casualty of the Great War, Mutti told me, most likely from exposure to poison gases. Many of these men were still quite handsome. They carried their blights as a sign of valiance, it seemed. To me, it looked as though they had great secrets they were carrying. But I noticed this too: they always looked me straight in the eye, with pride.

We lived in Charlottenburg, a "borough," I suppose you'd call it, close to the city center. It was a wealthy borough with large homes built a century earlier, and the streets were lined with expensive boutiques:

stores selling hats and men's suits, fancy chocolate shops and bakeries. We lived on the Windscheidstrasse, and I took the S-Bahn to school each day. "S" for street train. Then there was the "U." The U-Bahn, the underground train.

Our home was grand, but it was grand in a city sort of way. It was a *Wohnung*, a large apartment, on the third floor of a distinguished house. There were five floors in the building, and it was built of stone with decorated windowsills and a large oval-shaped front doorway with a dark vestibule where it was always slightly cooler than it was outdoors. Inside the vestibule was a floor made of white marble, polished bright each day by our house manager, with a wide marble staircase leading to the homes above.

The rooms in our Wohnung were larger than any I'd ever seen in Swinemünde. Each of our bedrooms—and there were four—had a table in the center with chairs, where Dieter and I would sit together to study and write our school papers. On many of these nights, Papa Spaeth sat with us and helped with our school problems, especially with the Maths, which, for me, was difficult.

When Papa Spaeth wasn't there, we would talk to each other when we studied; we'd help each other, too, when it came time to memorize. Learning poems from the old masters and reciting them by heart was an art we were all required to learn. There was no question. How I wish it were still true! Those poems come to you when you need advice; they remind you of consequences and what is evil and what is kind. My favorites were, of course, those from Schiller and from Goethe, and Dieter and I practiced them at night. There were others, many of them, that I can still recite.

The ceilings in our Wohnung were taller than I'd seen before too, and there was sculpted crown molding around the edges. The doors were majestic—nearly twice as tall as a person—and had brass handles that required both hands to get the door to clink and swing open. Above the latch of each door was a keyhole with a huge brass key sticking in it.

## III.

As early as 1933, when Hitler formally banned all parties other than the Nazi Party, the custom of raising the right arm in salute and pronouncing, emphatically, "Heil Hitler" was highly encouraged of all public employees. This included teachers. Each teacher was supposed to extend his right arm straight out in front, raise it at least to eye level, and shout loudly, "Heil Hitler!" And of course, we students were supposed to respond in like manner, especially when singing the national anthem.

However, some of my teachers refused. It was 1938, and it was Berlin. Things would change soon enough, but for now no one wanted this. My Maths teacher, in particular, was one who loathed this new thing, this right arm thing, this *wrong* thing, as he saw it. "What? Am I now sick?" I heard him say once, as he was explaining himself to another man. "Ich bin doch nicht krank!" and he stood his ground. As *Heil* also means "heal" in German, he was playing with the words. This Maths teacher kept his job, but only for a few more years, and then was sent into the *Wehrmacht*,[6] surely against his will. I wonder if he survived.

Sometime later, after I was already finished with my *Abitur*—the exam that, if I passed, would allow me to go to university—our school changed dramatically. All teachers in all schools were replaced by loyal Partei teachers then. One in particular, a teacher Dieter had as a student, joined the Nazi Party just so he could keep his job. It was a sad thing, because, much later, after everything was finished and Hitler was dead and the war was over, this man could no longer find work. No one would hire a former Partei member. He hanged himself in his living room, right where everyone—his children and wife and others in his house—would surely see what he had done.

Although things were still rather loose in my school, and our principal was not fond of our regime either, we had been told that we should always salute with the Heil Hitler arm when we saw the Brownshirts, as we called the SA men, or the Blackshirts, for the SS uniform. As we often saw these men marching through the streets, my friends Hilde and Ilse and I just laughed at them. We thought they looked so strange with their self-importance. I mean, wasn't this a city? With fashion and taste? And now this? Men in uniforms?

We preferred to cross the street whenever we saw them, so we would not have to be bothered. We were not about to Heil Hitler to anyone, anyway. Besides, once, one of these Brownshirts whistled at me and said, "*Hallo, Fräulein!* Wouldn't you like to become a German mother?"

I didn't understand what he was saying, but I knew it wasn't meant kindly, that it was probably a sort of curse, something I should be frightened of, and I turned my eyes down to the street and crossed over to the other side. I did this very quickly and then took a deep breath. My face was red. I would never trust one of these Brownshirts; I wouldn't. I would stay away and stay quiet. "Stay small." That's what I told myself, and it became important in days to come.

Walking along the Kurfürstendamm one afternoon, my friends Ilse and Hilde and I passed a store with male mannequins in the window. All of them were dressed in soldiers' uniforms. There were the black ones and the brown ones, and the Luftwaffe uniforms that were a handsome gray wool, and even those for the Hitler Youth: brown shorts and shirt, and a tie and white kneesocks.

"Ah!" Hilde said, and giggled, remembering our principal's directive. "I understand everything now! Look. There's a brown one and there's a black one too. I believe this means we should now salute the mannequins, right?" And then she did it, just as a prank, and we laughed so hard we nearly peed in our pants. We Heil Hitlered the mannequins in the window.

Had we only known what could have happened if we'd been caught, we never would have dared.

So my life as a fourteen-year-old in Nazi Germany, in 1938, was still relatively free. And I learned I was quite good at sports. I ran well until my running instructor told me I was not to run so fast. "It's not good for a young woman to run too fast," I was told. I swam well, too, and my swimming instructor said, "Just not much faster, Margarete. You'll hurt your female organs, and you'll not be able to bear children." It was always like that: Women could train, but only so much.

I entered a number of competitions. Each one had medals like the Olympics—gold, silver, and bronze. In the summer of 1938, I competed in a national championship in Mecklenburg in West Pomerania, not so far from Berlin by train. We had to swim for sixty minutes, any style we liked—my favorite was the breaststroke—and I won my division. There were other sports, too, that I competed in. Running, 75 meters. Diving from the high board, 4.2 meters. I won the bronze medal for all sports combined.

Berlin had the Reichsportfeld, and it was not far from my house. It was the stadium Hitler was so proud of and the very same stadium where the 1936 Summer Olympics had been held. I wouldn't know until years later what had happened there: Our Führer shook hands with only the German athletes and then left the stadium abruptly, presumably so he could avoid shaking hands with Jesse Owens, an American black man who had won four gold medals.

Now that I lived in Berlin and so close, within S-Bahn distance, to the Reichsportfeld, I wanted only to swim and become good enough for the next Olympic Games, which would be held in 1940—only two years away. I was strong and I was an athlete. That's how I saw myself.

## IV.

The Wandervogel, a name that meant something like Wandering Birds, was an organization with a long history. It was where young people learned crafts and songs, and they hiked together, and even

Girls' sports team, Mecklenburg. Margarete is at the bottom left.

camped in tents and learned to build campfires, much like the Boy or Girl Scouts.

By the time I came of age to join, at fourteen, the Wandervogel had already been renamed the Bund Deutscher Mädel, the Organization for German Girls. And for the boys it was called the Hitler Jugend, the Hitler Youth. They were nearly always referred to as the BDM and the HJ.

Joining the BDM was something I had longed for, not only to learn crafts and songs, but because I would be allowed to stay with my friends after school on those days we had our meetings. We met once a week from three to five o'clock. I learned to knit and crochet, and sometimes, on Saturdays, we went on long outings.

There was a song about the outdoors we learned that Dieter and I sang as we walked to catch the train to school, repeating the refrain over and over again until we reached the S-Bahn, singing and waving our hats about as we walked:

> *Faleri, falera, faleri,*
> *Falera ha ha ha ha ha*
> *Faleri, falera,*
> *Und schwenke meinen Hut.*

Later, the songs we learned in the BDM and the HJ were less about hiking and more about the Partei and our Führer and our loyalty to both. Later, it was even mandated that all children join at age fourteen. Here is where I could have seen what was happening, but I didn't. At fourteen, I was thinking mostly of myself—and of boys.

Hilde was half Jewish, and she was not allowed to join the BDM.[7] She said she had gone to the leader of my group and asked permission to join, and she was told, unequivocally, no. And now I must confess my response to Hilde's tearful complaint: "Why do you fuss? Why bother crying? It's only one day in the week."

"But I'm only half Jewish," she wept that day as we walked down the street.

Margarete, right, with her friends in Berlin. "There was more to Berlin than school and sports and the BDM."

"Don't join, then," is all I said.

Oh, how I've regretted that answer, that I didn't pay attention that day, or on any of the days that followed, when I didn't really listen to her pain.

My life, at fourteen, was ruled by dos and don'ts—"Margarete, you must do this" or "Margarete, you mustn't do that"—and my focus was on obeying my parents and doing well in school. And so I dismissed Hilde's pain. I can use the excuse that I was too young, and young people are often cruel to one another, but I just didn't understand. I should have. Hilde was my friend, and a good friend, and the only one I had who was a Jude.

❧

There was more to Berlin than school and sports and the BDM. I could now join the *Tanzschule*. It was a finishing school, literally a "dance school" for young men and women, and the idea thrilled me. It was here that we learned not only how to dance but all the facts that went along with it, the etiquette. The boy learned how to ask the girl to dance—he would bow slightly—and she would learn to curtsy and accept. Boys learned how to kiss a woman's hand. We were always so nervous when the time came for this, but we got used to it and, in time, it was quite fun.

Ilse, Hilde, and I were inseparable. We attended the Tanzschule together, and we talked and gossiped. We flirted—we were allowed to do this here. And one time, a boy—his name was Karl—even gave me roses for my birthday, but that would not be for a few more years. We often teased each other, as we walked to the S-Bahn, about which boy liked whom better. "I can tell he likes you!" "I saw how he looked at you!" "He's got love in his eyes! I can see it, the way he stays with you too long at the doorway, the way he watches you. I can see it!"

"Oh no! You're wrong. You're wrong!" And we'd blush because we knew we were, in fact, quite right. The boys were looking at us much too long, and this was exciting.

# 5

# THE NIGHT OF BROKEN GLASS

## I.

It was now 1938, and I began to see signs everywhere that said JEWS NOT WELCOME or JEWS NOT ALLOWED. I thought it was something that existed only in big cities like Berlin, because I had never seen such things in Swinemünde. But, in fact, signs against Jews suddenly appeared everywhere in Germany.

Across from our home was a store with a show window where one day I noticed such a sign had been pasted, large, across the front, saying JEWISH ESTABLISHMENT. DO NOT DO BUSINESS WITH JEWS. Next to it was another sign with very large letters, written in a peculiar style that gave the name of the owners: Friedleid, or Friedstein. And often now, next to both of these signs, there was an SA man standing, looking important in his brown uniform.

The store was a leather shop, which I passed every day on my way to the S-Bahn. They sold leather handbags and leather gloves and belts and things, and this sign puzzled me. What did "Jewish establishment" have to do with anything?

I decided I would find out. One afternoon, as I had just gotten off the train and was walking past the store, I stopped and turned, and then simply walked in right past the spot where yesterday I had seen that man with the strange-looking cap. A woman, kind, with a gentle smile, asked me how she could help. Her husband—I assumed it was her husband—stood by her side and smiled as well. There was a fragrance in the air of something expensive, like the shoes my Mutti liked to buy. It was the smell of leather, and everything was arranged elegantly. A purse with a silk scarf draped over it. A belt next to matching gloves in the same soft leather.

"Can we help?" they both asked in unison, and both of them came around the counter to shake my hand. Suddenly, I had no idea what to do. I wanted to say something like, *My Mutti likes to wear soft gloves, and wouldn't she love a leather handbag, and the silk scarf is so lovely . . .* but nothing came to me. I realized I had no business whatsoever in a shop like this one. I had not a single Pfennig, and even if I did, what would I, a fourteen-year-old girl, want in a store such as this? I said only "Guten Tag"—"Have a good day"—and ran out the door. I was shy and ashamed of myself, and I was scared I would be scolded. For all I knew, Karl Spaeth could have been standing at the parlor window and seen what I had done. And so, red-faced, I ran. That was the last time I walked on that side of the street.

I still wonder: *How did those shopkeepers feel? Weren't they scared?* If I had had the courage, I would have asked these things. I would have said what was in my heart. But I got no answers to those questions, because I never asked them.

They were quiet people. This I knew about them. I never saw them walking in the street as I did other neighbors. In fact, I never saw them other than that one time, and my parents never brought them up at the dinner table, either.

## II.

I find it interesting that "Spaeth" also means "late" in German. It was the name of my stepfather, and I tell you this because I was becoming a woman. My body was growing up, and there were moments when I saw Karl notice. He was an unhappy man—this I knew. He was difficult, and he brooded often. His voice had become colder when he spoke to me. Sometimes I would see his eyes turn tiny and peer strangely at me from around the corners of the house. It frightened me, and so I stopped looking at him. He now often turned away from me, too, as I talked, as if what I said offended him. And so I stopped talking to him. It seemed he spent his days now finding reasons not to like me.

It came to this: He would beat me. It didn't happen all at once; it came sporadically at first, and then, only a hard slap across the face. I thought it was because Mutti had allowed me to cut my hair short, and it was no longer in braids like a girl. Or perhaps it was because I had started attending the Tanzschule and was interested in womanly things, like the lipstick I wore once to a dance. Or that there were boys my age who sat beside me on the S-Bahn. Perhaps it was all these things, and I thought so because too often I heard him say, when telling a story about something he was displeased with, "And such behavior from a woman …" I began to believe all his stories were about me.

Then something happened. He surprised me at the door as I was coming home. The bird eyes of Karl Spaeth were squeezed into a squint, and he was holding a cane in his hand.

"What are you thinking, with your coat open like that?" he shouted, and then stepped forward and hit me across my back. I ran that time to my room and closed my door to him. I slammed it shut, and I began to hate him.

A week went by. I avoided him. I took my breakfast alone whenever possible. I tried to arrive home early and run to my room quietly. Perhaps being on time would make him less angry. But then it happened again. He was at the door when I came home, and I wasn't even late. Eventually it became a common thing, seeing him at the door. He would use whatever he could find just there in the hallway when I walked in. A cane or an umbrella. "Why?" I would ask sometimes, as I hid my face from him to keep it from becoming bruised.

It was, I assumed, if not because I was late, then because my coat was open too wide. Or because my hair was messy, or because I laughed too loud. I never quite knew. The only answer he ever gave was "Because it's time again."

A day came when the authorities from the school wanted to know why. They came to our home and wanted to speak with my parents.

They were concerned, they said, because I was always so black and blue and my eyes were always so swollen. Was there a problem in the home? I only heard about this visit when I came home from school later that day. The authorities had come and gone and Karl Spaeth was at the door once again, holding his cane. He beat me hard, and he ran after me and beat me even more. This time he said it was because I had turned him in to the Nazis.

It was rumored (I had never heard it, but I never paid much attention either) that we, the members of the HJ and the BDM, should listen well at home and report any discussions of "anti-loyalty." Anti-loyalty? To what? To the Partei? I never listened much when these talks were held at the BDM either. They were always such nonsense. *Quatsch*. My girlfriends and I always sat in the back and played Käsekasten or a game we called *Schafskopf*, "sheep's brain," but its meaning is more like "dumbass" or something else. It must have been the "anti-indoctrination game" because we seem to have played it a lot during these meetings. We really never paid attention. It was all too stupid to listen to. Once our BDM leader caught us playing and she took our cards from us, but that was the extent of my involvement in the meetings.

To report my parents to the authorities, the idea of it, never crossed my mind. I was a grown-up girl, and I had my own ideas of right and wrong. The Nazis and their ideals never impressed me much, and neither, it seemed, did they impress my parents. My parents never spoke about the Nazis at home, or about Adolf Hitler. (Except that day I was beaten, when Karl Spaeth—I could no longer call him Papa—screamed that I was a "Nazi traitor," of all things.) Not since we had moved to Berlin, anyway, did they speak of the Nazis, and besides, it was known now that opinions had become a thing of the past. Speaking out was against the law. Mutti had learned that all too well from the unidentified phone caller when we were still in Swinemünde.

## III.

Again, I'll tell you what I knew about the Jews. It was not much, and it was even less that I understood, but I did see this once. It was on the Kantstrasse, a fancy street with expensive shops: clothing stores and confectionary stores, stores for briefcases and leather coats, and pastry shops. The Kantstrasse was just around the corner from my S-Bahn station in Charlottenburg.

A girl stood at the intersection of the Kantstrasse and the Kaiser-Friedrich-Strasse with a sandwich board strapped over her shoulders. From the front and from behind, everyone was to read, I SLEPT WITH A JEW. That's all it said, and this girl stood there, day after day, for many days, perhaps a week, and maybe even longer. I felt so sorry for her. Did she have food? She cried sometimes, I saw her tears; I think she was scared, and I was certain she would never do it again. I was scared too, for I was beginning to see what this "new regime" really meant.

~

Then this happened. The date fell in the middle of the school week. It was November 9, 1938. I had gone to bed early; there was to be an exam the next day in Geometry and, as everyone knew, I hated the Maths. Mutti and her husband had retired early, and Dieter, who had just turned thirteen, was the only one still awake. He happened to be in the parlor, doing something, writing perhaps, when suddenly there was commotion down below in the street, and it caused him to run to the window and draw the curtains aside. What he witnessed made him run to my room quite out of breath and shout, "Margarete, hurry! You must come! Come and look! It's a terrible thing! *Komm her! Schnell! Guck mal was da los ist!*" He couldn't believe what was going on in the street. I ran with him down the hall to the front room.

There, outside our parlor window, we saw it with our own eyes, the men in brown uniforms, the SA. They were screaming at the leather shop people: "*Raus! Raus! Ihr sollt raus! Ihr seit Juden. Raus!*" We stood with our mouths wide open and watched. As they were screaming, they smashed the store window with sacks filled with rocks, the window that displayed the lovely bags and the pretty gloves, the same window that had the sign that read JEWISH ESTABLISHMENT. DO NOT DO BUSINESS WITH JEWS.

This night would become known as Kristallnacht, the Night of Broken Glass. I didn't see the woman or the man, the couple who so kindly offered me their help that day. I never saw them again, nor did I know what to do about what I had witnessed. Tell my parents? What would they do? The room would become silent with anxious looks. I already knew this. Tell the authorities? It was the authorities that had done the window smashing. I could only think as a naïve young girl could think—these people must have done something very, very bad.

At school the next day, we were dismissed early. It was my confirmation class, and Pastor Jentsch told us to go home. "The Synagogue is burning," he said. That was all. He didn't say why; he only looked worried. His face was white, stern. Or scared. I didn't know which, but I knew something had gone wrong. Later, on the radio, we heard that synagogues were to be destroyed, because the Jews were holding secret meetings in them, and secret meetings were against the law. I supposed that meant all of the synagogues had to be burned.

The next day, again, we were dismissed early. This teacher told us to leave, to go home, to study. This was the same teacher, the Maths teacher, who had always refused to say "Heil Hitler" when he entered the room and we stood in response. Rather, he simply said, "Setzt Euch"—please sit—which now was not only improper but against the law.[8] He too looked very worried, but he still did not raise his arm or say "Heil Hitler," and I can only wonder what ever happened to him.

I left my class and walked down the street from my school in Schmargendorf, and as I passed it, I saw that the retirement home for elderly Jewish people was empty. All the windows and doors were wide open, and there were SS men everywhere. That building never again had people in it. It would stay empty until it was no longer there—only a few more months.

⁓

A German diplomat had been killed in Paris. This was the story we were told over the radio in the following days, and the killer was a Jew. This was the propaganda we heard and the reason we were given for purging the Jews.

You could feel it. There was something terrible in the air, something that never went away again. It was fear. I felt it, and I saw it in the eyes of others as I passed them in the street. No one spoke about anything anymore. Anything relevant, that is. Speaking, we all knew, would land us in a prison somewhere. Even telling a joke against the regime could get you picked up. So no one spoke, and I could not ask questions of anyone. Not my parents. They didn't speak about things. And to ask Karl Spaeth only meant he could get angry at me again. For the first time in a very long time, I wept because I missed my real Papa, the man named Werner.

# 6

## The Announcement Came

### I.

My membership in the BDM allowed me to get close to the Führer one day. It was 1939 by now, and it was his birthday. A huge parade, one such as Berlin had never seen, had been planned to celebrate it. Germany had just marched into Prague, and the Sudetenland was to be German once again. There was euphoria everywhere in the streets. To have taken back the land that had been disputed since time immemorial was, for us, a great accomplishment. It meant, for one thing, we would stop repaying France the unbearable debt the Versailles Treaty had required of us and use the money instead to rebuild our own country.

You must understand, we in Germany had had a very difficult time. We had hyperinflation, and everywhere neighbors, people we knew, were out of work. There were long lines of men, men like Bertha's father, who wanted work but could find no work. The Versailles Treaty that was signed after the Great War was intended to ensure we would never be a world power again. Germany was being counted on to rebuild the European infrastructure that had been badly damaged during the Great War, but to do so would take another ninety years. And paying off the debt we owed, as we understood it, would take more money than Germany even had in its gold reserves.

It was, in truth, an impossible task, and it threw our country into chaos. The new German regime stopped making the payments, and Hitler saw to it that our six million unemployed men had work again. People were elated. Men began building new roads and railway lines. There was such enthusiasm, such euphoria, suddenly. There were many people who spoke, in the early days, with excitement about Hitler. The radio talked about it, constantly. No wonder the air around this day, April 20, 1939, was a festive one.

One day earlier our building manager, Frau Schulz, had come to our door to deliver a flag with the new swastika on it. "It's been implied by the law, Frau Spaeth," she told my Mutti when she was asked why. "I believe it even *is* the law that this flag is hung where it can be seen. I was notified of this. *Each house with a window facing the street must hang our new flag.*"

When she saw Mutti's hesitation, she added, "Take it anyway, Frau Spaeth. It was a gift, no one asked for money," and so Mutti hung it in our parlor window, the one facing the street. On the day of the big parade, I noticed that everywhere—lampposts and houses alike—there was a swastika hanging. Every window was bright, everywhere there were red banners, and the atmosphere was filled with excitement. For me, it was even more so because my particular troop of BDM girls were going to be very near the parliament building, the Reichskanzlei, just there on the Friedrichstrasse.

We were each given a large bouquet of roses, red ones with long stems that we would throw onto the Führer's car as it drove by. With any luck, I could be in the front line, as I hoped I would be, and I would see this man, the one who said he was going to save our country.

And it did happen. I did stand in the front row, and I was able to throw roses onto Hitler and into his car as it drove past. Tears were in my eyes, and I was euphoric. I cried the same tears Bertha had cried: tears of joy. *What joy?* I wonder now. I never even knew what all the fuss was about anyway. I'd had a good life, no one in my family had suffered up to that time. We had money, we had food, we even had a telephone when no one else did, and my Papa always had work. But I was moved by the feeling that day, just as so many other people were moved by it, and as the Führer's car drove past me, I saw him wave, and I even imagined he was waving to *me*. This man who looked much too small inside his large Mercedes, and I do remember I was surprised to see *he* didn't give the Heil Hitler salute at all, merely a bent arm with his hand held as if it hurt—the one I thought might be waving at me.

Later, years later, Papa Spaeth told me Adolf Hitler always had such terrible breath. "It was impossible to be in the same room with him. You would want to find a window somewhere and open it wide and then stand very close to it so that you could at least have a moment of fresh air," he said. He told me this after the war was over, but talk like this would have been impossible now, and even though my Papa Spaeth would have preferred to serve another man, an egalitarian man, a righteous one, he said nothing. He did what he was supposed to do: his work.

So Hitler had bad breath! All that shouting and waving, all that stuff he did to make himself look so important, his screaming, not to mention that silly *Schnurrbart,* that idiotic patch of a mustache he wore, and no one could even get close!

## II.

We were at the Wannsee when the announcement came. It was a Sunday, I remember it clearly. Mutti, Dieter, and I had arrived early that day at this lake with its long white beach that ran all along the Grunewald Forest near Potsdam, just south of Berlin. It was our favorite place to spend our Sundays.

There was a low and rather long building at the entry to the beach, a pavilion of sorts, and it was surrounded by a wooded area. We could change our clothes in this building, and we could buy milk and Brötchen with cheese there. It had been built at the turn of the century, and it had that majestic feel of times past: a lazy time when things moved slower and women still wore dresses when they entered the water, every one of them carrying a parasol, and men wore straw hats.

*Strandkörbe,* large chairs made of woven rattan, with high backs and a curved roof, stood here and there in a sort of disorganized fashion all along the otherwise tidy beach. Under the roof of each was a blue striped cushioned seat where two people could sit comfortably and enjoy looking out over the water at the other sunbathers and still have some protection from the sun. There was even a sort of curtain—also blue-and-white striped—that you could shut if you needed to hide yourself to change into swimwear. Under the seat was a drawer where you could put your towels and hats, and Dieter and I always filled it with the books we brought to read. The Strandkörbe were much in demand and could often be found fully occupied, so we had come early that morning to be sure we would have one—Mutti leading the way, Dieter and I running behind with our picnic basket and towels. We had made sandwiches with Schinken and thick smears of lard, and we brought pickles Mutti had made from cucumbers.

Our towels were laid out, our books placed into the drawer, and Mutti was fussing with a long scarf she was trying to tie around her hair. Children were running along the water, screaming at each other about something, and a ball was rolling by just as the announcement came. It was loud, blaring from the speakers that were mounted high on the roof of the pavilion and pointed toward the beach. We all heard it, clearly, and everyone stopped what he or she was doing.

"As of 5:45 this morning, we are returning fire for fire . . ." It was only a part of Hitler's speech, but we already knew what was to come next. We already knew. We were, as of 5:45 that morning, at war with Poland. It was September 1, 1939, and Poland was our new enemy.[9]

This early morning announcement gave reason to what my aunt in East Prussia said she had witnessed during the weeks before: trainloads of soldiers, every day, and several times each day. And all the trains were heading east. "We all said to one another, 'Isn't it odd? It certainly looks like we're going to war.'" Tante Emma had told Mutti this only days earlier over the telephone.

This early morning announcement also gave reason to something else we had heard over the evening news broadcast. It was the last day

Helga with her children at the Wannsee. "It was a Sunday. I remember it clearly."

of August. There was nothing particularly special about that day, but we would all learn in the years to come that it was a day that would change the world forever. A radio station near the Polish border, Sender Gleiwitz, broadcast the news that night, news that Hitler said was clearly anti-German propaganda. And he said it made it clear that Germany needed to attack Poland. We had heard it all on the radio, shouted at us in his whiny voice.

I was now fifteen. I had had my birthday in July and I didn't know what all this would mean. Would I need to stop my studies and go to work? Worst of all, would I never be able to fulfill my dream of swimming in the Olympics? Would I be needed for the war? Mutti began to cry. "Wasn't one war enough? Wasn't it?" she kept sobbing as she hurried us to gather up our belongings. We were going home, and it was still so early in the day. With our bags and towels and sandwiches, the three of us ran past the signs that read NO JEWS ALLOWED and took the S-Bahn back to our home, Mutti's face now frozen. No more tears, no more words, just hurry hurry, and the sandwiches we had made just lay there on our table in the kitchen. No one had the appetite to eat.

～

"The first dead ones have been reported on the front . . ." came over the radio the morning of the second of September, and yes, it became clear, we now had more than one front: the western one with France, the front where we had just fought for the Rhineland, and now the radio let us know we had a new front. The eastern one with Poland. On the third day of September, we heard this: France has entered the war, and England has done the same.

## III.

Our car was requisitioned. That was the first effect of the war we felt personally. Some men from the SS came to our door and told us they wanted our car. They would pay us something for it, of course, but it was "for purposes of the war effort." Anyway, it would be impossible to purchase petrol from now on, they told us, as it too was needed for "the war effort," so our car would be useless even if we were to keep it.

The second new thing I noticed was that Berlin was to "stay dark." Suddenly, everywhere there were posters that read THE ENEMY SEES YOU. PUT OUT YOUR LIGHT. Leaflets were circulated, and everyone was instructed to know exactly what to do in case of an attack. Shutters were to be closed over the windows; blankets were to be hung to block out any stray light; the streets were to be black all night, no headlamps on our bicycles.

And yet life went along as if none of this mattered. We did what we were told and we rode our bicycles without headlamps. At night we closed our shutters. Even Unter den Linden, that lovely avenue of flowers, suddenly had camouflage netting spread over the top so it was as if we were now strolling under a huge tent, and we could no longer see the clouds. Still, none of this seemed to matter.

What did matter was the food. As soon as the war began, food rationing began as well. Suddenly we were supposed to use margarine instead of butter. *Margarine!* And it smelled so bad; just try to fry potatoes with that! Restaurants started serving soup made of everything they had. This became commonplace; all of them did it. And why all the soup tasted the same, I don't know, but it was, across the board, icky. Gray, tasteless, sometimes not even hot, with barely anything recognizable in it. This soup was served all over the city, sometimes even out in the streets. It came in large vats on wheels that we called *Gulaschkanonen*.

Although our ration cards with the tear-off coupons, *Essensmarken*, said we were allotted a certain amount of bread and meat per person each month, and for each person in the household there would be soap and clothing, based on what was deemed to be sufficient, there never seemed to be enough.[10] On the black market, of course, this was not true, and everyone began to look for what they needed there. The most famous area for the black market was right under the Nazis' noses! Right in front of the Reichskanzlei.

The food rationing was unsettling. Sometimes we were hungry—Mutti just couldn't find food to buy, even with our ration cards. Other times there was more than plenty of something, but only that one something—grapefruits, for example. Bread was not what it used to be either, and sometimes it wasn't even available at the baker's. A sign would hang in the window saying NO BREAD TODAY, and that was that. Our table was often more bare than we were used to, or, at the very least, we had to be more creative to make do with what we could get.[11]

For example, once Berlin's markets were flooded with curly endive. Every night, night after night, we ate *Endiviensalat*, something I will never eat again. Night after night I stayed hungry, refusing to eat it. This went on for weeks, it seemed. Then suddenly we had cantaloupe, lots and lots of cantaloupe, and I don't know where we got them all, but we had to eat cantaloupe.

Mutti tried. She shopped every day, looking for what was available. She knew the bakery family well, a man and his wife and their young son. Every morning Mutti would walk down to the bakery—it was only at the end of our street—to buy our morning Brötchen, and she would always hear the latest news from Frau Ritter, who would already have been awake since four in the morning, baking.

"Frau Spaeth! How are things with you? And your children?" And Mutti would ask the same of her. "How is your son? He's grown so much. I saw him just the other day on his bicycle! My, but that boy learns fast. It seems only months since you were pushing him in the buggy!"

"And what will it be for you this morning, Frau Spaeth? We haven't got much, but I know Dieter loves these *Mohnsemmel*, and we happen to have received poppy seeds just yesterday. I saved some for you."

Oh, how Dieter always loved the Brötchen with poppy seeds on them, and Frau Ritter, the baker's wife, had a special place in her heart for him. She had lost a son in childbirth, and he would have been the same age as Dieter. Always she asked about him. What is he learning? How are his manners? Is he becoming a gentleman?

Mutti told her about his studies and that he loved reading, and then, even when there was no flour, or the bread they had baked had already been sold, or the baker had to hang a sign in the window saying NO BREAD TODAY, Mutti still walked there each morning. "I do it for the ritual. What else will I do with my morning?" she'd say.

No one had coffee anymore. No one! Can you imagine? We were to drink *Ersatzkaffee* now. Always the reason was that the coffee or the bread, or the meat or the sausage, was needed for the war effort. Was it being shipped to the front? I wondered. But then, I thought, why can soldiers have coffee but we can't?

Ersatzkaffee looked black like coffee but tasted like hot dirt. It was not made from coffee beans—there was not a grain of coffee in this Ersatzkaffee—but there were other things in it, like chicory or, even worse, burnt wheat grains. The Ersatzkaffee never had the aroma you expected to have with a pot of brewing coffee either, nor did it have caffeine. *Muckefuck* is the name we gave it, and it was a funny name, and we said it jokingly and with a smile on our faces. Everybody had it, and because everybody had it, it didn't feel so bad. No one had caffeine, and so everyone was "in a bad mood," as Mutti put it. "It's just the way things are now."

Mutti did her best to provide for the family—she'd get a bag of potatoes and cook a soup with them, or beets and try to do the same— but I wasn't grateful for her efforts. I was a young girl who wanted her freedom, and besides, my Mutti had become my enemy since I turned fifteen. Hadn't she failed to defend me all those times when Karl Spaeth held his cane up against me? Hadn't she stood by, watching? Gloating, even, as if she were getting back at me? "Why am I being beaten?" I would ask. "For what?" And he would answer, "Because it's time again."

And she? She just looked on and had her own answers. "Because you've become a woman" may have been one of them. Because I was a woman and she was growing old. Perhaps that was why, but I stopped caring about what she thought and hated her instead.

Then there were the clothes Mutti bought for me. Those too were rationed, with each family having enough "points," supposedly, to provide adequately, but they were never adequate. Our clothes were always too small or too large or very ragged, and our shoes never fit. The points that were allotted were enough for one pair of shoes per child per year, according to Mutti. And only enough for one outfit per child per year. So, Mutti decided, *my* clothes had to be "unisex" so that my brother would be able to wear them after me. My sweaters should be brown, and my blouses buttoned down the middle. My shoes stayed on my feet until well past being too small, and these, too, needed to fit Dieter when I was done with them. My toes grew crooked, my feet always hurt, and the shoes were brown.

## IV.

No one really noticed, or, I should say, we tried not to notice the changes. They came slowly, and as Berliners have a certain Berliner sense of humor, we tried to laugh our way through them, believing these conditions would last only a short time.

Across the street from our home and to the right was a restaurant with a *Biergarten* behind it, a patio of sorts, where the men in the neighborhood would sit and drink a *Krug* of beer during their lunch hour in times past. Herr Stichler—perhaps that was his name—owned the restaurant, but I should really call it a tavern, because it was a place where everyone came to sit and talk and have a drink and maybe some food as well. Herr Stichler was a particularly amusing man, always laughing at something funny he had just told a guest, and he always had a kind word for me.

On an evening when Karl would want a Krug of beer for himself or a bottle of wine for the family at dinner, he would ask me to run over to the tavern, and I would do it happily, as Herr Stichler would always make me laugh. "Na, so was?" he would say, acting surprised, every time I came into his tavern. "What do we have here? Fräulein Margarete again?" And he'd smile broadly, taking Karl's Krug, the pewter mug with his Bavarian family crest painted into the porcelain finish, and, lifting the top with the thumb handle, he'd open the tap and fill it for me. And on days when my assignment was to fetch a bottle of wine, he'd say, "*Ach ja!* Again a festive night at the Spaeths!"

Herr Stichler had a thick mustache that hung low over his mouth and always made him look like he was about to sneeze. His eyebrows, too, hung low over his eyes, and I thought he looked like St. Nikolaus with his white hair and red-checkered shirt and round red cheeks like Christmas balls. His wife, Frau Stichler, stayed small and quiet most times, but she too would come forward with a joke or two if she saw the opportunity.

In the days before rationing, Papa sometimes asked me to fetch a *Bauernplatte* from the tavern. This "farmer's plate" was served on a wooden board, which was piled high with whatever meats and cheeses the restaurant had that day: sausages, *Schmierwurst*—a soft sausage, much like liverwurst—and cheeses from Holland, like Edamer, or even that stinky one from the town of Limburg. And there were pickles and capers and mustards. This is what we would have for our dinner on many nights. Oh, if I'd known how I would miss having a Bauernplatte for dinner!

❧

It was *Sylvester*, the last day of 1939. New Year's Eve, and the war was already four months old. Germany had defeated Poland and the Sudetenland was back in our hands, and we were now bound by a "nonaggression pact" with Russia. Everything seemed to be coming to an end. We all believed the war would be over very, very soon, and that we would have peace—and a life without food rationing—once again. No one lived as though the changes, the food shortages, and the automobile requisitions would last.

Our house was still red with the air of Christmas from a week before. Mutti had brought out all our Christmas tablecloths, which were fully embroidered in red, and little Swedish elves made of straw, called *tomtar*, with tiny red vests and red elf caps, adorned our mantel. And, as with every Christmas holiday, every room each evening was aglow with candlelight. In the middle of our parlor stood the tree, which, even though a week old, was still festive. It looked magical, this Christmas tree, with its angels and dwarves—*Heinzelmännchen*, we called them—made of gold and silver foil that hung from its branches, and when Mutti lit all of its candles each evening, it seemed to come alive.

Papa Spaeth decided we should have a party. It had been a horrific year and 1940 surely would bring better news, so it should be brought in with celebration. Our cousins, our *Onkel* and *Tante*, and all the neighbors from the building would come.

I was sent to the tavern across the street to buy red wine, four bottles of it, so Mutti could make her glögg. It's called *Glühwein* in German and is made with red wine, a cinnamon stick, cloves, sugar, and lemon slices, peels and all. All this is heated to just below boiling and then served in mocha cups. Blanched almonds and a few cloves are placed in the cup before the glögg is poured, and when you're finished with your cup, you can tip it up and eat the almond, which has now turned pink. You can imagine what it took for Mutti to have all these ingredients! But it was to be a great party, and only the best would do.

It had snowed hard that day, and it was desperately cold. I tied a scarf around my neck and put on my wool hat and mittens, my boots, heavy socks, and a big overcoat just to run across the street to the tavern for the wine. I held my scarf up against my face and ran quickly through the crunching snow.

Herr Stichler was, as usual, in a humorous mood and immediately made a joke about "what a lush this young girl must be to be running through such nasty weather just for some wine." He smiled, and then he handed me the only bottles of wine he said he had. "Your Mutti told me about the Swedish wine, and I've been saving these for her," he said as he reached under the counter and produced the bottles.

Only days earlier, all over Berlin, placards had been posted. Sure, I had seen them, but I had not paid much attention. Herr Stichler certainly had something to say about them, though.

"Can you believe this?" he exclaimed, mostly to himself, as there was no one else in the tavern, but he was looking me straight in the eye.

"What is it?" I asked, sure it was none of my business. He was an adult, after all, and I was still just a girl.

"Those placards we now have all over the city!"

Oh, yes, the placards. The ones that stated: NO ONE SHALL BE HUNGRY. NO ONE SHALL FREEZE. I asked him if those were the ones he was talking about.

"Of course!" And of course, Herr Stichler had something more to say about that. "Yes. Right. Now we're not even allowed to be hungry anymore!"

I had to laugh. Things were desperate—we read in the paper that a man had been found frozen in the street, and coal was being rationed. But this man could still be funny.

"Yes, true. I have seen them. And yes, now even that's *verboten!*" We both had a good New Year's laugh over that.

"Please pass along to your parents wishes for a very happy Sylvester evening," Herr Stichler said then, winking. And while he did that, he reached under the counter once more and handed me yet one more bottle of red wine, saying, "Just because it's time again!"

So the last night of the year 1939 was festive and full of laughter. The Schulzes and the Ahlbecks from upstairs, our cousins and Tante and Onkel, who took the train in to Berlin for the evening, and us, the

Spaeths and the Doses—we all gathered to have what we never would have believed would be our last celebration together in that house.

It was the only time I ever saw Papa Spaeth drunk. He joked till tears rolled down his cheeks, and someone began to sing a folk song and we all joined in, and before the last refrain we were suddenly all holding hands and dancing. We danced through the house, up and down the stairs, and around the spindly Christmas tree with its foil hangings and magical candles, Karl Spaeth in the lead. He was in such a good mood, making everyone laugh. How easy it was to be around my parents when everyone was happy and no one was concerned about things. No one scolding or telling us what we had done wrong.

Dieter and our three cousins, Hans-Hermann, Gerhard—Gert, as we called him—and Fritz, and I all sneaked back into the kitchen several times during that night when no one was paying attention, and we filled our own cups with the glögg. We probably filled them too many times, but why not, we said, we can celebrate just as well as they can.

Dieter was very good at showing off how well he could run the entire length of the hallway runner, stepping only on the flower patterns and never in the spaces in between. We all tried it and of course we were too drunk to succeed, and so we fell over and then tried it again, the next time trying to step on only the leaf patterns, which was even harder. Fritz kept falling, and we'd laugh some more.

When we finally tired of our game, and I finally managed the runner without falling, we returned to the front room to join the adults. We arrived just in time to see that our Papa Spaeth and Herr Schulz, the house manager, had decided that the Christmas tree, which was still standing in the middle of the room, should be removed, and it seemed they had been in a rather serious conversation about it for quite some time.

It was our stepfather who stood with his hands on his hips, then stepped over to the window and opened it wide to the street below.

"Out!" he said, pointing. That was all it took for Herr Schulz to grab the top half of the tree while Papa Spaeth took hold of the trunk and the two of them half sang, half giggled the words, "Eins. Zwei. Dreiiii!"—and out it flew, candles and all. We children ran to the window to see where it had landed.

What a sight! Snowflakes falling so heavy you could hardly see to the street below, candles still burning, and a dead Christmas tree lying in the street like a corpse.

The next morning, Papa Spaeth and Mutti were still in a party mood, still talking about how fun the night had been, and suddenly Papa Spaeth, with a puzzled look on his face, exclaimed, "What happened to the Christmas tree?" There was a bare spot, still scattered with pine needles, where that tree had been. And then Dieter, grinning from ear to ear, said, "But, Papa. Look. Look outside!" He took Papa Spaeth's hand and led him to the window and pointed down to the street.

"There. See?"

"How terribly odd!" Papa exclaimed. "How on earth did the tree get there?"

"But, don't you remember, Papa? Last night? You and Herr Schulz threw it out the window."

"No, no. That's impossible!" He must have been pulling our leg, but he forever talked about that Christmas tree lying in the street as if it were a great mystery. He always ended his story with, "I can't understand why there was a Christmas tree lying in the middle of the street!"

# 7.

# THAT'S JUST HOW IT IS NOW

## I.

As the spring of 1940 rolled into summer, food became more and more scarce, or strange. Sometimes there would be strawberries for days on end, but there would be no milk. There would be exotic new vegetables, but no bread. A time would come when we could remark once again, "Look at all the lovely jams. Real fruits!"—but not now, and not for six years yet to come. We called our jams "I.G. Farben," the name of a famous German chemical factory, because there wasn't really anything recognizable in them, just colors that looked more like chemical compounds than anything edible.[12]

The milk farmer still came around with his dairy truck whenever he could, and Mutti would tell me to run out to have our milk can filled or to purchase some cheese from him. But even his supplies were needed to go to the front first. Less and less, we heard the *clip-clop, clip-clop* of his horses' hooves on the cobblestone.

## II.

Dieter was now fourteen, old enough to join the HJ, the Hitler Youth. He was still a soft boy, young for his age, and his voice had not gone through the change yet. He wore glasses already, because, as Papa Spaeth said, he read too much.

And I was beginning to figure some things out: Hitler was not our ally, and the war was no longer making sense. We had invaded Poland, and no one seemed to know why. No one was ecstatic the way they were when we "liberated" Czechoslovakia and the Rhineland. Things were beginning to feel wrong and frightening, and all I could think and wonder was, *Won't this war be over soon?* And my close friends felt the same way. We began to listen to the BBC, but this was not an easy thing. It was illegal, and we knew that. It had been outlawed at the start of the war to listen to *any* foreign station; to do so and get caught could land you in a prison, a work camp, or worse yet—dead.

Ilse and Hilde and I did it anyway. We hid in our basements and put a blanket over our heads and listened. They broadcast in German, but it was the British news, and it didn't sound anything like what we were hearing on our German propaganda stations. The German radio played symphonies, which were lovely, and then schmaltzy polkas, which didn't interest me in the least, and then the boring speeches of the Führer and of Göring about all the "victories" our brave German soldiers were accomplishing. But the BBC told us something very different. Britain was hoping the United States would enter the war *against us*, when we were still hearing propaganda on our radio stations that America was fully behind us!

❧

Dieter often brought friends to our house—something I rarely dared. Somehow no one got angry with him, only with me, and my bringing a friend home would only cause trouble with Karl, or at least that's what I believed.

One of Dieter's friends was Otto Lippert. Otto told me one day that he wanted to become an insurance mathematician.

"Where did you get a crazy idea like that?" I asked. "There's no such thing as an insurance mathematician!"

"You don't even know what you're talking about," he said. "Of course there's such a thing as an insurance mathematician!"

"Well, then, fine. I'd like to become a beautician mathematician," I shot back at him, and we both had to laugh.

"Bakery mathematician!"

"Veterinary mathematician!"

"Musician mathematician!"

"Swim instructor mathematician!"

"Farming mathematician!"

"Butcher mathematician!"

"Street-sweeping mathematician!"

"*Street*-sweeping mathematician?"

Both of us stopped and looked at each other and held our sides for laughter.

"*Street*-sweeping mathematician? *Right-o*," I said—something I'd heard on the BBC, and something I realized I'd better keep my mouth shut about. How would I know such a phrase? So I stopped myself, and we continued the banter.

"Of course. One must sweep just so, and pile the rubbish just so, and piles should be organized just so. And of course this must be done precisely at the right time," and we drew out patterns in the rug as we joked. And every time we saw each other from then on, we winked at each other as if to say, *Yup, that's the job for me: street-sweeping mathematician.*

These boys were only a year younger than I, but they seemed so very innocent. And stupid, really. I would have arguments with them, and Dieter would take their side. "Can't you see what's going on around us?" I'd say, and they'd say, "Yes, of course we can see what's going on around us," and there was no end to it. They saw only good intentions, a quick end to the war, and a victorious outcome for our country.

I, of course, didn't let them know that my friends and I listened to the BBC. Even to breathe a hint of illegal activity could bring trouble. A friend of Dieter's, perhaps someone who really believed in our government or who was just dumb enough, could call the officials to report me. It was easy to do. You didn't even need to identify yourself or have proof that the deed was actually done; you just needed to say you saw such and such.

A young Dieter in uniform.

You just needed to pick up the telephone or walk into the government offices and report something you thought *might* be illegal.

Dieter came home one day with his new Hitler Youth uniform on, and I spotted him as he stood in the front hallway, observing himself in the mirror, so proud of himself. The brown shorts and the white kneesocks and a tie and, of course, the swastika emblem on his red armband. He looked up and noticed me in the reflection and said, "Margarete! Look at me. I'm one of our men now! I'll finally be able to serve my country!"

I stood shocked. "Oh, Dieter, Dieter! You're so wrong! You're so, so wrong!" We never spoke at home about the politics of our country. We knew it was verboten, and especially because my Papa Spaeth was in the navy and was serving our country, verboten was the law in our house. But I was old enough; I could see very well what was going on around me, and I said to him in a very direct tone, "Don't be so idealistic, Dieter! Don't you see what's happening? We're at war! We're invading countries we have no business invading! Food is being rationed, and who knows what else will come of this. Don't be such a fool!"

Dieter just stared at me, an amazed look on his face. "What are you saying? Hitler intends only to save our country. He has said so many times in his speeches. And that's exactly what he's doing. He has saved the Sudetenland; he has taken back the Alsace area, land that has always been German. People are working again. What are you saying?"

"Why, oh why, do you believe such nonsense? Don't you know the rest of the world is against us? France and England? Oh, Dieter, Dieter, don't be a fool!" And we argued and argued, and I never got through to him, and I was scared for his sake. He listened to all the propaganda that they fed those boys in the HJ, and he believed it all. We would argue when we came home from school, and we would argue when we did our chores, and then he would bring home the *Völkischer Beobachter*, the Nazi propaganda newspaper, to try to prove to me all the good things the Nazis were accomplishing.[13]

What we did together was go to church, and it was every Sunday, and afterward we would spend our time talking late into the afternoon—about God and what was true and what was false. Dieter was very devout—maybe this is why he refused to see there was anything wrong with the world. He thought everyone had good intentions, that all people had a good heart and that they only wanted what was good and that all intentions for this war were good and that things would all turn out just that way—good.

## III.

Karl Spaeth was home less and less. He had much to do at the OKM Oberkommando, and this should have come as no surprise. After all, Germany was at war. He was close to many of those in higher positions at the Oberkommando, and I met a number of them when they came to visit on occasion. These men would join us for dinner and then withdraw to what they called their "salon." They would stand around in the parlor with their cigars and discuss things that I was never included in.

But I did overhear some things. "*Ja*. Well, he says, 'Even Chamberlain and Dadalier gave glowing reports. Even they are happy we freed Czechoslovakia and Austria.'" Then, "That man's not to be trusted. He's doing things that no law in the German books would ever allow. How is he getting away with this?"

I could hear from the tone of their voices that these men were serious and they were not pleased with how our Führer was handling things. As these meetings continued, the talks became more serious. Many years later, when I spoke with Papa Spaeth about these nights—and yes, I did come to call him "Papa" again—he confided in me that these "salons" were a small part of what was a loosely knit organization of German officers called the Schwarze Kapelle, the Black Orchestra.

❧

Maybe it was a day when the family was expecting guests—Karl often invited them—I can't remember, but Mutti had baked a cake with whatever ingredients she could find. It had been baked in a Bundt pan, and who knows what she used to make it smell so good! Could it have been real flour and butter and eggs? I came home after swim training, and I was exceedingly hungry. As I was every day. Even before the rationing, I was a child who liked to eat, but now I was twice so. I saw the cake sitting on the stove to cool, and I don't know what got into me, but I took a knife and cut myself a healthy chunk and ate it. Boy, *that* tasted good! As if it had real butter in it and real sugar sprinkled over the top, and it was still warm, and just the smell of it made my mouth water for more.

And then, just as I was about to swallow the last bite, bent over the stove, knowing it was a wrong thing to do, Mutti entered the kitchen and stopped in her tracks. She looked at me, horrified. I turned around with crumbs still hanging off my chin when she let out a scream. "*Ach!* What have you done! What have you done! My cake . . . my cake! You've ruined it!" She burst into tears, her hands wringing the apron that now had several mended spots on it.

Oh, how sorry I was for what I had done! I knew immediately I was in deep trouble, but what could I do? The cake was already in my stomach, and how was I to change that?

Karl Spaeth heard her scream and immediately came running into the kitchen from the desk in his office, and he had one of his *You're about to get it* scowls on his face. I was relieved to see he was not holding his cane, but I could see too that he was not about to let that stop him.

"You ate Mutti's cake?" he shouted, staring straight at me with his blue beady eyes. "The one she's been baking all day? The one she worked so hard to get the ingredients for? You? You, you filthy cow, you should have that cake?"

He used the word *Vieh,* which is worse than cow, a dirty farm animal, but at least he didn't say *Hure,* which he had flung at me once before, but because Mutti was standing here in the kitchen listening, the word "whore" did not come out of his mouth, a word no one of his gentility should ever use. He used that word only in private when I came home with my coat open and Mutti wasn't looking.

His face became redder and his hands began to shake. I knew something was coming, but I didn't expect this. He took the cake in both his hands and lifted it high over his head, then smashed it into my hair. When that was done, he rubbed what was left of it all over my face and chest with his slimy hands. Yes, my chest. This, too, he began to do now—touch me there. I looked down at my feet and felt so bad because of the wasted cake and the crumbs that were lying all around me on the floor.

I was not going to cry, though. Those days were gone. He could beat me all he wanted, but he was not going to see me cry ever again, so I stood there and watched while he did this. *He's making such a fool of himself,* I thought. What a waste it was that now there was no cake left at all. All that butter, all those eggs—gone. *Couldn't Mutti have at least sliced the rest of it up and served it on a nice plate?* I thought. But no one was asking me.

That evening, when the guests arrived, I was sent to my room as punishment, without dinner, and I was not allowed to be with the family guests. I don't think there was a dessert, though. The ruin of yet another night.

❧

My birthday in 1940 would be my first of five during wartime. Of course, I believed it was to be the *only* one during wartime. I was turning sixteen. I was becoming a woman, and I had only two more years of school before my Abitur. I wondered how it would be celebrated. Would anyone remember? It was, after all, wartime. Mutti always made such a fuss over food, and there was no doubt now that Karl Spaeth hated me.

I got out of bed in the morning and made my way to the kitchen. In times past I would surely have been greeted with a delightful surprise. A cake and a gift would have been sitting on the kitchen table. Certainly, I thought, Mutti has done *something* for me? Gingerly, I walked in. No aroma of coffee brewing. The tiles of the kitchen floor felt cold. No one else was awake. And there, on the table, I saw what I thought I remembered to be the old drapes that had adorned our living room windows when we first moved into this Wohnung. They were heavy drapes, a dark maroon color, made of velour.

"These are *hässlich!*" my mother had exclaimed back then. "Take them down immediately. They're ugly and they make the house much too dark. Ugly, ugly, ugly," she had said. I stood at that table and heard those words again: *hässlich, hässlich, hässlich.* My face fell. Could she have meant this to be my gift? I looked and I looked again, and I picked up the material. It had been cut and sewn and made into a bathrobe. A heavy, maroon—and ugly—bathrobe. And I assumed it was to be mine. In July?

How I hated her, then.

## IV.

From my street in Charlottenburg, I could take the S-Bahn all the way into the city center and get off at Potsdamer Platz and be able to shop. I, of course, had no money, but I loved to "shop" anyway. And so did my friends. Near there, at the Leipziger Platz, was a grand old department store several stories tall that could be reached using elevators, beautiful ones with wrought-iron gates, and each car had its own operator, dressed in a gray uniform, operating the elevator wheel. This store, our favorite, was once named Wertheim. It had a glass-topped atrium and a café that served nougat cake, and the higher up we went on the elevators, the more fancy and the more expensive the goods became. Mutti, when we first came to Berlin, shopped there for her dresses and hats and coats.

One day the name of the store, which had been owned by a Jewish family, was suddenly changed to AWAG. The acronym stood for something like "General Products Retailing Organization." When he thought he was out of hearing range of "busy ears," Karl Spaeth joked that AWAG also meant something else: *Aus Wut Arisch Geworden*— Because of Anger, Became Aryan!

Karl Spaeth knew things weren't going well for the Jews. His Jewish friends had left Germany long ago for Hungary and Romania, or the United States or Canada. One family he knew even emigrated to Palestine. And the other Jews? We never spoke about them at home. We always assumed everyone had emigrated, just as Karl Spaeth's friends had done. I don't believe he knew that the Jews in Germany, or in the rest of Europe, were being sent away to concentration camps and killed there. He was in the Kriegsmarine, the navy—not the SS, which was in the Nazi Party.

≈

There were five or six Jewish students in my class. I didn't know any of them, except, of course, my friend Hilde. Hilde was half Jewish, which I didn't think meant anything. Her mother was Jewish, and the family always hid her inside the house. I understand this now. At the time, I only felt sorry for Hilde's mother, always sitting at home. I can hardly remember what she looked like. Her face was always gray, and her eyes seemed far away in the distance behind a wall of cigarette smoke. I never really grasped the terror this woman must have lived in.

One day two SA men knocked on Hilde's door. Hilde was the one who answered, and she told me the whole story. They had come to confiscate the family radio, they said. The conversation between the two SA men who stood in her doorway, dressed in their brown uniforms and polished boots, and her mother went something like this:

"You are Jewish. We've come to confiscate your radio. You're no longer allowed to listen to radio broadcasts."

"Hilde was half Jewish, which I didn't think meant anything."

"And why not?"

"Because you're Jewish. We've already said this."

"But my husband isn't Jewish. What about him? Can't he listen?"

"Well, yes, if he's not Jewish, then he can listen."

"Then what about my children? They're half Jewish. Are they allowed to listen, or are they not allowed to listen?"

Both men stood in the doorway and looked stunned, and then they laughed. One of them came up with this answer: "Well, if they're half Jewish, I suppose it would be all right for them to listen, but they can listen with only one ear." And with that all three of them had a good laugh. Both men sat down with Hilde's Mutti and shared a smoke with her and then left the home, saying only, "Guten Tag."

Anyway, it wasn't permissible to listen to a foreign radio broadcast after the war started on September first, and listening to Hitler's endless speeches wasn't all that interesting. That's what I told Hilde when she told me her story. Oh, that she put up with me in my ignorance!

It wasn't only the Jews who had problems, though. It was anyone who was not German. Mutti's friend Katherine came to visit one day. The two of them were sitting in the kitchen. Katherine had her face in her hands and kept wiping her eyes and mouth with her handkerchief when I walked in. I sat down with them at the table, which was very large and in the middle of the kitchen, and Mutti poured me some tea. I tried to take Katherine's hand in mine. I wanted to let her know I'd listen.

"I'm supposed to divorce my husband," she cried into her hands. "They'll take me away, and they'll take my husband as well, if I don't do it. We've been married for twelve years! *Mein Gott*, what am I to do? Where am I to go? And he? What's to become of us?" Mutti couldn't console her; neither could I, and she spoke with such a heavy accent. What were we to do about it? Mutti and I sat as we watched her weep.

Katherine was British, but she had a German passport. The problem was she was married to an officer in the German army with a rather high rank, and although they were both citizens of Germany, marriage to a person stemming from an enemy country was no longer allowed. Katherine had been ordered to divorce her husband immediately, and that was the final word. The end of this story? She divorced him, as was proper, and they went their separate ways, as was proper. She moved to the country to live with her parents-in-law. Were they ever reunited? I don't know. Mutti never talked about her again after that day. "We all have our problems, this is war, and that's just how it is now." That's what we would say.

⁓

I noticed something from an experience I had on the S-Bahn, which I rode at the same time every morning. There were some young people my age who always sat in the very back of the train car. I thought to myself how arrogant they were that they never spoke to me. As we all rode the same train every day and were all the same age, wouldn't you think someone would introduce himself? Say hello? What school do you attend? Who are you? I suppose I could have made the first move, but I was too shy and I was alone. They were many.

Then one morning I noticed that they all had a yellow star sewn on the outside of their jackets. A few weeks went by, and I suddenly realized they were no longer on the train. Never again did I see them. It was war. And people disappeared. That was all I knew. I noticed it, but I thought no more of it. And then a time came when I just didn't see Jewish stars at all anymore.

That's when I should have begun to understand the significance of the *Ahnenpass*. We all had one—my Mutti, my brother, and I. It was a book that provided full identification of its holder. On the first page, the person's name, permanent address, and the parents' names appeared, with the official stamp of the Reich stamped at the bottom. Thirty-four pages were blank and neatly organized and numbered where all immediate relatives' names were to be entered, including the parents and the parents before them, and before them and before them. These entries were then officially verified and given the official stamp. To me, it was just a boring document. I did not think to draw any connection between the Ahnenpass and those disappearing stars.

# Part II

## Bombs on Berlin
## 1942–1945

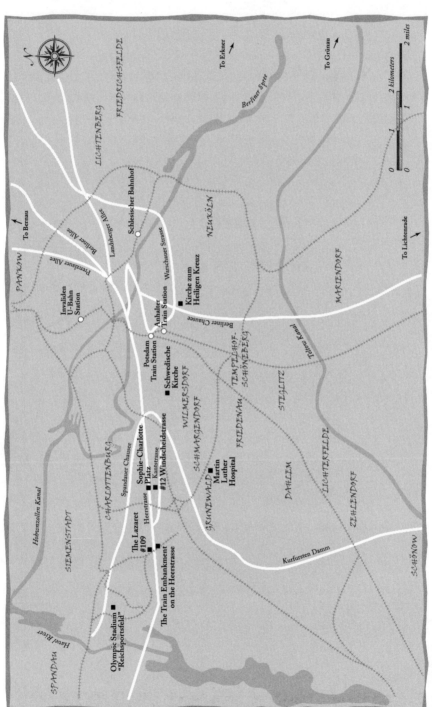

GREATER BERLIN, 1943

# 8

## IN THE BUNKERS

### I.

The news about the fronts, the new occupied territories, the places we always heard had been "liberated"—France, Czechoslovakia, Poland—was always announced with great enthusiasm. Joseph Goebbels, the propaganda minister, often came over the radio, giving his long and boring speeches, and the *Völkischer Beobachter* told stories of victory here and victory there. There were some who doubted, who had seen a war before and how terribly it had ended. Mutti was one of those. She said the news was not always what it appeared to be, but she never said more than that. She merely looked worried.

We, in Berlin, feared for ourselves. With the British having entered the war, wasn't it possible our city, the country's capital, could be attacked? Goebbels had an answer to this long before we even dared to think it: "If a single bomb drops on Berlin, my name shall be Meyer," he announced. It's a *Schnack,* a nonsensical saying—"My name shall be Meyer." He could have said, "If a single bomb drops on Berlin, I'll be a monkey's uncle."

When the bombs from England did come, the first one landed right on my street, the Windscheidstrasse.[14] It was August 1940 and it hit the house just across the street from us. A giant hole had been blown in one of its walls, but I don't think anyone was hurt. Those first bombs, in 1940, were not so significant yet; the bad ones would come later. However, from this day forward, Goebbels won a new name, Ober-Meyer, among us Berliners: the Super-Monkey.

Days later, new bombers arrived. This time, bomb sirens blared all night.

From leaflets that were circulated throughout the city and from our neighborhood supervisors, we had received instructions on how to run to our basements in an orderly fashion and what we were to bring. We each carried a small sack packed with a change of clothes and our important documents, our passports and birth certificates and, of course, the Ahnenpass, if we had one. All bathtubs were to be filled with water in case the house caught fire, gas and electricity were to be turned off, and we were to stay in our basements until the all-clear sirens rang through the city.

I was still in school when the bombings began. This disturbance— staying up well past midnight—made classes and studying a near impossibility. The sirens went off; you packed your things. You ran out your door half asleep, your ears were ringing. You'd run to the basement; you'd see your neighbors doing the same, each with his little sack of belongings. And the sirens kept blaring.

I will never ever forget the sound of those sirens. They would start off slow, like a ticking alarm clock, and then faster—saying hurry, hurry, get into your shelters—and then it would become an endless wailing, no stopping, and get progressively louder as the minutes passed. The whining could be heard from all parts of the city.

We would sit then, in the black, a few garish lights hanging here and there, everyone's face looking ashen and afraid as we waited. On many nights we stayed in our nightclothes. Some of us would wrap a blanket or coat around ourselves. Others paced all night. We could hear the planes overhead, the sound coming closer and closer, the whirring of the machines filling the sky, and we heard, too, when a building had been hit. *Boom!*[15]

## II.

One night, after the bombs seemed to have come extremely close to our house, perhaps even hit it, and it was already very late or very early the next morning, Dieter and I were sent to the upper floors to inspect the damage.

It was a rule, in our house at least, for the children to be sent up into the house first. The reason? We were young and we could stomach the destruction. The older people might take such a fright they'd have a heart attack. Dieter and I were to report back if it was safe for the rest of the neighbors to come up. That was our assignment.

Oh, the fear. I led, with Dieter close behind. "I'm here with you," Dieter kept saying in his little-boy voice. "I'm here. Don't worry, Grete. I'll protect you. Don't worry," and I imagined him at Christmas again. *Don't worry . . . Just step on the flower patterns . . .*

Floor one, the vestibule, was intact. The marble stairway was still standing. There were bits of plaster lying around, but nothing more. Floor two was intact. Floor three, which is where we lived, the hallway was all right. So far, so good. We opened the front door and walked around. A cabinet had fallen over and some cups had broken. In my bedroom a few books had fallen to the floor, and Dieter noticed that his desk drawers were standing open. So far, though, all seemed well, and I felt encouraged. No smoke, nothing smelled of fire, and we left our Wohnung to climb the stairway to the next level.

The doors had been left unlocked. This was the rule, right along with leaving the bathtubs full of water and the gas turned off. We let ourselves in and looked around. We then opened each door, each closet. It was such a different home from the one that we lived in. So old-fashioned! The same space, and yet old, old things. An old couch and a chair that was worn to a thread. Nothing matched. The lace curtains were old-fashioned. Dieter looked at me impatiently. "Come on! What are you doing? Looking around like this? We have work to do."

We walked around, went through the entire house, opening all the doors to all the bedrooms. Several framed photos had fallen, and I picked them up and placed them back on the bedside table. I didn't want Frau Ahlbeck to have a fright. Dieter had already gone on ahead to inspect the floor above, and suddenly I heard him yell, "*Aei!* Margarete, come quick!"

I hurried. Dieter was standing in the open doorway of the bathroom in the top-floor Wohnung. He looked at me, his eyes large as moons. Neither of us knew what to do next.

We stared, and looked away, and stared some more. There, in the tub full of water, like a monster, was a bomb: dark steel and pointed on one end, lying silent and unexploded. I had no reference, no knowledge of what this discovery would mean. I was only a girl of sixteen, but at that moment I felt like I was three. I wanted my Mutti, and I wanted someone to hold me, and I didn't want to see any more of this war.

"Come, Dieter. We should go back down and tell the others." I grabbed his arm. We weren't sure whether we should run or walk, or if our running could rattle the bomb enough to explode it, so we tiptoed down the steps quietly. *Let the monster sleep.* We made it down the steps, and as soon as I saw my Mutti, I fell into her arms and sobbed.

Herr Schulz called the neighborhood officials whose job it was to make sure all the homes were safe after a bombing raid. It was soon decided that the bomb would not explode, because, in fact, this monster had "drowned." There was, though, a broken window through which the bomb must have entered. It had simply slipped into that tub and peacefully gone to sleep.

"It's our great luck and the grace of heaven and of God that we are still alive," Herr Schulz, looking rather shaken, told the rest of us who were still waiting in the bunker. The monster was later removed, and we were all given one more day.

That day of bombings took many of the important buildings in Berlin, including the Reichstag and the Propaganda Ministry. But most sadly, many residential neighborhoods were decimated too. And still our street, the Windscheidstrasse, had no damage other than the broken window in our house and the house across the street with the big hole it in.

Bombings soon became a daily event. We would sit together in the dark, and there we would wait. Some of us prayed; some of us just fell asleep. Sometimes our house would shake and we would hear furniture falling in the upper floors. There were sirens and more sirens, and then we would hear a wall falling somewhere. We could hear bricks crashing—it was a horribly loud noise—entire houses falling, and we never knew which one had been hit. And there were loud explosions, some off in the distance, some very near. We would usually discover later it was a gas line that had been hit and the gases had caught fire.

When all was clear, it often was morning already. We students were so tired, we just fell asleep in class; some of us would fall off our chairs in the middle of a lecture. And, more and more frequently, a classmate or a teacher would simply never show up again. We never asked why.

## III.

We had all been in our basement shelter since about six one night, and it must have been early on in the war years, because Dieter was with me. "Did you hear *that?*" Dieter gave me a good shove. No, I had not heard a thing. I was sound asleep, and if a bomb should have dropped on us, well, I would not have known.

"Did you hear that? We must have been hit!"

Everyone in the bunker stood up from their seats, some pressed their ears to the walls, hands trembling with fear. "O Gott, O Gott!" Frau Schulz kept wailing. Her kitty had been left behind in her apartment, because she would never come when she was called.

Then it came again. A violent shudder; everything shook. Mortar fell from the walls. "Good God! Oh God! We've been hit! We're on fire!" No one could move; the fear simply stunned us.

And then the world went silent. We had to wait for the all-clear to sound, and all we could do was wait. And cry. Certainly there were those of us who did. I heard a whimpering coming from the corner of the room, but there was no light anymore. I only sucked in my breath and prayed a quick *Thank you, God.* After all, we were still here and alive, all of us.

It was so late, maybe three in the morning, when the all-clear sirens finally sounded, and we were going to be able to see what had happened and what was now gone.

Again it was Dieter and I who were sent to inspect. This time, Dieter bravely took the lead. *Stay inside the flower patterns . . .*

I ran up the stairs and into the first-floor Wohnung. Everything was broken and covered in dust—the chandelier was lying on the floor, chairs were tipped over. Everywhere there was glass. Broken wine glasses, a cabinet that had fallen over face-first. Everywhere, a silent, dusty darkness. Each Wohnung looked to be the same—a mess—but the building itself seemed still to be intact.

We had a small hatch in the ceiling of the top floor that opened to a roof garden. It was where we hung our laundry to dry and where the women of the house would go to shake their rugs. This hatch had a ladder with a rope on it, and Dieter said we needed to open it. What if the roof were burning? That was always a great danger, because if the roof caught fire, the whole house could come down, even after the bombings had stopped.

It was I, then, the older one, who had to do the climbing, and I took my first step, though I was filled with fear after what we had just seen inside the house. I climbed up and carefully pushed open the hatch.

What I saw filled me with terror. Red! Red! Nothing but red! The calm I had tried to maintain as we made our inspections instantly became hysteria.

I took a deep breath. I had work to do. I was the one who was standing on the ladder; I was the one who would now need to climb up farther onto the roof to see. *How much was on fire? Where was it burning?* It wasn't courage that made me go up another step. I was *supposed* to do it, and that's what drove me.

Outside, on the roof, the noises were unbearable. And yet, I could finally feel relief: The red I saw was the sky burning, not our building. It was filled with flames, and all the houses around us were burning.

A house on fire in Berlin. "What I saw filled me with terror." (akg–images)

Tall buildings with fires leaping up higher than twice the size of our building. I looked over to my left and saw that an entire city block was on fire. Explosions everywhere. I could hear them, but I did not know where they were coming from.

The air was hot, like on a midsummer day. I tried hard not to shake, but my knees threatened to buckle. I stepped back down and shut the hatch door. "We're safe, Dieter." I heaved a large sigh, and I hugged him. Then I wept.

Adults came soon; they had heard my screams. No one had a heart attack, and school would begin in only a few hours. The neighborhood fire inspectors arrived and everything was checked to make sure no gas lines had been hit, no water lines. As everyone was busy with *something*,

Dieter pulled on my sleeve and said, "Come on. Let's go out. No harm can come to us now. The bombings are done, and shouldn't we be the ones to see what has become of our neighborhood?"

Funny to say, but this invitation brought some relief. It was something to do. And we quickly walked down the stairs, stopping first in our Wohnung so that I could get my scarf and a coat. Dieter already had his boots on, and he was in a hurry.

Oh, what a shock to see everything burning. I mean, everything. The house kitty-corner from ours, completely up in flames. All the windows had exploded, and behind them was nothing but red, fires burning on every floor. And where were our neighbors? I didn't know; I never would know, but the building was going to be gone very soon. Our block would begin to look the way so much of Berlin already looked, broken and empty. We made our way down the street, stepping around debris, piles here and there, burning, and walked in the direction where I had seen the block of houses on fire. Trucks were standing askew, blackened or burning; trees were burning. As we rounded a corner, a sudden blast of hot wind hit me in the face so hard I had no time to even tighten my scarf, and it blew right off my shoulders! I screamed, sure no one heard me. I clung to a lamppost. Dust was blowing everywhere, and the winds were blowing backwards, headed back *into* the burning houses! I saw a baby buggy, and I watched as it was suctioned up into the wind and then ignited.

Through the dust and the wind I saw that, up ahead, Dieter too was holding on to a lamppost. He too had his head ducked down against the wind. *Aei! Aei!* I screamed at him, and from under his arm that had been shielding it, his face appeared as he tried to look in my direction. He waved one hand and together we turned and ran back home as fast as we could.

I would learn later that what we had experienced was a firestorm, and I would never again leave my house just after a bombing.[16]

❦

When I came home from school the next day, I learned from Mutti that the bakery had suffered a direct hit, a *Volltreffer*. The entire house was gone, every brick of it. Gone. Mutti went that morning, hoping to buy her usual Brötchen, and found nothing but a crater in its place where the baker and his wife and their young son had lived.

Mutti said she just stood there with her net bag in her hand, the one she had hoped to fill with Brötchen, and stared at the gaping hole. Others came, other neighbors who had survived, all with their sacks hung around their arms, and they too just stared.

The family had lived in the rooms behind the bakery. There was no basement, so there was no bunker. The baker, we learned, had decided to stay with his family until the raid was over, and that's how they died. I pictured him, this young man with a small boy who had only recently learned to ride a bicycle. I pictured him kissing his boy, saying, "Sleep, young man. The noise will soon be over." And I thought of Frau Ritter, and I wondered, *Where will we buy our Brötchen now?*

## 9

## I'll Be Home in No Time

### I.

Then things were quiet in Berlin again. Oddly so. We all thought the war was coming to an end. No more bombers flew over our city for nearly two years. We still had the food rations, and some of our buildings had been destroyed, but there was a strange sort of calm before the devastation that no one saw coming.

Signs of our changed times were certainly still there. There were more and more uniformed men on the streets—the SA men who wore brown uniforms, and the SS in black. Both were frightening, but the SS in particular were the men we stayed away from. Even their hats that stuck up so weirdly in the front were intimidating. We got to know who our "friends" were—the soldiers we could speak to—and whom to avoid. The SS and SA had the eagle emblem on their collars. Regular soldiers wore the eagle on their chest. This is how I could tell them apart, because even they had brown uniforms. We distinguished them like this: "Bird here, good," pointing to our chest. "Bird there, bad," pointing to our collar.

On the radio we heard only good news: "Another successful campaign on the Eastern Front . . . Another successful campaign in the deserts of Africa . . ." And I continued to study for my final exam, the Abitur, which I took and passed in March of 1942.

Although no one knew it at the time, my class would be the last one to take this exam. After our class graduated, the big bombers would start to arrive over Berlin, daily, and all the schoolchildren were evacuated to the east to be further educated there in what was called the *Kinderlandverschickung,* or the KLV.

The teachers in all schools were supposed to wear the Nazi insignia on their lapels, showing their loyalty to the Partei, but oddly, in my school, I don't remember that any of them did. We called it the *Bonbon*, the "candy." It was a round red button with, of course, the swastika on it. I have told you about our Maths teacher, the one who refused to give the Heil Hitler salute, as he was supposed to do when he entered our classroom, but our director was not a Partei man either. He was a religious man, and he let us all know it. He encouraged discussions in class—about what was righteous and how one should serve God. This man did not stay long. After my class graduated, he was replaced by a Nazi headmaster. Who knows what happened to him. He was probably sent to the Wehrmacht.

## II.

Dieter turned sixteen while I was busy with my Abitur. He was old enough now, he said, to fight for his country, and he enlisted in the Wehrmacht of his own free will. "Idiot!" That was my only reply to his announcement. In two years he would have been drafted anyway, and by then the war would have been so close to over that he might have avoided combat altogether. But, of course, we didn't know that.

His friend Otto Lippert enlisted too, and so did Hilde's brother. Her brother came home one day after having already spent time in service to his country. I was at her house when this happened. I heard him exclaim, "Das ist aber gemein!" "Mean!" is what he said about the new laws.

He was not allowed to enroll in the officer's training school, which is something all the boys hoped to do. He said he was told he could only be a foot soldier if he wanted to fight, because he was a half Jew, and half Jews were not allowed to become officers.

Dieter packed his rucksack. "I won't need much. They'll provide." He was sure of himself. He'd stuffed a few changes of underwear into

Dieter in his uniform, age sixteen.
"He was old enough now, he said, to fight for his country."

his pack and an extra pair of trousers, a comb and a toothbrush. His face shone with the pride of a boy who knew he was about to become a man. His eyeglasses were polished, and he stood at the front door waiting for Mutti and me to go with him to the train.

Mutti was trying hard to fight back her tears. This was her baby boy, after all, and she knew what war could do. Had we not already seen too many of those one-legged men with eye patches and empty sleeves? I tried to be positive. *He'll be all right. With luck, because he's the son of an officer, he may stay away from the front lines. Maybe even get a desk job.* I prayed to the secret place I had created inside of me, the place that had protected me, so far, from bombs.

Dieter was to leave from the Schlesischer Bahnhof, which would take him east to Frankfurt an der Oder, not far from Berlin, where he would receive his training. With its numerous tracks and platforms, it was a bustling train station. Everywhere there were soldiers and crying women, people hugging each other, waving white handkerchiefs as trains rolled off. The air was filled with a constant drone of train whistles and loudspeakers announcing arrivals and departures. Mutti and I stood there on the platform, in the midst of all this, and we watched our boy board the train. He was confident, smiling a huge smile. Mutti held her handkerchief to her mouth with one hand and waved with the other. I cried, and slowly the train moved forward.

Dieter and a man who would soon become his comrade leaned their bodies halfway out an open window. "Don't look so worried, Mutti! I'll be home in no time!" His voice drifted away as Mutti watched, and when his waving arm was merely a speck, she broke down in sobs. "It's not possible . . . It's not possible . . . ," she kept muttering.

"Mutti, *komm,*" I told her. "In two weeks, Dieter will know where he'll be sent. And we can visit him soon."

Then we made our way home, a place that would now have one family member fewer.

## III.

My mother was stupid. She always decided things for me. And I should have just once said, I won't do this. But I didn't. She sent me to the *Frauenschule*. She thought she could get me out of the *Arbeitsdienst,* the work service, this way, but instead I ended up doing both.

So, I went to the Frauenschule for a year. That was the school where women learned all things to do with women's work: childcare, cooking, ironing, and the like. I didn't do well in those subjects. I didn't want to be a *Hausfrau!* I wanted to be an athlete. I still had dreams of competing in the next Olympics, whenever that might be. But I did receive the highest grades in Leadership and Cultural Folklore. For those I got an A.

I finished that horrible year, and I was finally able to return home in April of 1943. I had learned how to iron clothes, and I had wasted a year because Mutti's plan to keep me out of the Arbeitsdienst didn't work. That's how I saw it. I still had the Arbeitsdienst before me, and it would take another six months, but it turned out to be some of the most fun I'd ever had in my life. I wished I had simply gone straight there and Mutti had not meddled. After all, I was a grown woman. I was eighteen.

The Arbeitsdienst was one of the things Hitler created, when he first came to power, that actually helped our industry. He formed the Labor Service, which once again provided work for the people who had been unemployed as well as for the young people. We were needed to work, and we were happy about that. It provided us with something to do. The youth of the Arbeitsdienst built roads and canals and cleared away swamps for farmland. We lived with families or in barracks and received a small allowance for our work. And some, like me, got a uniform. For me, the work was on a farm, and it was a wonderfully healthy life.

The farm was just south of Hamburg, and here I learned everything about farming. I was outdoors all day long, and how I loved getting my hands dirty! The farmer's wife showed me how to plant kohlrabi, cabbages, potatoes, and carrots, and how to heave hay with a pitchfork. I'd get so hungry that I'd pull carrots right out of the ground, wipe the mud on my pants, and eat them just like that, dirt and all.

I learned, too, how to weed the garden and how to milk cows and goats, how to make butter from the cream and leave the buttermilk for drinking. I also participated in the butchering. I learned what parts of the cow are cut first and how a butchered cow is drained of its blood. I was taught how to make blood soup and blood sausage, the soup being thick and dark, the sausage having something added to "fill it out," like barley, as the farmer explained to me. I wrote notes in a cookbook from this time on the farm, and for many, many years,

The farm just south of Hamburg. "I was outdoors all day long, and how I loved getting my hands dirty!"

my favorite recipes were those I learned from this farmer and his wife.

There were several girls on the farm with me, also fulfilling their Arbeitsdienst obligations. Three of us became quite good friends, as we all shared the same space, with our bunks pushed up against three sides of the room. It was a blissful life. Early to wake, hard work, early to sleep. Good air and, most of all, good food. Lieselotte was one girl's name. The other was Anneliese. They had similar names, and they even looked alike. Both had dark blonde hair that they wore cut short and turned under, as was the fashion. Both had straight teeth that showed often, as they both liked to smile. Lieselotte was from Köln and Anneliese was from the north, Schleswig-Holstein.

One evening my two friends and I shared a bottle of wine. It was a Saturday night, and we sat in our room and talked Quatsch. Silly things. We laughed and got tipsy and were just happy to be together. One of us—I can't recall whether it was Lieselotte or me—told a joke.

"Adolf Hitler, Josef Goebbels, and Martin Bormann were all in a boat" is how it started. We felt safe joking about our leaders, because we were among friends. "The boat tipped over. Who was saved?"

We looked at one another.

"Who? What's the answer?"

"The German people!"

Oh, we had a good laugh.

And we laughed and talked until early in the morning, and then went to bed still giggling.

The next morning, Anneliese came to both of us and said she couldn't sleep all night. "I'm so upset over all the things I heard you say last night," she said. She was frowning and knitting her fingers together. "I'm afraid I have to turn you in." She stood with her back straight and her eyes on us. "I have to do this. It's the law, you know."

Lieselotte and I simply stared, open-mouthed. "Anneliese! Do you know what you're saying?"

"Yes, of course I do."

"But do you really know? We'll be sent away to a prison camp. Don't you know that? We could even be put to death!"

We were both stunned. My mind told me to run, immediately, out into the countryside somewhere. I imagined hiding inside chicken coops, running from farm to farm during the nights until I could return to Berlin somehow. But then what? They would come find me there, too. But I would have to run, all the same.

We pleaded with her, and she cried, and then we cried. And finally she just left the room. She never did turn us in, but we didn't speak again, either. The lesson I learned from that night was that no one could be trusted, ever.

## IV.

One night, when I had been on the farm only a short time, I heard planes flying overhead. I ran outside to see. There, above my head, was

Lieselotte and Anneliese. "We felt safe joking about our leaders because we were among friends."

an entire sky full of planes flying toward us from the north. It could have been five hundred or more. I had no idea what was about to happen. The war had seemed so far away from us out here in the country.

The planes flew by and then out of sight, but I knew this was going to be a terrible night. I kept looking to the north, and suddenly it became brilliantly red. In the distance, I heard explosions. The sky became redder, and there were huge billows of smoke. *They must be bombing Hamburg*, I thought. It was the only possibility. Hamburg was only twenty kilometers away.

The skies continued to be red, and walls of bombers kept coming from the north, for days. We were all so frightened, but no news came our way. We only surmised that it was Hamburg being bombed, but we had no idea how bad it was until trainloads upon trainloads of refugees began to arrive at the station in our village. All were running from Hamburg, which was still burning. It was women, mostly, with horror all over their faces. Women who had lost their children. Children who had lost their parents. We came to learn that nine thousand tons of bombs had been dropped on Hamburg in the period of about a week.[17]

Some of these refugees stayed with us on the farm for a while. Many of them simply stared into the air ahead of them and never spoke. A few did talk, but with dazed looks on their faces. They talked of melted asphalt, people stuck in the asphalt, not able to move. Winds pulling people up into the inferno. People running with their clothes on fire. People jumping into the Alster River. The river catching fire!

❦

In the larger cities, the British had been dropping leaflets saying the war was a lost cause, that they were prepared to rescue us from our oppression, and some of us wanted to believe that. I was frightened. I was young; I wanted my life to move forward, to learn and study and, one day, have a family. And yet, there was the war.

We heard reports of bombs falling in Berlin, day and night, and I worried about Mutti. All alone on most days. Karl Spaeth was away much of the time now. No son or daughter there at home with her. How was she holding out? I asked permission for a morning off one day and rode my bicycle down the country road to the train station to make a phone call. I felt a need to talk to her.

The station was filled with trainloads of soldiers and more trains full of civilians leaving their destroyed cities. I took the few Pfennige I had in my purse and went to the public telephone to make the call to Berlin.

"Mutti! *Ja, hallo!* It's me. Margarete. I can't speak long, I haven't enough *Münzen*, but please listen to me . . ." Mutti was saying something, but I heard very little. "Ja, Mutti." I needed to speak quickly, my money wouldn't hold out long, so all the things I would have said in a letter—things like "I'm enjoying myself tremendously" and "Yes, I'm healthy and eating well, and yes, the farmer and his wife are treating me very well"—these conversations didn't take place. All I said was "Mutti. Come here to the countryside. You'll be much safer here than there in Berlin."

I heard only what sounded like a sigh. Perhaps a cough, nothing more, and then, "No, no, Grete. No. I'll be fine here . . ." Her voice seemed so far away.

"Mutti, do you understand how dangerous it has become? I mean, I hear it from the soldiers and the refugees coming from the west, from Hamburg and from Köln, that we'll be bombed much, much more. And that Berlin is to be decimated. I've heard this!"

Mutti seemed not to believe me, or perhaps she was simply too scared. She said very little. I tried then to convince her. I saw what had become of Hamburg. Would Berlin be spared? She needed to leave.

"Mutti. I beg you to listen. Yesterday I saw a British propaganda leaflet. I saw it with my own eyes. A refugee had it with her and she showed it to me." And in a final moment of desperation, I exaggerated what little I knew: "Mutti. They say they are going to bomb Berlin to pieces. That's what they've said." And then, "Mutti, it will be our street next, they said so, they said the Windscheidstrasse—"

I heard a click. Mutti was no longer on the other end. Only the silence of a dead telephone.

So it was true. Even the phones in the public places, at the train station, were tapped. I quickly looked around me to see if there was an SS man standing somewhere off in the distance, smoking a cigarette, pretending not to notice me. I didn't see anyone, but I took off on my bicycle, quickly, and I took a route in the opposite direction of our farm in order not to draw suspicion on Herr and Frau Federmann, the farmers who were so kindly taking care of me. Their name sticks with me because it means "Featherman," and as kind as I imagined a "feather man" to be is exactly how they treated me. It took all day to return home, and I was hungry. What had I accomplished? I was still frightened for Mutti, but I didn't know what to do.

## V.

Papa Spaeth received a letter on the nineteenth of August, 1943. Dieter was concerned for all of us. He knew that Berlin had been bombed, and he had received my letter describing the burning of Hamburg. Still, he wished "Mutti would not worry so."

*Dear Father,*

*Thank you for your letter: wireless radio is of course a better invention than the loudspeaker or, in fact, anything else. Today I passed the first listening class and can now type at a tempo of 50 (words per minute). I've even begun my duties working the radio. In any case, it's quite fun to be able to type on this machine and even more fun when the connection actually happens and I'm in a real conversation with the other party.*

*The higher level of horse riding does, on the other hand, bring its downside, like stall duties. And another distasteful side job is that of cutting hay. And, so often, we have roll call and no one answers because of all the incorrect names that are listed! But be at ease: I have, as of yet, not been punished.*

*And, about my comrades, and my superiors, I have nothing to complain. Even if we're sometimes handled in a rather "rough" manner, I have to admit, it's only for the good. It usually works anyway, as in most cases they don't really need to use the technique of "giving him hell" or "giving him a slap." Often I think of swearwords to say, but then I stop myself. You must always keep in mind the spirit of the men, and why we're here. That way you create your own form of discipline.*

*Does Mutti really want to leave Berlin? Grete's first impression of Hamburg really did her in! I read all about it in her letter. But I'm sure Mutti will know what's best and make the right choice as to whether she should leave Berlin or not.*

*I wish you good health and recovery during your time off and I hope you return refreshed. I especially wish that Mutti would not worry so.*

*Best wishes,*
*Your Dieter*

From what she shared of this letter, Mutti must have been considering coming to be with me in the countryside after all, although she never said anything to me. Perhaps it was her way of saying, *Don't worry so much.* Time, after all, was too short, and the time it took to make a decision already meant new problems had occurred.

But Dieter was proud, and she was proud to tell me about it. He had been trained in Morse code, something he talked about to his Papa. And his position now, at the fronts, would be to report.

# 10

## You'll Study Medicine

### I.

The Arbeitsdienst was done and it was 1943. I still hoped to compete as an athlete one day. But wars don't need athletes, and this one was no exception. What this war needed was medical staff. Hospitals were desperately short of medics and nurses, and doctors were greatly needed for the front. With most of the men being drafted to fight, there was a huge vacuum of able personnel in that field. My heart wanted to study sports, and the sports schools still did have openings. But it was wartime. I told myself, *There will be a time after war, and won't I be able to compete then? Or at least teach then?* But when would "then" be? Three years? Five? Twenty?

Mutti decided for me. It would be medicine.

"It's what's best for you. You'll likely be married soon anyway, and if you were to become an athlete, even if you were a good one, which you aren't, or if you could get a position as a teacher, which you won't—those positions hold no rank. No status. So? You'll study medicine. End of discussion."

I wanted to ask, *What have you ever made of yourself, you who have no more than horse ribbons to show for yourself, and silk dresses? You should know, Mutti, it's a new era, and I can think for myself.*

Then I applied to medical school.

Jena, 1944.

## II.

I was to begin my studies in September, and it would be in the lovely, lovely town of Jena, where Goethe and Schiller lived and wrote and taught at the very university I was to attend. Its architecture dates back to the early years of the Renaissance.

When I arrived in Jena, by train, the weather was still warm. I registered for classes as soon as I arrived. There was Anatomy and Chemistry, which I loved; Physics, which I hated; and Stenography, because my Mutti said I needed *something* to fall back on if I were to fail. But I was a student! I was about to study what would become my life's work, and for the first time in my life, I was on my own. Free to dress as I wanted, open coat or not, free to decide where I would go, with whom, and when, and free of my stepfather, Karl.

Jena did for me what Berlin had done when I first arrived there: it took me into its arms. Jena was a relatively small city, everything was within walking or S-Bahn distance, and in the center of town was the old city square.

Jena's *Rathaus*, the town hall that dominated one end of the square, was built in the late 1300s, in medieval times, strong and dramatic. There was an astronomical clock in its tower—something all the *Rathäuser* of that era had—and every hour a little door opened and a comical little man we called Schnapphans appeared, dangling a golden ball in front of him. This ball was supposed to represent the soul of man, and Schnapphans's antics during his show were to try to catch the ball, something he never succeeded in doing, until he just disappeared behind his door again, only to reappear and try, once again, to catch the soul an hour later.

I stood there that first day, filled with awe at the thought that these were the same antics that Schiller and Goethe might have watched as they stood in this square, this same little man attempting to do what no man could ever do. *Was this where Goethe imagined Faust?* I wondered.

Opposite the Rathaus was an old apothecary where I often shopped. It was a quaint store filled with shelves upon shelves of brown bottles organized in neat rows, holding homeopathic remedies for rheumatism, circulatory problems, headaches, and other, unnamable things. The proprietors looked to be nearly as old as the shop itself. Both had brilliant white hair and strong white teeth, and both wore white lab coats, as was the custom.

In the center of the square was the statue of our school's founder, Johann Friedrich I. Long ago the students had shortened his name, and we referred to him only as Hanfried.

My living quarters were with a widow named Hanna, whose son was at the front, fighting in Africa. She was lonely and needed the extra money, so she gladly rented rooms to students for a few Marks each month, and she took me in as if I were her daughter.

The university was beautiful in a lazy sort of way, with a large courtyard in the middle, and the street alongside it was tree-lined and shady. The rooms were large and imposing, the way university rooms ought to be.

It wasn't difficult to make friends in Jena. The town was small enough, and most of the population was made up of students or those otherwise associated with the university. Within a week I had made five good friends, all of them medical students: Heidi, Anne-Marie, Klaus, Helmut, and Franz. All of us seemed to have the same professors, the same lectures, and the same attitudes. We were here to study and wanted to forget about the horrors that were going on around us.

The Schwarzer Bär became our favorite student tavern. It was hundreds of years old, with Gothic arched doorways, low ceilings, and dark paneled walls with tapestries. One tapestry showed Martin Luther sitting at a long table, holding his hand up while speaking with friends, a Krug of beer and a plate of food before him. Jena was a town that was particularly moved by the Reformation, and Martin Luther was known to have frequented this very same tavern.

After a day of studying, we would gather in the Schwarzer Bär to gossip about our teachers, and in particular we would joke about our

Anatomy professor, Professor Schmitt, who was always quite humorous. You could tell he loved his field of study. He'd give his lectures as all professors gave their lectures, but his mannerisms always made each sentence sound especially funny, especially sarcastic, so that we always left the hall nudging each other, repeating his jokes.

An added dash of humor was a pair of heavy gray boots that he shuffled around in, a statement that complemented his air of impropriety. We admired him, too, because he was not fond of the Nazis. He said only "Sit"—not "Heil Hitler"—and he'd click his boots together and give a wry smile and then go on and teach.

As students, surely we thought about our politics and the situation of our country, how dire it was beginning to feel, but we wanted our lives too. We wanted to study, and so, rather than speak of politics, we spoke instead about philosophy—Nietzsche and his theory of the *Übermensch*, the true Superman—and religion. And, of course, we spoke about Faust, Goethe's character who made a wager with the Devil to sell his soul in exchange for knowledge. The part of this tragic play that would stay with me for a long, long time was when he chose, because he suddenly heard church bells ringing, to live rather than take his own life. It felt like an omen by which to live.

⁂

Like any student, I needed pocket money, and I did what many did—I donated blood. I could do so once a month, and for this I would receive twenty Marks. Plenty for a bottle of wine or a glass of beer at the tavern after class. My other job was obligatory—volunteer work for the war effort. It was called the *Kriegsdienst*. As a medical student, I was able to work in one of the science labs of the well-known optical manufacturer Zeisswerk, which made instruments for U-boats such as periscopes, specialty binoculars, and rifle scopes. Here, in this lab, I noticed that some of my coworkers did not speak or understand German. They spoke among themselves in a language that sounded much like Polish. I didn't know until years later that they were most likely prisoners. And possibly even Jewish. I assumed, as I had in Berlin, when I saw people like this, that they were simply *Fremdarbeiter*, foreign workers, with poor hygiene and ragged clothes, and that they had come to Germany of their own free will to work.

⁓

In October my first letter arrived from home. Mutti asked very little about me but talked much about Dieter, telling me all about what he'd written regarding his training. I knew she feared for him and worried tremendously, and in her angst she told me what he had told her, that his life was going well. He'd made it sound like a boys' camp: "Please send me my swim trunks. And I hope you'll be able to take some of my laundry home to wash the next time you come to visit." The next letter said he was now in full regalia. He had new riding trousers and high knee boots and was being sent to Brest-Litovsk, in Russia.[18] I think talking about him in this way helped her to accept the fact that he was a soldier now, and gone. Mutti finished her letter to me with "Please phone soon."

Two days later another letter from her arrived, and her request for a phone call sounded much more urgent. It wasn't easy to phone, for Hanna didn't have much money and phone calls were expensive. But I promised myself I would call on the weekend coming.

But when the weekend came, I was busy and I didn't call. I really didn't think of home much. I was living the student's life in Jena, and my friends were more important to me now.

## III.

One bright autumn morning I was restless, excited about my future—and I wanted more than anything to play hooky. My first lecture would be with the professor my friend Heidi and I had nicknamed Herr Langweiliger, or Mr. Boring. We made a plan: We would show up at the lecture hall, stay long enough to be counted in the roll call, and then sneak out the door as soon as the professor turned his back. I had made sandwiches with salted lard, and we decided we'd "study" on the riverbank. As planned, the two of us sat toward the back of the room, closed our books quietly, and stepped out of the room.

We walked to the Saale River and found a spot in the grass to lie down. There we looked at the clouds and talked and dreamed of a life in the future. We giggled about being married one day and having children and living in a little cottage far away from everything. "Keine Fesselballons. Keine Industrie," we both agreed, and we had to add, "Kein Krieg." No captive balloons.[19] No industry. And, most important, no war. We never once opened our books, never once mentioned Physics, and in a dreamy mood, late in the day, we finally walked back to catch the S-Bahn home again and parted ways at the train station.

The ride on the train jolted me back to reality. One of those Partei women with all her badges and political armbands was standing at the front of the car with her stiff legs and stiff face. She watched me with intent as I boarded the train. I could tell immediately that she wanted to engage all of us passengers in a pro-Nazi discourse. As soon as the train lurched forward, she started in: "Der Führer . . ." and "Der Führer . . ." All I heard was "Der Führer . . ." Loud and distinct so no one could ignore her.

I leaned my head back. I didn't want anything to do with her talk. I was sleepy, so I closed my eyes and I mumbled under my breath, "I'm so *sick* of this."

"Was haben Sie denn da gesagt? Fräulein?" the bitch snapped at me. It's not a word I would ever have used, but it's so appropriate here.

She *was* a bitch, and she decided to take it upon herself to make me her project. "What did you say? What did you say? What did you say?" Her voice rattled through my brain for days after that.

"Nothing," I said. "Nothing," and she continued her drivel.

⟐

Two SS men appeared at my door the next day wanting to speak with me. Hanna was terrified when she saw them. She ran to my room and rapped on the door. I was still in my nightclothes. "Come quickly," she said, with a very worried look on her face. "And don't say a thing! Quickly now. Quickly. Quickly."

"Hallo, Fräulein," they greeted me. Without any sort of further introduction, they came straight to the point. "Were you not on the train, headed north, traveling from the Saale station yesterday? At about 4:30? Were you not on that train when a lively discussion took place?" And, "Were you aware of what you did in participation?"

"Yes, yes," I admitted. "I was there. I meant nothing, sirs. I merely meant I was tired. I'm a student, you know, and have had many late nights of study. And, of course, sirs, I'm very sorry."

It was to be only a warning this time. They said they hoped I had learned my lesson, and that I might contribute in a more positive way in the future. "Because, you know," they said on departing, "you could be needed to work, and of course there are consequences if you don't comply ..."

The fear I had not felt since leaving Berlin beat in my chest. I understood. Even breathing, even in Jena, was no longer free.

From that day forward, I became aware of a professor who always seemed to be around—peering out his window at me when I walked the hall. Staring at me, with his Nazi nose up in the air, as I sat on the stone bench where I pretended to study, as I left the lecture hall, as I walked down the street. Always there, this man with the upturned nose and nothing better to do than to frighten me. Those SS men must have told him something like "Watch that girl. She's a loose one. Just keep an eye on her." He made me terribly nervous, and I found another hallway that led to my classroom so I could avoid his foul office.

Then a call came from Berlin. It was November, early in the morning. I was preparing for exams when Hanna came to my door to tell me it was my Mutti. I ran to the parlor to answer the phone, feeling guilty for not having called her first.

"Grete!" Her voice sounded tense. "Are you all right?"

"Yes, yes, Mutti. Yes, I am. And you?" Was that fear in her voice?

"We were bombed again last night, Grete. It was terrible. All of Charlottenburg was on fire . . ."

Suddenly I realized that all those requests for me to telephone had been her calls for help. She had been living with the inconsolable dread of the nightly bombings, something I had let slip far to the back of my memory. I only thought she had been worried about me and needed reassurance that *I* was all right. Oh, how selfish I felt, that I never thought of her!

"But tell me! Are you all right, Mutti? How did you survive?" I thought of our Wohnung and the days we sat together in the bunker. I thought of the monster in the bathtub and the night of the burning sky. Then, I asked the question you never wanted to hear the answer to: "Is anyone we know dead?"

"Grete. It was terrifying. But, by the Lord's hands, everyone in our house is still alive. Our building is still standing, but all the floors down to ours are gone. The Schulzes lost their home. The Ahlbecks lost theirs. Frau Schulz's kitty is dead. No one lives above us anymore, Grete. Above us is only sky."

I couldn't speak. I could only try to make myself imagine what Mutti was saying. Our house had been hit?

"Most of our block went up in flames. Most of it is now gone. The butcher shop is gone." And she gave a whimper. "I'm so lost, Grete.

Papa keeps saying not to worry. The war will soon be over. But I fear he is only trying to make it all feel not quite so bad. And he's gone all day, off at work . . ."

"Mutti, come here. Come to Jena. Please do!"

There was a brief silence, and then she sighed. She said she felt somewhat relieved, and then said no. "If most of the neighborhood is already gone," she reasoned, "why would a bomber drop another one here? Why would he waste a bomb on our little Windscheidstrasse?"

Our telephone conversation lasted for a long, long time. It was so good to be speaking with her. She said Papa was fine, that Berlin was trying to pick up its pieces, and the radio was giving positive reports from the fronts.

Neither of us brought up Dieter. I knew what she was thinking: Was *he* still all right? As far as we were both concerned, we should keep him in our minds as enjoying his "boys' camp," in exactly the same way he kept describing it in his letters, hoping to be home soon.

A week or so later, I heard over the radio that Berlin was bombed again, by the British, and that more than seven hundred bombers had passed over the city. Seven hundred bombers!

Mutti called once more to reassure me she was all right and that the Windscheidstrasse was still as it had been left from the last bombing. "Don't be shocked when you come home, though, Grete. You'll not recognize it. It's a hell here, I'll not deny that, but we are managing. Concentrate on your studies."

And that's exactly what I tried to do.

Even in Jena we heard bomb sirens and the shrill voice of loudspeakers announcing, "The enemy has been sighted and is advancing from a northerly direction." But, for now, the planes just passed over us.

It was assumed that the British would want to bomb the Zeisswerk if they could only target it, so the city of Jena was surrounded by a circle of ghastly-looking Fesselballons that would release gray hazy "thick air" when enemy planes arrived. So far, this seemed to work, but it never let us forget we were at war.

# 11

## The Professor with the Gray Boots

### I.

In the Schwarzer Bär one night, I was sitting at the end of a long wooden table with Franz, a fellow student from my Physics class. He was a handsome boy, blond, with strong hands. I remember his long tanned fingers wrapped around his glass. He leaned across the table toward me and lifted his beer while looking me straight in the eye. I raised my glass too and tried to make a small toast, "To another boring lecture with Herr Langweiliger!" Franz laughed, and we started a conversation. I liked his smile, his teeth. He was a personable man.

After another beer, our talk began to touch on politics. We were feeling each other out, without giving too much away. We had to be careful. I had certainly learned this from the experience with Anneliese back on the farm! And yet, Franz seemed different, kinder and more easygoing. I felt I could trust him.

I began to tell him about a conversation I'd overheard, and I checked his eyes to see if he was with me. He was. It was about a teacher, a woman who was told she would be let go from the university because she had a French boyfriend.

"I overheard this discussion, just the other day. I was passing her classroom when I heard her shrill voice. I could tell she was upset. I slowed down and looked to see who it was that she was yelling at. It was our director!"

Franz looked as if he might have his own stories to tell about our director, and so I continued.

"'You should be fired,' the director said to her. 'Don't you know people will talk? Don't you know enemy boyfriends are illegal?'

"She shot back at him, 'You have no business telling me what to do!'

"'Yes, I do. It's my duty to fire you. You should be quite happy you're not being sent away to a prison camp on top of it all! I have the power to do that, you know!' He seemed to be overly heated. I was surprised, because I always took him to be such a reasonable man.

"Then the woman replied, 'But there'll be an after-war time, and a time when people won't talk anymore, and all this won't matter one squat bit!'

"I have no idea what came of that conversation. I don't even know the teacher. She's not one of mine."

I stopped there. There was more I wanted to say, but I was nervous.

To my surprise, instead of the usual pinched mouth and change of subject, Franz put his face close to mine and whispered, "Do you know, there's a camp not far from here?"

"What?!" No, I didn't know, and it wasn't something I wanted to think about.

"Shhh. Don't tell a soul. I believe it's a prison camp where they're busy building war machinery. And it's being done by prisoners! But shhh!"[20]

His bluntness stunned me and frightened me. I quickly looked away. There were so many questions I wanted to ask. *Who is there? How do you know all this?* But, of course, this would have been illegal, and so I stopped myself and bit my teeth together. I changed the subject and talked about my day at the river with Heidi. I left the tavern that night with a terrible stomachache.

## II.

I stayed late the next day at the chemistry lab. I was working on the dissection of a dog, and the project fascinated me. But, to be truthful, I was so bothered by what Franz and I had talked about that I didn't want to go home to Hanna's just yet and be alone with my thoughts. Better to be busy.

Suddenly the sirens blew. "Thick air" or not, it seemed the British had finally found us. The bombers were not passing over us this time. *We* were their target. I sucked in my breath, threw down my instruments, and did the only thing I knew to do. I ran. I left my books; I left everything and ran as fast as I could to get to the bunker that was just outside the main entrance.

I yanked open the hatch and quickly made my way down the steps. There I found, already seated, a number of professors and students I had not yet met. Everyone looked bewildered, scared, and no one said a word. Briefly, we all nodded a Guten Tag to one another, and then I took a seat on a bench and I squeezed my thumbs—a wish for luck.

As I became accustomed to the light, I saw I was sitting next to the Nazi professor, the man who loved to glare at me. Would he take this opportunity to scold me? To teach us all the virtues of the Partei? I hoped not. What we needed now were prayers. I did not get up to change my seat. Instead, I put my face into my lap, my arms over my head, and prayed, "God, carry me."

*Boom! Boom!* All around, louder than I'd ever experienced. *Boom!* The walls of our bunker began to rattle. More noise, glass breaking. I thought, *They must have hit the Zeisswerk!*

≈

When finally the all-clear sounded, we simply sat for eternally long minutes. Nothing moved.

The silence was broken by a commotion outside the bunker door, then a loud rapping. "Open up, open up! We have a wounded man!"

Someone opened the hatch, and in the blinding flash of light from the outside I saw two men with another one between them. One was holding the man's arms, the other his waist.

The man's face was contorted with pain. He was moaning and rocking his head back and forth. His jacket and tie were splattered with blood, his trousers soaked. Then I saw something I'd never seen before: The man's pants went only to his knees; what was left of them was in shreds. Bloody bits of skin hung like tassels, and there were no feet.

"There are medical students here, aren't there?" one of the men shouted.

"Yes, yes! Of course!" I was terrified, but I mustered all the confidence I could manage and said, "Bring him down into the bunker. At least we can lay him down somewhere and keep him warm."

We quickly made a bed with a few blankets and jackets on one of the benches and made him as comfortable as we could. I proceeded to do the very little I knew how. I checked his breathing and his pulse. Both were reasonably good. Some of the other students were tying tourniquets around what was left of his legs. Then my heart sank to my knees. I saw what one of the men had brought in with him when he ran into the bunker—a pair of gray bloodstained boots. I then looked into the man's face and recognized him. It was Professor Schmitt. Next to him were his gray boots, the two things he would never ever need again.

## III.

The bombers were gone, the air was still except for a few remaining sirens, and Professor Schmitt was lying on our makeshift bed. Surely an ambulance would soon arrive and take him to a hospital. I had done all I could, and I felt depleted. It was time to leave the bunker.

Slowly I emerged and looked about in the dust-filled light. Smoke was everywhere, and as my eyes adjusted to my surroundings, I realized that there was nothing left. Where there had been buildings only hours ago, there was now nothing. Burning craters with freestanding walls. This was something I had already seen in Berlin. But in Jena? And then my mind began to grasp what had happened, something I was not prepared for. My university was gone, and with it my future.

I wandered through the rubble, stepping over books and pieces of furniture, a pair of eyeglasses, and suddenly I thought of my friends Franz and Klaus, Heidi, Anne-Marie, and Helmut, and I became scared. Where had they hidden? Were they still alive? I picked my way to the city center, the square where our founder's statue was, the Hanfried, and where Schiller's house was, and our tavern. The tavern. That was my destination. I thought, if anyone survived, he or she surely would go there.

I knew I would have to leave Jena now. There was no question. Studying was over; dear Professor Schmitt would forever have no legs, if he lived at all; and Jena would no longer have its university.

A few students began to appear from out of the smoke, and, one by one, we gathered in front of Hanfried. No one spoke, but we wept. We wept for the friends we knew we would never see again. We wept for the professor whose booted feet were missing. But mostly we wept because our dreams were dead. We would no longer be able to study, and we wept deeply for that.

A young man, a student I had noticed in my Anatomy class, stood opposite me, and I watched as he peered up into the eyes of Hanfried. From an inside pocket of his jacket he pulled out a flask and offered it around. And as the eight of us took our drink of schnapps, one after another, we gave our last toast to Hanfried. We said things like "Thank you" and "I'll miss you. I'll be back." And "Until better times"—a phrase we had by now learned to use frequently. We hugged one another and promised never to forget each other and never to forget our studies. And we turned to go to wherever we would now call home.

For me it would be Berlin. I had not eaten all day, but with the food rationing, hunger had become such a familiar companion that food was not my first thought. Home was, and I made my way to the main train station near the Saale River. I took one more walk to the river's edge, picked a few flowers, and threw them in, begging the river for its blessings "until better times." I would never see or hear from my friends again. Heidi, Anne-Marie, Klaus, Helmut, Franz . . . I don't know if they survived.

The Hanfried statue. "Until better times."

꧁

The station was full of people—students, professors, women with their children—and all was in chaos. Some people knew where they were headed. Some had lost their homes and had no relatives to go to. They only knew they couldn't stay here.

There was no true train schedule anymore. Trains were often delayed. Tracks had been destroyed, stations no longer existed, so we simply waited until a train came along that had the name of our city on it.

Darkness arrived. With my sweater I made a pillow for myself on a bench and drifted to sleep. As each train approached, I opened my eyes to see where it was headed, and I'd see, again and again, it was not to Berlin.

Morning came and still the same scene, only fewer would-be passengers waiting like me. Many had found transport through the night. I began to feel hopeless. So many trains had already arrived; so many people had already departed.

I suddenly thought of Hanna and realized I had not said goodbye. It really had not occurred to me until just then. In times of such chaos, one sometimes forgets about things that are important, and remembers the silliest things, like "Did I remember my scissors?" But now, suddenly, I realized that I needed to say goodbye.

I walked the few blocks to her house, through streets now looking so much like Berlin: rows of houses in ruin, but right next to them rows left untouched. I was happy to find Hanna's house fully intact. Her neighborhood had been spared. But she was shaken.

"Margarete! Where have you been? I've been worried sick. I thought you were dead!"

I cried then. "Oh, Hanna. You've been so kind. I need to go home to Berlin, as you must know. The university is gone."

She told me how much she would miss me, and I was filled with regret and sorrow and a deep sense that I had no idea what would come next for me. I stepped forward and gave her a long hug goodbye.

I went to my room and packed the few things I had brought. My books could stay, I decided, for I promised myself I'd be back one day. Then, with a light suitcase and a heavy heart, I walked back to the train station and took up residency on my bench once again.

Another night, another day. Trains arrived sporadically. Day three, and I'd had no food. Finally a train approached, and I saw it was going to Dresden. Dresden was two hundred kilometers south of Berlin, meaning another four-hour train ride to get there. But Dresden was such a beautiful city, it had been nicknamed the Florence of the North. And because it was so beautiful, we all believed Dresden would never be bombed. I began to rationalize that I could just as easily wait there for a train to Berlin as here, and in any case I'd be waiting in a city that was safe.

Another good reason to take this train to Dresden was that it had a food car. I had twenty Marks or so on me—plenty for train fare and even some for food. By now I was terribly hungry, so I decided to board. I picked up my bag, walked to the train, and then, for no reason at all, I stopped. My mind blanked for a moment, and as quickly as I had made the decision to board, I also decided not to.

*What's another day without food?* I asked myself. *And either way, I would still have to wait for that final train to Berlin.* I turned around and walked back to my bench. I'll never know why I did this.

The following day, when I was back in Berlin, I would read in the paper that that train full of passengers had been hit by a Volltreffer. Full on. Not a soul survived.

That's when I knew I had an angel.

# 12

# You'll Not Recognize It

### I.

I stepped off the train and out into the light of Berlin. My first impression was this: All the flowers were gone. And then this: The trees were black and leafless. Buildings I used to know were gone. There and there, blackened walls silhouetted against the blue sky, a bathtub hanging in midair, a house with corrugated paper over its holes. Large puddles of water filled the streets. I was amazed by this realization: *Someone still lives there, in that decay.*

The air was still. I could hear no dogs barking; there were no children laughing, no birds. Slowly I made my way around the ruins

A street scene in Berlin after an air raid. "Buildings I used to know were gone." (akg-images/ullstein bild)

and through the piles of rubble to the S-Bahn station. There, somehow, I managed to find a train that would take me to Charlottenburg and to the Windscheidstrasse. I wondered how on earth Mutti had survived all this. There was so little left. What would Charlottenburg look like?

I got off at my stop, the same one Dieter and I used to get off at when we came home from school, the same one Hilde and Ilse and I used to get off at after our Tanzschule. Here too, nearly everything was gone. Empty. "You'll not recognize it, Grete," my Mutti had said. As I stumbled over piles of rubble and looked around, I wondered if I would even find my house.

I walked by a church I had passed a million times before and saw that its ancient Gothic stained glass of blues and reds was missing, and plain windows were in its place. When I arrived at the Windscheidstrasse, it was no exception: more puddles and piles of rubble.

But up ahead, my house still stood, just as Mutti had said.

And, as she had said, it had shrunk in half. The window Dieter and I had looked out of when we witnessed the SA men smash the leather shop with their sacks of rocks, the same one I always worried Papa Spaeth would be looking out of, was now on the top floor. The upper levels of the house, the homes of the Schulzes and the Ahlbecks were gone. For a brief moment I wondered where they might be living now, and then I spotted Mutti. Standing like an angel in the doorway. Her arms were raised, her head was tilted to the side, and she looked, to me, as she must have looked at twenty. Her face gleamed with tears of joy. I dropped my bag, ran to her, and we held each other for a very long time.

"Mutti, Mutti . . ."

"Grete . . ."

There were no other words. *How are you? How have you been?* would have had no meaning. And to talk about what had happened . . . well, *so much* had happened. Where was one to begin? And so we just stood in the doorway and held each other. We knew, in that moment, that we were two of the lucky ones.

## II.

I had nothing to do now that I was back in Berlin. My student days were over, and I was back home, so I did what I was supposed to do. I registered, once again, for the Kriegsdienst. I reasoned that, since I had been a medical student, I could certainly help the war effort by tending to wounded soldiers.

So, I went to the German Red Cross station on the Berlinerstrasse, not far from our house. Here I received a temporary Red Cross certificate and a Red Cross uniform. I was to work as a medical assistant in whatever capacity was deemed necessary. My new certificate read: "All military personnel and public servants are hereby required to honor the Red Cross uniform and, upon request, shall provide all necessary assistance." I felt proud, useful, and even hopeful that I now could make a difference.

With this certificate and my new uniform, I was to report to a small train station in the southeast corner of Berlin, where my job would be to change the dressings of the wounded and bring them tea—and cakes, if we had any.

I rode my bicycle to work, as it was much easier and quicker than trying to find an S-Bahn that might still be functioning. Mutti came with me, riding her bike as well. She too, in the past months, had been working as a train station nurse and told me the trains were always packed full these days. There were the men being shipped off to fight on the Eastern Front, and soldiers were returning to their homes on leave. Sometimes there would be wounded men who would need to have their bandages changed, but mostly, Mutti said, they only wanted a cup of hot tea and some conversation.

When it comes to the wounds? "You just do what you have to do," she said. "You'll know what to do." It was the only instruction I was given.

The train station was a small one. Just two sets of tracks and a narrow platform. There was a little hut to the side with a small potbellied stove where we could boil water for the tea, and there we were able to warm our hands, too, as it was spring and the weather could still be cold. I grew to enjoy my work. I enjoyed meeting these men. So many of them looked so young—no older than Dieter—and talking to them made me miss him terribly.

When the trains came through, we looked first to see if there were women or children on them. Sometimes there were. They always looked frightened and helpless, often no more than a solitary bag to their name. They were traveling because they had been bombed out, and we knew this, so we took particular care of them. We gave them extra cakes, extra tea, and I'd take my handkerchief and wipe a child's face, which was nearly always dirty and tear-stained.

&#8766;

My days went like this: Up early in the morning, after not much sleep. Hurry, hurry. Dress in my Red Cross uniform, take what I could for food, some Muckefuck, some bread with the "IG Farben" jam. Then I'd jump on my bicycle and pedal to the train station. On my morning ride, I'd see what had disappeared during a night raid. Houses that now had sky visible through the holes that had been windows only a day earlier. Walls that now appeared like giant ghosts looming over my head. Walls that only yesterday housed a family.

My job offered me warmth and it gave me tea when otherwise I'd be hungry, and it gave me something to do. Above all, it allowed me a view of the war as seen from one man and then another.

"It's a terrible mess in the east," I heard again and again. "I was in Russia." "I was in Poland." And they would shake their heads and say again, "It's a terrible mess." "We should be out of there soon. Otherwise this war is a lost cause." I believed this; I understood it all too well. All I had to do was take a look around my own city, what was left of it. All I had to do was listen to the BBC. And now the Americans were fighting us, too. Indeed, they could be right. Indeed, it could be a lost cause.

## III.

I was alone at the station one day. My job had become routine: I knew when to be there, what to do, but also when to leave. The air raids continued. We were so used to them by now. The Americans arrived around six o'clock, followed by the British, and we knew we should be close to a bunker when evening rolled in, when the sirens began their wailing.

It was a day not unlike the others, when there were many young men and even more civilians who needed my attention. A sweet little boy, blond with brown eyes, told me quite earnestly that he was coming to Berlin because "There is a very nice school here for me!" I glanced over at his mother quickly and saw the strain in her face. *Oh, that dear boy. May he only keep believing!* I gave them both a cup of tea and a warm smile and said, "Macht's gut!" I wished them well and moved on to tend to the next man.

It was a soldier who said his home was in Jena. Oh, my heart fluttered when he told me that, and how I wanted to talk with him more. But suddenly the sirens went off. We quickly said goodbye to each other, his train took off, and I turned to run. I left my bicycle where it was, as I knew I would need to run for cover somewhere if the bombs actually fell before I made it home.

Oh, but the wailing! It comes and then it comes louder. Slow, then it speeds up. Then comes the final *tic, tic, tic* that we always waited for in the bunker, the one that screams at you, *They're here!*

I could hear the planes overhead already, and the thud of bombs falling in the distance, and I knew I was nowhere near my home. The sky became black with a wall of at least one hundred planes, maybe more, all flying in formation. It was what they called a "carpet bombing" raid, something both the British and the Americans did.

I heard them drop then. *Thud! Thud! Thud!* But I was still in the street, still running. Parts of the city were already burning, and I knew I needed to get to safety fast. I ran down some steps into a U-Bahn station as fast as my legs could take me, and in the darkness I looked for where I could hide. It was behind the stairwell, a tiny space, but large enough to cover me. I could barely breathe; my eyes were blinded by fear. I turned to brace myself against the wall, and then it gave way. It felt soft, not hard, and I realized I was leaning against a man who had also found this space to take shelter. Without thinking, I grabbed his coat lapels and buried my face inside his jacket, right up against his chest. Then this man whispered the Lord's Prayer into my ear and he held me tight around the neck.

Sometimes bombings lasted only twenty minutes, but at other times a second squadron would fly over us, right behind the first one, and the whole terror would start all over again. This was one of those times.

When it finally quieted, the man breathed deeply, and then he spoke. He said, "It is finished."

"I believe it is finished," he said again.

And then again.

Under normal circumstances I would have collected myself. I would have apologized for my rude behavior. I would have been embarrassed about hiding my face inside his coat. But this day was not normal. In times like this, the unimaginable can happen and you do unimaginable things. We wished each other farewell, gave each other a little nod, and then we walked up the stairs to go back to our lives.

As I emerged from the subway and saw what was before me, I quickly grabbed his hand one last time. I closed my eyes and said once more, "Dear God!" Fire was burning everywhere. To the right, to the left. People running, stumbling over ruins, holding bags, some clutching a child with one hand and a handkerchief to the mouth with the other. The sky in the direction of Charlottenburg was engulfed in flames.

I ran back to the train station where I had left my bicycle and found it was still leaning against the railing, as if it did not have a care in the world.

The winds had begun, and I remembered the horrible night when Dieter and I went out after a bombing. I tied my scarf tight and pedaled as fast as I could. I needed to get to Mutti.

At the Windscheidstrasse, everything was burning. But, once again, our house still stood. Our Wohnung was still the top floor, and quickly I said a prayer of thanks. When I got to the door, they were all standing there—Mutti, Frau Schulz, and Frau Ahlbeck. They were terribly shaken, and of course Mutti was terrified because I had not been home.

Then, all of a sudden, as if it was just another day, our telephone rang. I couldn't believe it still worked. It was Papa Spaeth. He was worried for our safety. He was fine, he said, but then he never seemed concerned for himself. The Oberkommando had a bunker deep beneath its floors where the officers and the personnel hid during these day raids. We merely had our cellar as shelter, and it was *our* home that would go next if the house were hit again. Mutti tried so hard to stay calm while she answered his questions. "Ja, Karl. We're all right. We're all right. Yes, we can breathe again. Yes, our Wohnung is still standing."

❧

A day or two later, a phone call came from my friend Ilse, who lived in Wilmersdorf, three U-Bahn stations from our home. Her house had been hit.

"Think about this," she said. She was trying hard to be calm, not hysterical. "I was in my Wohnung. It was, as you must remember, on the top floor of the building . . ." I knew what was coming. "I was busy trying to pick up after the bombing. Furniture that had been knocked over. A wind came through the hole where a window had blown out and a whirl of sparks flew in. Quickly I ran to the tub to fill a pail of water so I could douse the carpet that had caught fire. Then the drapes caught fire, and suddenly I looked behind me and everything was burning. I could only run down the steps as fast as I could. I took nothing with me, not even my purse. As I ran past the other doors, I saw neighbors in their homes trying to gather up their things. I screamed at them, 'The house is on fire! Run! We're on fire!'"

She paused. I knew what she was about to say; she did not need to ask.

"Ilse. Come to me. Come right now. Walk if you must; take the U-Bahn if you can. I'm here."

She began to cry. "Grete! I've lost everything! Everything! Not a scrap of paper! Not a comb!"

"I'll be waiting for you. Don't worry. I'll help you."

It was not long before she was at my door, her face dirty from tears, her hands shaking, and she fell into my arms.

"Come, Ilse. Quickly, before Mutti gets home. I'll help. Of course, I'll help."

I took her to my room and together we filled a suitcase. I went through my closet, took a dress and said, "Yours." I left the next one for me. The next was "Yours." I went through all my things—stockings, gloves, hats, and sweaters—"Yours, mine, yours, mine," until I had given her half of all I had. We then went to the linen closet and I put a few of the pillowcases into her suitcase as well. We shut it, set it next to the front door, and made some tea.

"Ilse, breathe," I told her. "You're safe. The war will one day be over, and we are each other's best friends."

But I didn't let her stay long. I told her to go quickly, before Mutti saw what I'd done. She'd want to take some of the things back—"because it's good quality, because we might need it"—I could already hear her say this.

"Go, Ilse. And trust in God."

She thanked me, we hugged, and then she left. Ilse, like all of us, did what she had to do. She moved in with the neighbors who lived below her. That's just how it was done.

## IV.

The destruction didn't happen all at once. It was gradual. The Tiergarten, the Alexanderplatz, Kurfürstendamm—they had all been hit, and their ruins were constantly crumbling, long after the bombings were over, when their walls couldn't hold out any longer. More and more of the neighborhoods became larger and larger piles of rubble. We understood it as a way of life. Like boiling frogs. Put a frog into boiling water, it will jump right back out. "No, no," it will say, "this is wrong." But put the same frog into cold water and slowly bring it to a boil, and it will stay as if it were meant to be there forever, and even die. This is how we lived in Berlin.

My stepfather worked in the OKM Oberkommando every day. He was a Kapitän zur See in the Kriegsmarine, and he came home most nights like a man with an ordinary job. Sometimes it wasn't safe, and he would stay in the bunker they had there, underneath the government buildings.

He'd been home the night I returned from Jena. I hadn't seen him in more than a year, and he looked distinctly gaunt in a way I had never remembered him. His fat cheeks had hollows in them now, and his face, although he shaved religiously each morning, had a shadow on it.

That night he was waiting for me in the parlor. It was just before we were to begin our dinner, and he asked me to come in and sit. In his formal way, he wanted to welcome me home. I was nervous, as I had always been nervous around him, but times had changed. This man was no longer a threat to me; he was merely a man who had married my mother and had lived in my home for half my life.

"Margarete, come for a moment and sit." His eyes looked like they did when he used to help me with my Maths problems. Stern yet focused and clear about what he was about to say. If there was anything different about him, it was that he looked sad.

"Child . . . ," he began, and he let his sentence drop. He only looked into his lap and seemed at a loss for words. This was unusual. I waited.

"I want to apologize to you." He lifted his head and his eyes met mine in a way they had never done. "You are a woman now. You are no longer a girl. You have experienced things no human should ever experience. And at such a young age."

With a sincerity I'd never before seen in him, he said, "I'm sorry. For all of it. That our country is in this mess. That your dreams of becoming a doctor have been shattered. I am sorry for it all. If only I could make it better for you. You will be a great doctor one day. I know this about you. You are a kind person and a giving person and your patience is an asset. You are strong . . ."

Tears welled up in me. I had not, in my wildest dreams, expected this from him. Memories came. Memories of the cane, of his temper, of running to my room to hide. I stood up from my chair and walked over to where he was sitting, rather more hunched than usual. I put an arm around his shoulders, and I said something I would later regret: "It's too late."

I was about to leave the room then, when I saw him drop his head into his hands and weep bitterly.

"Oh, Grete. I don't blame you. I've had remorse over our relationship, the way I was with you, for so long. I realized, once you were in Jena, and when we received your letters, the stories you heard from the refugees from Hamburg, what a great woman you are. And that you are but a young girl.

"And I've realized, too, how I've failed as a father."

I was not prepared for this. I saw a kindness in him that I'd never allowed myself to see before, and in that moment I forgave him everything.

"When I was growing up, it was not easy, you know. My father was away, often for years. He too was in the Kriegsmarine. My only dream was to be as important as he. Why do you think I've always worked so hard? I never felt I had done well enough. I always wished for more, to be better. And I always felt like a failure."

I sat down. He turned and lit a lamp. It was getting dark outside.

"My mother? She ruled with a paddle. It's how things were in those days. Children were to be dealt with strictly, and that defined good parenting.

"I tried to raise you as I saw best. I wanted for you, and for Dieter, to make me proud. To do well in school and in your duties. I see now that, in that respect, I've succeeded. You have done well. And I'm proud of you. And I have failed. But you have always been a daughter to me. I am sorry."

The eyes of this man, the ones I only ever saw as bird eyes, now had honesty and regret in them, and they looked soft. His hair, which had become much thinner in the last year, was wet and sticking to his forehead.

"Forgive me," he said, again and again. And the man wept. I sat there and said nothing. I feel sad about that now. But I knew that our relationship had changed. He would never take a cane to me again. This I knew, and I knew he would be someone I could call "Papa" again, and feel proud.

# 13

# THE TWENTIETH OF JULY

## I.

Letters from Dieter still arrived regularly. He still sounded well, and it all still sounded like boys' camp. But he hinted that often there was no food, or very little of it, and Mutti sent him her food ration stamps, writing he should use them to purchase meat.

Dieter had been sent to Gross-Born, in western Pomerania. There he was to be trained in artillery for the Wehrmacht, and because Gross-Born was close—only a day's train ride—I decided to visit him.

How happy we were to see each other! He was taller, that was my first impression. And he had become a man. He had turned seventeen while I was away, and he was shaving now. His face, which had become harder than I remembered, had the shadow of a day's beard on it. His eyes looked hollowed like those of the men I saw on the transport trains going to the east. Yes, it was clear, he had seen some things already, things I did not want to know about. He had seen battle. He mentioned it only briefly in a letter once, saying only that it was difficult to ride his horse well because his saddle had no stirrups. But I wanted to know about him. How was he doing? Who were his new friends? How was "boys' camp"?

"Grete, you'll laugh! I had the best Christmas Eve! I went to bed. That's all. All these men who use any excuse to drink and laugh long into the night and dance and feel terrible the next day from their hangovers, they puzzle me. I took all my schnapps and all my cigarettes—you know I don't smoke and I hardly drink—and traded them for eggs. I now have food, and I had a good sleep!"

"Here's something else that will make you smile. I get my shoes polished for me each morning, for which I get an extra twenty minutes in bed. They do all this for me! I just trade and enjoy myself."

Then he looked up at me, as if for the first time. Maybe he noticed how thin I had become, how strained my face was. "Grete. How is it for you?" I knew he was thinking about Jena and that I had, just like Mutti, seen too many bombings. His eyes met mine, and he asked again, "Grete? Are things all right?"

I shook my head no, but I said I was managing as everyone was managing. I told him how I had shared my clothes with Ilse, and he was genuinely pleased. I told him about my work at the train station and how much I felt I was doing something to help, and he nodded his approval at this. Then I told him that I wished I wasn't always so hungry.

"Ja, ja. Grete. I know. We're all in the same boat. I too am hungry, and the soldiers here are all hungry. Sometimes we even go with no food for an entire day, but we still have to go out in the field and it often goes for ten hours or more. I do believe this war will soon be over, though. Just think, Grete, and believe in this, we'll be celebrating Christmas together again, and it will be this year yet. I'm sure of it. I'll be home, and we'll all be able to put our lives together again, soon."

It was reassuring to see him in such high spirits. He was a dear boy, and all those thoughts I used to have, about how gentle and soft this boy with glasses was, passed through my mind, and I thought, *Surely, God will protect one as innocent as he.* I prayed and I believed, along with him, that we would spend our next Christmas together, in our home on the Windscheidstrasse, and all this mess would be over.

We walked for miles that day, our arms linked, talking and reminiscing about happy times. When it was time for me to catch my train home, he said his last words to me, words that reminded me again that this boy was far too sweet for a soldier's work. He said, "Enjoy, Grete, what God has granted you," and then he turned away. Why I remember the look of his back, the wool of his jacket, I don't know.

It will be a picture that will stay with me forever. My brother with his soldier's cap on and his uniform and his knee boots, with his skinny body, walking away on the platform.

～

Two weeks later, he was sent to the front, in Italy. Even then, his letters said no more than this:

> *Dear Mutti,*
>
> *Could you please try to find a small Italian phrase book for me?*
> *The landscape here is breathtaking. From the window in my room, I can see the blue Adriatic Sea. A cooling breeze blows constantly, so it is never hot here. The cherries and strawberries are just now in season and the roses are blooming. One liter of wine costs twenty Lire—that is about two Reichsmarks. Yesterday we bought two liters. Things are going very well for me. I'll write again soon, and send my best wishes to the family.*
>
> *Your Dieter*

## II.

Dieter was promoted. He was to be trained as a lieutenant. This was wonderful news! This meant he might stay away from the heavy fighting at the front, and he would have a position when the war was over. Mutti was delighted. His station would be in Küstrin, straight east of Berlin, and we could visit him often.

> *Dear Mutti,*
>
> *The day after tomorrow, you will celebrate your birthday for the fifth year during this war, but I believe your next one will be in time of peace. I know you worry; please don't worry. You are my mother, and I love you dearly.*

*I am strong. You must believe this. Be happy for me, as I am happy that I don't need to stand by and watch. I am here to save our country. I know it is difficult for you; perhaps more difficult than anything you've ever had to do. Be proud of me.*

*I will be home soon.*

*Your loving son,*
*Dieter*

Five years of birthdays, and Berlin was being bombed as he was writing.

Then came the weekend that Dieter visited. It had been nearly three months since I had seen him, and I'd asked for the time off from work.

He was already home, sitting in a chair in the parlor, when I came through the door. I flew to him and he took me in his arms and we twirled. He smiled so broadly, his mouth was nearly as big as the glasses on his face.

We sat and smiled at each other for a long, long time, and we squeezed each other's hands. He started to talk about small things, like had I been to the Wannsee lately and how much he missed the "fine Italian air." I think he talked about unimportant things because he didn't want to make things hard for anyone, to leave behind tears.

And then, when all the chatter had come to an end, he paused. He looked at me through his two thick lenses, and said, "Grete, will you trust me if I tell you this? I am a soldier, first and foremost. I fight to defend our country. You trust this, right? I have given my all; I enlisted at sixteen, a time I should have gone to study, as you went to study. But now I realize I believed in things I no longer believe in."

He dropped his head. He seemed at a loss for words. And clearly about to weep. He set his glasses on the desk next to him, and pushed at his eyes the way he had as a child. Then he threw his head back and these words blubbered through his lips: "It's not what I thought. It's not what I thought. Oh, Grete. We have been so betrayed!"

"Dieter?" What was it he wanted to tell me? What had he seen that had made him react so? "My brother. Tell me. I can hear it. There's hardly a thing I haven't seen. Hardly a thing I would not believe by now. Tell me. What is it?" I sat on the divan, not far from his seat, and he leaned toward me, now beginning to convulse as he tried harder to hold back his tears.

"Grete. He has betrayed us. I never knew this. I always believed. He said he was not against the Church, and yet the things I know now are not of God. They are of the Devil." And he wept. He wept and wept, and I tried hard to keep from letting that place behind my own eyes let loose. I wanted to be strong for him, but I was losing ground. "He has betrayed us, the German people. Hitler is not who he said he was. He is the Devil ..."

He would not say more. He straightened his back and put his glasses back on. He brushed his shirtfront, smoothed his pants, and said, "Will you come visit me now that I'm in training in Küstrin? Will you come on the weekend, maybe?" His voice was imploring.

I said I would, but I knew I wouldn't. I knew, when the weekend came, I'd be too tired. I'd want to find an excuse. I'd want to sleep. But I said, of course, and we hugged a brotherly, sisterly hug.

We spent two happy days together, trying to pretend there was no war. I told Dieter about my job and how much I loved medicine, and that I intended to go right back to studying as soon as all this was done. "This is true," I told him. "I even left my books in Jena!"

And when the bombs came, we ran to the bunker together, Mutti, Dieter, and I. Now there was one more in our cellar, and he was a man from the front. Those of us who had been there for so long together talked with him and loved him and gave him wishes for a safe return to his duties, and we did as we always did. We prayed and looked to the ceiling.

That Sunday afternoon, as he was preparing to leave, Dieter recited a verse he loved, from his favorite poet, Rainer Maria Rilke:

*Life has not forgotten you.*
*It will hold you in its hand.*
*It will not let you fall.*

I knew this poem, and I repeated it back to him. It was our farewell.

～

A week later, a telephone call came from Dieter. His voice was soft and not quite as proud as it had been. He told Mutti his officer training in Küstrin had come to a halt, because men were needed at the front. He could not wear glasses as an officer, he explained to us, so he was being sent out to fight.

We talked a long, long time on the phone. Dieter must have been lonely. Again he asked, "Will you visit me, Grete? I'll be gone soon to the front. I mean, I'll be home soon, I'm sure of this."

I said, "Yes, yes, of course," while he talked on and on, rapidly, as if he himself didn't believe what he was saying. "They keep telling us of German victories and—will you visit me?"

There are some regrets one can never overcome. Dieter phoned on Friday to remind me of our weekend together: "Are you coming?" I said, "Yes, yes," though I didn't mean it. My work had been hard. I had sat in the bunkers every night that week, and sometimes all night long. More than once I simply fell off my chair, fast asleep. That's how it was, but it was no excuse. I lied to Dieter. It's the regret I'll live with for the rest of my life. He said, "Please," and I said, "Yes," but I didn't come.

## III.

A letter came from Dieter dated July 24, 1944. He did not know yet what had happened.

On the twentieth of July, Mutti had been in the city and came home, much out of breath, saying, "Everything at the Reichskanslei has been cordoned off. There must have been another assassination attempt!"

There had been many failed attempts on Hitler's life, going back as far as 1939, and she was right. There had been another one. But once again, Hitler did not die. Once again, it was only an "attempt."

The evening radio program announced, "Our Führer is alive and well and will come on the air shortly."

We were aghast, horrified, and, in some deep place inside ourselves, we were also hopeful that the radio was only, once again, broadcasting propaganda, and that possibly this time it was true, he was actually dead. The war was such a lost cause by now; our entire country was up in flames. Our soldiers carried on bravely, although we no longer knew what cause we were fighting for. The belief, the one Hitler wanted the German people to stand behind, that our country was under attack, was false.

His voice came on the radio. That unmistakable barking voice: "Providence has saved me!" he shouted. "*Götterdämmerung.*" The twilight of the Gods.

This wild man who believed even God was on his side had the Devil living inside him!

⁓

The news of the assassination attempt did reach Dieter a week later. He wrote home, asking about the family of his friend Paul, whose father was the Commander of Berlin. His name came up often in the news as having been implicated in the assassination attempt, and Dieter wanted to know if we had heard any further news. Yes, we had. On the radio, and all over the newspaper.

Paul von Hase, the father, had been put to death. Either hanged or shot. In fact, all the high generals and high officers and old members of the Reichstag who were involved in the assassination attempt were put to death. Hitler called his retaliation the *Sippenverfolgung*, a purge of all family members of all the suspects. Several thousand people were either hanged or shot after this as punishment.

Many of my stepfather's friends who had been in our parlor, speaking in hushed voices only a few years earlier, those members of the Schwarze Kapelle, suddenly disappeared. We had no idea where they went; we merely assumed they had been involved. And we just sat at home and kept our mouths shut, very tight. Even a whispered word could put us in jeopardy.

The twentieth of July changed everything. Jews, who were once able to leave Germany, were no longer allowed to go. Everyone was to be drafted into the all-out war, even old men, even women. All universities were closed. The Heil Hitler salute was mandatory and failure to do so punishable.

And we would forever, from that day on, refer to it as the Twentieth of July.

# 14

## Horse Carts and Children

### I.

Anne-Marie was a new woman who arrived one day in our cellar. She was a bit older than I was, a chemist by trade. She was frightened for her life after the Twentieth of July. Her uncle, who was an officer, had been involved in the assassination attempt and had been one of those put to death. This was her uncle she was talking about! She had no idea what would happen to her now. After all, she was his niece.

Then the news came: They took her job away, and she would no longer be a chemist.

We sat together during these long, loud nights, listening for directions. It was direction, after all, that mattered most. We'd hear the sound of bombers coming from the north, so we imagined them having crossed the North Sea. Then we'd wonder, would it be the eastern part of Berlin they'd be targeting this time? The west? Would it be, once again, Charlotttenburg? I mean, we couldn't even shoot back! Those bombs would just fall on us, they never even saw who we were, and we couldn't see them.

They liked to throw *Feuerplätchen*. Plates, like saucers on fire, would whirl out in all directions. Some would come flying through open windows or open doorways, and in an instant the entire building would be engulfed in flames.

But the Feuerplätchen weren't the worst of them. The worst were the Americans. They would come with their planes in huge formations, a hundred at a time, blackening the sky with their presence, filling the air with a dense drone. And when they dropped their bombs, if one of them hit your house, you could only pray that you'd die quickly. Those bombs would go straight to the bottom floor and then burn straight up, bringing the house down within minutes.

Our night skies brought what we called "Christmas trees." British planes would circle the area and drop flares, so the bombers could see their target, and from this we knew exactly who was going to die. Everything in that neighborhood would glow red, and minutes later the bomber formations arrived, dropping their death loads.

Anne-Marie and I sat together and said things like "How on earth will this all end?" and "How much longer can this go on?" One night, one very dreadful night, she told me she had a guardian. She said it was a man, an angel, with wings taller than she, and she could see him often when things were really bad. He would stand behind her and hold her shoulders with his hands.

This is how we survived. We talked and told each other our secrets for survival. Everyone just had to figure out how to make it through another day. How to find enough food, how to keep their spirits alive. It had been five years already.

We would sit and count the minutes some nights. Sometimes we'd say, "What's going on? Where is he, that Brit? He's late."

If we were relatively at ease, relatively sure it would not be Charlottenburg this night, we might have tried to make a joke of it: "He's probably found a girl over there in France, probably still trying to zip up his trousers." But on most nights we simply clenched our teeth and prayed it wouldn't be us.

It was on one of these nights when Anne-Marie and I were huddled in our corner with our suitcases underneath our feet. Everything outside was burning. Doors were slamming and windows were shattering when suddenly, with a blast of hot air, the door to our bunker blew open and a dog came flying in from who knows where, frightened out of his wits. I opened my mouth and thought words had come out, but they hadn't. I was as surprised as the dog. He took a quick, frightened look and then ran around the room, circling it as fast as his little legs would go, and he never stopped. I suppose he had a right to that, what with all the panic, the terror, the need to run it off. He was no different from any of the rest of us. We sat and watched the poor thing until he finally fell over dead. From exhaustion or a heart attack, or because there was really nowhere else for him to go.

## II.

More and more, there were refugees arriving at my train station. People fleeing from the Russians. Children and women. But the first were of a different sort—well-dressed families, fathers and mothers with children on their laps. Who were these people in their fancy first-class cars?

The Partei people. The "Hundred Percenters." The ones with their nice little Bonbons on their lapels and their women dressed in smart hats and gloves. The very ones who, only days earlier, warned the villagers they would be shot if they tried to leave. They were the mayors with their families who had left their villages in the middle of the night.

Days later, when the real floods of refugees arrived, I heard stories. Bad ones that I don't want to tell. About children being murdered . . . no, I can't tell.

But I can tell this one, from a refugee I became friends with:

"We could already hear the artillery from the Russians, and we still weren't allowed to leave. If we did, they showed us exactly what would happen. They would kill us. It's true. A neighbor was hanged from a lamppost, right in the village square only a few days ago. I knew him. He used to bring the feed for our horses. Just a man, a farmer. He tried to leave with his horse and cart. They hanged him. Just to show us what would happen if we tried to do it ourselves.

"We heard women screaming from a neighboring farmhouse. It was a woman I'd known my whole life. With her were her sixteen-year-old daughter, her mother, and some others. People who were staying with them. I recognized the voice when she screamed, 'Please!

*Nyet!* She tried the only word she knew in Russian—No!

"But it was to no avail. The screams continued, then I heard gunshots. And then all was quiet . . .

"We packed a bag. I didn't even have time to take my fur coat. I ran so fast, through the fields and into a ditch. On the road I saw horses with wagons attached to them. The horses were dead. The wagons just stood there, some tipped over. People were trying to run, but the snow was so deep—up to their knees in places.

"The roads were completely clogged. Nothing could move. Horse wagons, people running with wheelbarrows. Snow began to fall, and it fell all day and all night. It was so deep, and the air so cold. Children. I saw children, dead, alongside the road. The parents were either dead or, somehow, had gone on alone . . ."

She was missing a finger. I only noticed it when she began her story. Her hand was wrapped in a scarf, fully brown with dried blood. It was the finger that had once worn her husband's gold band. She had arrived in Berlin without family. Her mother, her father, grandmother, two nieces and a nephew—they were all missing.

"My family fled when they saw the Russians advancing. I hid in the barn and didn't run until late in the night. I thought it would be safer to run when I couldn't be seen. But I had such a fright! As I made my way to the barn door, I heard a noise behind me. There had been a Russian soldier in the barn all this time! He was asleep, possibly drunk, I don't know—maybe a defector? I don't know. Maybe it was just an animal who, just like me, was scared.

"I ran so fast then, in the darkness, and my ring caught the latch on the barn door. I was delirious. I had to run."

And then she showed me the stump that was leaking pus. Horrified, I brought bandages to her and washed her hand in warm water. I helped as well as I could and told her there was a *Lazarett*, a military hospital not far from us where she should go to be treated for tetanus.

This poor refugee woman needed help that I couldn't give her. She was sad beyond words, but she was also hungry, so I gave her some tea and we sat by my stove. I told her to stay as long as she liked. "But Berlin is no safer," I told her. "We're being bombed nearly every night. You should continue on if you can. Somewhere north. I hear from other refugees that they are trying to get to the Baltic, where they hope to make it onto a ship."

I heard later that one of these ships was sunk by an American bomb.[21] Was that good advice to give her? It was the luck of the draw. Stay here, you'll die; go, you'll die. Stay here, you'll survive; go, you'll survive. It was just dumb luck, either way.

## III.

On the twenty-sixth of January—it was now 1945—I received my official certificate from the Red Cross that would allow me to work in a real Lazarett. I was to do real work in a real hospital. I would see real emergencies, and, I felt, I would be able to help much more than I had been doing by handing out tea and a few bandages.

My new place of work would be at the Lazarett number 109 on the Heerstrasse, where I would treat soldiers coming directly from the front. I was to assist the doctors in whatever capacity I was needed—in the operating rooms or in the recovery rooms.

I was excited about my new position—and fearful. I had been promoted, yet my appointment had been mandated by the "medical emergency law," which had an ominous sound to it. But this was war. Everything was ominous.

The Lazarett on the Heerstrasse had been a boys' school, converted to a hospital about a year earlier. By the time I arrived, it was already filled to capacity: one hundred patients on each of the three floors. The rooms that had been classrooms once and the auditorium we called a *Gymnasium* where lectures had been held were now filled with beds of dying men.

One level down from the main floor was the "OP," the operating room. This was where all the severely wounded men would be sent to have their bullets removed or their legs amputated. It was a dreadful place, but we had a bright and caring doctor in charge. He was from Estonia, a short man with broad hands and a small sweep of brown hair that he combed over his otherwise bald forehead. He had gray eyes with heavy lids that often made him look like he was sleeping. His name was Dr. von Lutzky.

All the medical assistants were women, and they were all about my age. We soon became close friends. Christa, Gerda, Heidi, Trudi, Anika, and Ruth are some of the names I recall. At night, when our work was finished, we shared stories; we talked about what we had heard on the BBC. The toilet room on the second floor was a great place for talking. We sat here often, with a cigarette, and gossiped. We called it our *Zigaretten Klosett*.

Anika was a strong woman, one who would survive, and she had such fascinating stories. She had been studying medicine in Weimar when the universities were closed. She stayed on in Weimar but needed to figure out how to survive. She said it was wit that told her how to make money, but intuition that saved her life. She taught herself how to make donuts over the Bunsen burner she stole from the school. And she sold these donuts in the streets. Then the idea came to her to buy leather from a farmer with which she made bags and sold them on the black market.

Often she sought refuge in the lobby of the one of the grand hotels in Weimar. When the weather was bad in the winter, as it often was, she would walk in, sit on one of the lovely sofas, have a smoke, and pretend as though she belonged there. On one of these blustery days, when she was sitting in the lobby, she spied a newspaper on a table just across from her and got up from her chair to pick it up. Just in that moment a bomb crashed through the ceiling and landed right where she had been sitting! The sofa was demolished in the blink of an eye, but she was untouched.

We all had stories like this, stories that amazed even ourselves. I had my man in the U-Bahn station, the bomb in the bathtub, and I knew what we were all thinking. We were somehow, so far, the lucky ones.

⁓

Our friendships grew closer as the times outside became worse. Even the men who arrived at the Lazarett, the soldiers with their terrible wounds, became dear to me. We all clung to each other, each moment, each conversation, as though everything had a special meaning. When it was Ruth's birthday, all we could do was pick a few flowers from outside and light a candle for her, but just that held a meaning as if it was the most important event of our lives.

We were known as the *Schwestern*, the Sisters. Schwester Christa and Schwester Gerda. I was Schwester Margarete. At the Lazarett we had a bunker under the building where we retreated some nights, or even during the day, when there was a bomb attack. Just because this was a hospital didn't make the waiting in the bunker any easier or the fear any less. We only sat, as we did in any bunker, and prayed while we heard the walls falling outside, doors blowing open, the winds, the machines roaring overhead.

Among us were two nurses who never got along and fought openly. One of them, Schwester Gerda, was what we termed a "brown nurse," one of the *braunen Schwestern*. She was a proud member of the Partei, and she wore her Bonbon clearly visible on her lapel. The other, Schwester Jutta, talked on and on about the boyfriend she was madly in love with, and she talked too much. We soon learned that this boyfriend was in fact French. She called him a Fremdarbeiter, but in fact he was a prisoner.

Jutta talked too much about other things, too, things like the war and how foolish it was. How irresponsible the Führer was, how crazy it all was. And how eager she was to have it be over.

Weren't we all?

One night, as we were sitting in the bunker waiting out the sirens, Jutta began, once again, with her opinions about the war.

Schwester Gerda sat just beside me, Jutta across from us on another bench. Gerda was a tall woman with dark eyebrows who stood erect, and she called herself "a doer." I secretly considered her narrow-minded and shallow.

"How can you say these things?" she started in on Jutta. "You and your silly ideas of French boyfriends. You can't even call yourself a German! You! It's people like you who are betraying our country," she snarled.

Jutta was not about to let Gerda get the better of her. I was afraid of what I was witnessing.

"You? Who are *you*? If it weren't for that stupid little Bonbon you pin so proudly each morning on your lapel, who would you be? A nothing! What have *you* ever given? Do you think it's *you* who's saving this country?"

The brown nurse cocked her head and sneered back at her, "Now, tell me, Jutta. Tell me, honestly. Do you mean to say you really believe all this?"

And the two of them went on fighting as the rest of us sat in silence.

Poor Jutta. The morning came. I arrived for work and walked through the front door of the Lazarett in time to see a flash of uniforms and badges and Jutta being hauled off, held by each arm between two SS men.

Jutta was never sentenced, an intervention of fate. She could have gone to the concentration camp for this, but the war ended before her sentencing date. Meanwhile, we had all learned to keep our mouths shut tight around Schwester Gerda.

⚰

We were treated very well at the Lazarett. We were the Red Cross, after all, and we felt safe because of that. We moved about with relative freedom and a rather false sense of protection.

We received food in the Lazarett. Bread, and sometimes even enough that I could take some home to Mutti at night. My blood donation money also allowed me to buy extra eggs and butter, and sausage and Schinken, much of which I also gave Mutti.

We all made our monthly donations to the Red Cross blood bank, for which we received twenty Marks each. Mostly, if we could find it, we'd buy wine with this money, and on nights when we couldn't go home and we had to stay in the Lazarett, in the bunker, we'd bring bottles with us. We would light a candle, smoke a few cigarettes, pass around a glass of wine, and wonder to ourselves how this would all end.

❧

The Americans were advancing; they were already well into German territory. The Russians had begun their offensive against us, and it seemed from the news on the BBC that the German troops were rapidly losing ground. Often I thought of Dieter but said nothing. To talk about him would only bring tears. All of us had tearful stories of men we missed and worried about, and we all stayed silent about them.

❧

A soldier was brought to us by our *Sanis* one morning—*Sani* is what we called our paramedics. He was very, very sick with a fever, a cough, and a sore throat. It was something we all had, illnesses like this, poorly nourished as we all were and susceptible to all the sicknesses around us. Besides, everything was so dirty! Every street was filthy from rubble, and the dust of ruined homes was constantly flying around in the air we breathed. It's no wonder people were sick.

I approached this man who was lying on a stretcher, a blanket up close to his face, to help the Sanis move him over to a bed. I stepped back, shocked. I recognized the face. It was Otto Lippert! Dieter's good friend, the "insurance mathematician"! Oh, but I was happy to see him!

He immediately asked about Dieter, and we exchanged news about our worried mothers. Then I asked Otto about himself. Had he been to the front? What news did he have? His eyes lowered, and it took him a moment to answer.

"It doesn't look good, Margarete, but we are making some headway." Then his voice unexpectedly dropped to a whisper. "Grete. I have to tell you a secret. I've never even gone to the front! Can you believe this? I've tried. I've tried. And every time I try, another problem crops up. I broke my arm first. That was my first 'battle wound,' but it didn't even happen in battle. It was a silly thing. Just jumping up onto a train with my bag over my shoulder. Somehow it caught on the door and I fell backwards. When I landed, my arm lay behind me, my shoulder socket empty. It was in a cast for nearly six months. You know, they won't let you shoot if you have only one arm.

"When I was let out, I left to find my company, but I couldn't find it. Every time I was directed where to go, by the time I arrived by train or S-Bahn, my company was already gone. I followed, but again, when I arrived, they had moved on. I finally returned to Berlin and was given, once again, the orders to go out and find my company. I have never found them! Now I'm sick."

I took his hand in mine, gave a chuckle, and said, "You're lucky. Stay sick as long as you can. Stay sick!"

"What about the war? What about my duties?"

But I just said, "Stay sick." Then I said, "I have to go now."

I needed to tend to the other patients, but I went to his bedside and visited with him often. The other men probably were jealous. We were supposed to spend equal time with them all. Otto stayed with us

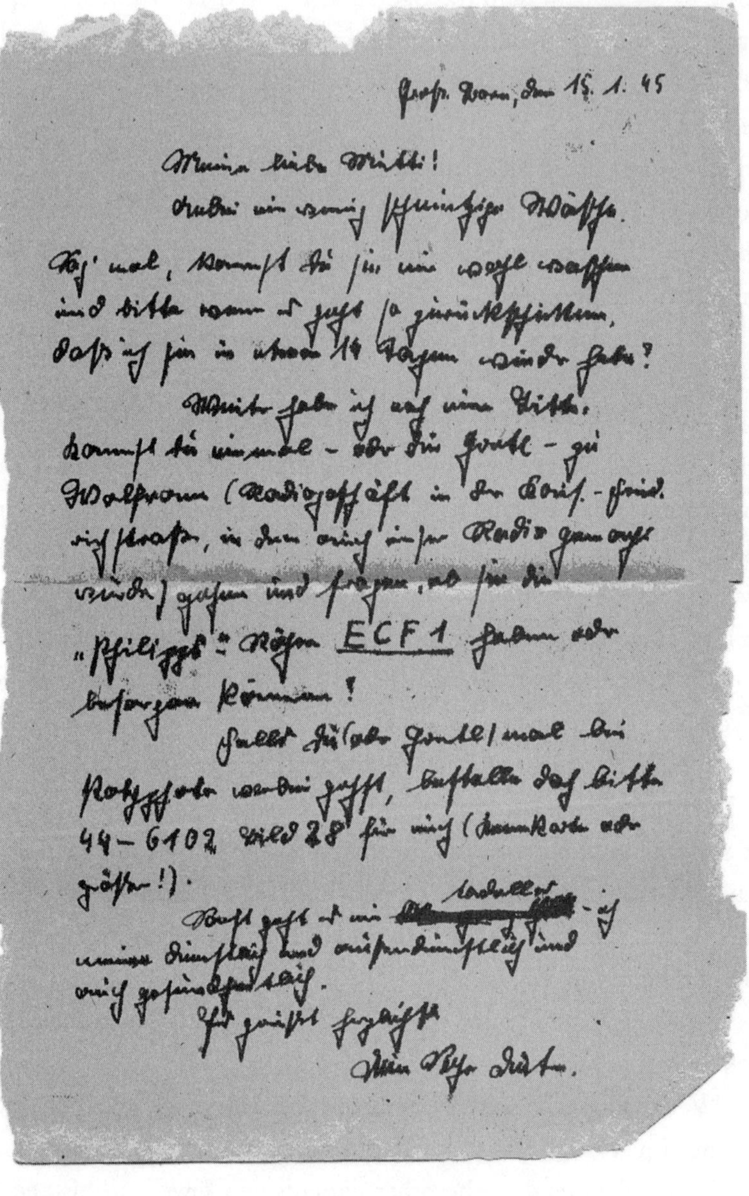

A letter from Dieter, January 15, 1945.

for several weeks, and when he had healed well enough to leave, they put him in an SS uniform and sent him out. We never heard from him again. I'm sure we would have, had he survived.

⮩

Berlin was a major target now. Britain was bombing us every night; the United States was bombing us during the day. The Russians were advancing, and the city kept burning. More and more I saw death—in the Lazarett, in the streets—but I continued to do what I was supposed to do: I went to work. And I did what everyone else did: I looked toward the Kaiser-Wilhelm-Gedächtniskirche. The church's steeple, visible from nearly every corner of Berlin, gave us hope. It was, for us, an omen. "If the Kaiser Wilhelm Memorial Church still has its steeple, Berlin will stand" was what we said to reassure one another.

⮩

At first, when it was still safe enough, I rode my bicycle to the Lazarett and then home again in order to be with Mutti during the night. It was easier than finding a train that still ran, but it also gave me courage to ride my bicycle, like I had some control over my fate.

## IV.

Signs all over Berlin had been attached to walls long ago with the initials LSR, meaning *Luftschutzraum*, bomb shelter. They pointed to basements under churches, houses, subways—anywhere that might provide a safe place to hide when the bombs came. But I began to see something new. Someone had painted graffiti on these signs, small print between the letters L-S-R, so that it now read: *Lernt Schnell Russisch!* Quick, Learn Russian!

The Eastern Offensive is what we called it. The march of the Russians into Germany. It began in late 1944, a bitter winter, and continued into the spring of 1945. In January the Russians had recaptured Warsaw, and they continued to recapture the rest of the territories Germany had taken, city by city—thirty to forty kilometers a day. Hitler's orders were crazier than ever. It was obvious we had lost the war, and yet he insisted on feeding the enemy more and more human fodder.

Königsberg fell to the Red Army in April, then Danzig, and when we heard that the Russians were already on the Oder River, we could not believe the fighting was still continuing. The Oder was only seventy kilometers away.

The bombing raids continued, and you would think, by now, there was nothing left to our city. But they bombed us all the same. The city was completely camouflaged in smoke as it burned, every day, all day long. The sky was an ugly yellow. We could not see the sun through it, so we kept our lights on nearly all the time. We walked with handkerchiefs across our mouths in order to breathe. Fires smoldered for days, and corpses lay everywhere. What a gruesome sight: a charred body shrunken to half its size or, most terrible, a charred baby you think must be a burned doll. Corpses of soldiers had been one thing, but now there were so many civilians.

When the bombings ended each day, bodies would be dragged out into the streets. I suppose the intention was so relatives would be able to identify them. So many of them had such ghastly looks on their faces. I would, when I could, take a jacket or a shirt and pull it up over a corpse's face, so at least it would have some dignity as it lay there.

On the Windscheidstrasse, Mutti saw victims, casualties, and corpses from the war, too. She did what she could. She helped those who were wounded, bandaged those she could, called for the Sanis to come help when it was needed. And it was needed all the time.

New friendships developed quickly in our bunker as we sat huddled together. One of the new people was a woman named Frau Götke, who had with her a young boy. She told us the boy had been born out of wedlock to a mother who was a nurse and could no longer keep him with her. The boy spoke German without an accent, though Frau Götke told us he was Dutch. He stayed quiet, with his large, terrified eyes watching her as she told her stories. We wondered about him, but we stayed silent. Frau Götke seemed unafraid to talk anymore, and as our friendship grew, she told us stories, terrible stories, about what she had seen. She said she couldn't hold these things in any longer, and that she didn't care what they would do to her. She had principles, she said.

She had been a member of the Partei, fully pledged, and she had worked most of the war years in the east as a secretary. She had been well paid, she said, and as a single woman, she enjoyed her position very much. It was high up, and she was able to be "in the know," as she put it.

She had witnessed something that finally drove her to leave the Partei, to run away, putting her own life in danger.

"It was the Jews."

Now I heard for the first time some of the terrible things happening to the Jews, and from a woman who'd been there.

"It was just on the outskirts of the city. It was a row of women. They were naked, all of them, and they were made to stand against a wall. Men in uniforms were there, with guns. I wondered if this was some sort of aggressive voyeurism. You know—because they were powerful men and the women were weak. It was bizarre and weird and frightening. No one else was there. Only the women and the men in uniform. I was a secretary. I was to take studious notes. The women had panic on their faces. Where would this lead?

"A lovely girl with thick long hair had enough courage to walk up to one man, an SS officer, who stood alongside others, barking orders. She had a pile in her hands, and as she approached, I realized it was the clothes she'd taken off. A thin dress and a pair of brown shoes.

"She looked at this man, walked up to his face, nodded, placed the pile at his feet, and then remarked, 'I never knew you Germans could be such pigs!' It was said in a heavy accent. She must have been from western Poland, somewhere there, but she stood tall as she made her way back to the line.

"And then they were shot. All of them."

We were horrified. Such a story did not even ring true, but she had told it. We were stunned. Then she told us this: She fled in the middle of the night. Running through forests and fields, it took weeks to get here, to Berlin. She knew she would be put to death if she were caught. No one runs from the Partei. From stories like this, and from rumors we were beginning to hear, we knew some terrible things were happening to the Jews in the east. That's all we knew.

Though no one ever spoke about it, it became clear that the boy she had with her was Jewish. No one said a thing. And, of course, no one turned her in. We all had our own worries. We had brothers and fathers on the fronts, our own lives to try to save. Shelter from the bombs.

## 15

# WHO WILL SAVE US?

I.

The ring around Berlin was rapidly closing in on us. The Americans were marching in from the West. Some of our people, the nurses and Sanis who worked with us, those who lived in the suburbs west of Berlin, could already see from their rooftops (the ones that still existed) the American troops. What they saw was surprising, because we had expected the Americans to come to our rescue, but the Americans were just standing around, smoking cigarettes and talking. They didn't seem to be making any effort to save us.

~

The night was late. I had much to do at the Lazarett, so many new arrivals, and it really was too late for me to leave for home. But I tried anyway. I didn't want to leave Mutti alone. I decided to run this time and leave my bicycle behind, just in case I would have to duck into a bunker somewhere.

The sirens had been blaring for some time, and the planes were already nearly sitting on top of my head. I put my hands to my ears and kept running. My prayer: *Forgive me, Father, for I know I have made a mistake.*

Suddenly, I heard *zisch!* A bomb had fallen just beside me, or just behind me. I nearly jumped out of my shoes. I screamed. I was confused; noise was everywhere and I had no idea anymore where to run.

I spotted a doorway. As fast as I could, I ran to it to take cover. Then—I don't know why I did this—in a split second I decided to run to the other side of the street to hide in another building's entry. Why did I do this? I'll never know. It must have been Providence, because in that moment the building I had just left was hit by a bomb.

I knew I had to run again, and I did, and suddenly the second building was hit by a bomb. Everything around me began to burn.

I looked back for just an instant and saw there were two people inside a building that was fully on fire. Their mouths were open as if they were screaming. Their hair was on fire. They were running down a hallway that was about to plunge to the ground. Their doom was so near, only seconds away. My only thought was *May they just die quickly.*

All around me was noise, and I had no idea where I was even heading anymore. I just kept running. Walls were crashing, bombs were whistling, sirens were screaming. The winds started. Suddenly I just stopped in my tracks and stood, looking around at that inferno. It all felt so insane and so useless, this running. Anyway, everything was gone by now.

This thought came to my mind, and I believed it with all my might: *I am the only one left alive.* Off in a distant part of the city, I could still hear the bomb sirens. But what good were they to anyone now? *Everyone else is dead.*

I lifted my head then and saw, just up ahead of me, something sway like a ghost. It was hard to make out in all the smoky air, but I recognized it as a tree, and I suddenly realized it too was alive. I made my way over to it and took its trunk in my arms. I held my face against its bark. I was so grateful that it was there.

Its branches seemed to respond. They seemed to reach down for me, as if we were in an embrace. I could feel life flowing through its limbs. I was frightened out of my wits, certain that I would die before the day was over. But this tree, it stayed with me; it did not let me go.

Then I felt something brush up against my arm. Something very gentle, very soft. And that's when I heard a voice. It was no more than a whisper—but you must understand, I heard every word of it. Was it the tree? No, it was an angel, I was sure of it. Who else would speak to me in a moment like this?

It said, "You shall have a child."

That's all, and then it vanished.

I dropped my arms. I stood for a long minute, and after that minute I knew something had changed in me. I was alive and I knew I would survive this war.

No sirens now, and I began to walk in the direction of home. I heard no dog, no soldier, not even a bird. I looked to the sky and saw no sun.

I looked to the east, expecting to see fire. Indeed, there was fire. But, to my horror, I did not expect this: the Kaiser Wilhelm Church was in flames, and the steeple was gone.

Berlin was finished.


## II.

At the Lazarett, we sat in our Zigaretten Klosett and listened to the BBC. We believed the Americans might arrive in Berlin by Sunday, and we made preparations for this. We kept hearing the reports of their progress. They had already entered Hannover. They had taken Thüringen.

Meanwhile the Russians kept advancing from the east. Daily, refugees were arriving by the thousands. People from the east—East Prussia and Pomerania—and everyone in the west was running too, because their cities had been bombed out. It was a terrible mess. Everyone was running, everyone was afraid of the Russians, but where were they to go? All the cities were bombed out. Even cities that once seemed safe, like Dresden, had been bombed out.

In Charlottenburg, Papa Spaeth walked through the door late one night. He looked tired. He kissed his wife and said, "Keep yourselves safe. This is all coming to an end soon. I'll be home in a few weeks." And with that, he took his attaché case and left the house. We would not hear from him again for a very long time.

We did not know who would enter our city first, the Russians or the Americans. We hoped it would be the Americans. At least we knew

The Kaiser Wilhelm church, destroyed.

the Americans would treat us with kindness. We were deathly afraid of the Russians. We'd heard too many stories of terror from the refugees from the east.

Mutti and I made a plan. If it became clear that the Americans weren't coming, we'd take off and run to the west, to Thüringen perhaps, like all the others. We never thought further than that, though. We never thought, *What then?* Because where would we go then? "Whatever we do, Papa will find us. But we have to care for ourselves now. He'll find us . . . he'll find us," Mutti kept saying, and we worried and planned, but we never came to a decision.

Then, one afternoon, a good friend of Papa's came to our home to talk with us. Maybe Papa had contacted him? I don't know. "I've come to tell you, it's too late," he said. "Do *not* try to leave Berlin! The circle has been closed in. We are completely surrounded by Russians. You will never escape. Your fate would be the worst imaginable. You'll be killed, or at the very least taken prisoner. I beg you. Please listen. Don't leave!"

Whether this was good advice or not I'll never know, because we decided to stay in Berlin.

❧

In the Lazarett, we had heard on the BBC that the American front had come to a standstill. The Russians, however, kept advancing. I stood in my uniform at the Lazarett and looked out the window. I wondered if this was going to be my last moment of peace. I remember how lovely the spring appeared. It was Eastertime, and flowers were springing up here and there through the cracks and the rubble. The sunshine was warm and pleasant. How does nature do this? All this ruin and destruction, and yet she still arrives in full bloom.

Dr. von Lutzky, the Estonian, was a smart man. All of us nurses still had our Red Cross passports, but they still had the Nazi signatures and the covers still had the Nazi swastika stamped on them. This could pose a problem when the victors entered Berlin, so he decided to write us all new passports, bearing only the Red Cross stamp and his personal signature. We were the Red Cross, he wanted the victors to understand, and we should, under the Geneva Convention and under all circumstances, be immune from war and kept under protection. But, of course, we had no idea how our captors would react. Better to be wise.

Dread and hope commingled in the air. The hope was that the war was about to be over. It was inevitable, although there was still fighting going on. The dread was the arrival of the Russians. That too seemed inevitable.

Schwester Christa arrived out of breath that Friday, running through the front door. "Listen to this! I just spoke with an SS man outside. He told me everything! He said the Americans are indeed coming, and they are coming to join what's left of the Wehrmacht. The British are coming to join us too, and together we will all fight against the Russians. It will take time yet before the war is over, but it will be over. The war will be over! The Americans will be here!"

It is true that there was an American general who was a bit more farsighted than the rest of them.[22] He did want to continue to fight against the Russians. He foresaw exactly what would happen. A division of the world, half of it going to the Communists, and the Soviets would be the world's future enemy.

The Americans arrived at the Elbe River, just west of Berlin, and did not budge. Nothing moved.

As we sat together taking our cigarette breaks, I recall saying, incredulously, "I can't even imagine the Americans would be so stupid as to allow the Russians to march into Germany's capital! It's unthinkable. Surely the Americans won't forsake us. It's unthinkable. Unthinkable!" We were already practicing our English. We were already talking about how to receive these men, our saviors. To let Berlin fall to the Russians seemed, to us, an impossibility.

And yet, the Russians were now in Bernau, only fifty kilometers east of us. And they kept marching and driving their tanks forward, ever closer.

❧

It was the weekend, then, I suppose. One of those fat Nazi men came to our hospital that morning and demanded all of our attention. The nurses, the soldiers, wounded men.

"Attention! Everyone! Announcement. The Russians have *not* entered Bernau! This is propaganda being disseminated by the enemy. It is a lie. And if a single one of you says that the Russian has come that close to our well-defended city, he shall be shot. Do you understand? On the spot. Then hanged right here in this schoolyard. Right here from the very lamppost outside your door. That one right there," he snarled, pointing to the door. "All the world will then see what a coward and a traitor he was. Does everyone understand this? It's an order! No one is to repeat these enemy-disseminated lies again!"

The man looked around the room, looked each one of us in the eye, and glared. With that, he made the Heil Hitler salute and strutted out. What we heard days later was that he boarded a train that very night and headed west for safety. He and his entire cowardly family nicely escaped the doom he wanted us all to deny. He was from Bernau.

Everyone in Berlin was preparing for the worst. It didn't look like anyone was coming to help, and the Russians continued to march in from the east.

Young boys, old men, and women: that's all that was left to defend the city. The *Volkssturm* was established. All men who had been previously deemed unfit for military service were called to join. It was a sad sight. The units we saw didn't even have proper uniforms. Some of the men wore their own fedora hats, others just a suit and tie. Many of them were mere boys with boy voices, boys who had been members of the Hitler Youth, only twelve years old. I saw invalids marching with their crutches, elderly men who probably had fought in the last war, the Great War, but were certainly not fit to fight now. Some carried rifles, but not all. We all wondered where on earth they were going. But it was a *Führerbefehl*. In other words, they were given orders from the highest command, something you could not refuse even if you wanted to. All men of all ages were to defend the city.

What would *they* be able to do once the tanks rolled in? Boys? Old men? And when did they have the time to practice for this? They created roadblocks all over the city using burned-out trucks and buses and furniture. It was laughable, really. But what else were they to do? Once one of those Russian panzers started rolling in, would an old broken sofa stop it?

Refugees from the east had brought stories of violent rapes. "They aren't satisfied just raping a schoolgirl, or her grandmother, or setting a young fourteen-year-old soldier to a woman, just to see how he'd have his first-ever and then laughing at his clumsiness. They will shoot the woman as soon as let her live, when they are done with it all." These were the stories we'd heard. Even more terrifying was what they did to the children.

## III.

I was still traveling home in the evening on my bicycle, and Mutti was brave. She would fight them if they came, she said. "Have no worries! I won't, after all this, let even one of those Russian *Buben* do anything to me."

Who knew if that would be true. I could only help her prepare. We pulled all the rubble we could find into our vestibule. Windows, doors, sofas and chairs, chests, all broken things, and then buckets of glass. Then we scattered the debris all up and down the stairs of our building, all the way up to our home, making it look as though there was no possibility anyone still lived there.

The idea was this, and it worked: We knew the Russians liked to drink their *Wodka*, as Dieter had so innocently described it in a letter only a year ago. And we knew they could get quite drunk. Wouldn't it be during a night of drunkenness that a Russian boy, who had not seen his woman in six years, would get the idea to rape? In such a state, and finding a stairwell so cluttered with debris, couldn't this deter that one *Bube*? Wouldn't he prefer an easier find, a woman on the first floor, for example?

⁓

Maybe it was Sunday. Herr Stichler, the proprietor from the tavern across from us, stood in the street and called out to all the neighbors. He just stood there and shouted loud so everyone could hear. He said he was pouring beer, and anyone could come and take as much as he liked. It was early in the day, and Herr Stichler seemed unusually full of fun for an ominous day like this.

Mutti handed me a large milk can—one of those impossible-to-carry metal cans with the two handles on either side—so I could have it filled up to take home. "He said it's free," Mutti said.

"Grete! How nice it is to see you. I always love when you visit." Herr Stichler tried to smile, but this time I did detect the worry behind his eyes. We all knew what would happen if the Russians found his taps full. He, in his own way, was also preparing for the worst: the Russians, drunk. We all knew what that could mean.

⁓

The Estonian doctor hung a huge sign outside the Lazarett entrance: EPIDEMIC HOSPITAL. It was written in Cyrillic. Thank God this man knew how to speak Russian. In huge, unmistakable letters, and on two sides of the building, he warned them not to come into our hospital.

And he did one more thing. He gave each of us nurses an ampoule with a lethal dose of morphine to keep in our pockets. "Just in case," he said with a wary and very weary mouth. There was nothing more he needed to say. We understood.

⤳

One night, when I arrived home from the Lazarett, Mutti showed me what she had found. She had come upon a man in the street, dead, an SS man, right in front of our house on the Windscheidstrasse. "Of course they stole his boots right away. It was such a ghastly sight, this man with bare feet. I wanted only to cover his face, to give him some dignity as he lay there. The entire street was full of corpses, you know, but this one just bothered me so. I couldn't look at him anymore. As I pulled his jacket up to cover him, something heavy fell out of a pocket. It was a bundle of knives. Nice ones, even. Look."

Mutti pulled out a set of table knives, maybe six of them, and laid them on the kitchen table. They had ivory handles with wide, sharp blades, the kind of knives used for fancy dinner parties. Then I saw why they had caught her attention. The initials LAH were engraved on the handles. Leibstandarte Adolf Hitler was what they stood for, the bodyguard of Adolf Hitler. I took a deep breath and stared at them. Was this SS man one of his bodyguards? Or was he merely a man who had stolen the knives? We would never know. He was dead, but now those things lay in our kitchen.

"Mutti, put those away! What will happen if the enemy comes into your house and sees what you have? They might misunderstand and think you had something to do with the Leibstandarte. Mutti, hide them! Throw them out! You won't even be able to trade them on the black market!" I think I was somewhat more aware of the potential danger because I had been so involved at the Lazarett and heard so much of the news.

She then threw the knives onto the stairway that was already so cluttered with debris, and there we let them lie.

A girl offers water to a young member of the Hitler Youth. (akg-images/ullstein bild)

## IV.

Very near the Lazarett was a large training center for the Hitler Youth. All the boys for the Volkssturm were recruited from there. As the battles in Berlin continued, many of these boys came to our Lazarett, sometimes just for a drink of water. There was a boy who was so small and his uniform so large that he kept tripping on the pants legs that dragged behind him on the floor. His steel helmet kept slipping down over his eyes. Again, it was Schwester Ruth who met him just as he entered the door. He was thirsty, he said in his little-boy voice.

"Where are you coming from, *Bübchen?*" we asked.

"From the Front!" he announced proudly, saluting. "From the train station, Ostkreutz!"

I brought him a cup of water and whispered to him, "Don't shoot at everything that moves, all right? Only the enemy. Understood?" I was half joking, but we had heard that now that the Hitler Youth were out there with guns, no one was safe. They simply shot at anything that moved. They played war as if it were a game. They were children, some no older than twelve, and we saw the results in our Lazarett. Horrible wounds. Legs and arms missing, gunshot wounds to the stomach.

⊷

I was in the lower level of the Lazarett and happened to look out the window, which was eye level to the street, and saw a pair of soldier's boots walking by. They did not look like those I'd seen on the corpses in the streets. Then, to my horror, I realized they were Russian!

I dropped what I had in my hands, maybe a bandage roll or an ampoule of morphine. I knew this was going to be a terrible night. I ran up the stairs and announced, "They're here!" Everyone pretended not to know what I meant. We continued to do our work into the night, but our hands were trembling.

"No nurse is to go near a window!" were the orders from Dr. von Lutzky. "And no one is to go outside. We will continue to conduct our business as we have always conducted our business." He was a man who stood by his actions, but I could see that he too was afraid. "And may God be with us all," he added, bowing his head.

Sometime later that day, a general walked into our Lazarett. He was in a green uniform and wore high boots. There was red piping on his sleeves and red insignias.[23] He was clearly not one of ours. He was Russian. We all pretended to go about our business, but we could not help sneaking peeks at this man. He looked not much different from us. Tall and slender, tanned skin.

The Estonian doctor, our savior, walked up to this man and began to speak to him in a low, controlled, and correct voice, in Russian. He waved his arm as he spoke, taking in all the staff and all the wounded soldiers around him. The Russian nodded and smiled in a way that seemed to relax our doctor. They both then gave a respectful nod of the head. The Russian straightened himself up and turned to walk out the door.

As soon as the door slammed, a cheer went around the entire ward. We understood that the doctor had told him we treated infectious diseases, and it would be unwise for anyone to enter without need. He had convinced the man in the green uniform that no Russian had any business entering our Lazarett *unless* he was wounded. And *if* he was wounded, we would take the utmost care of him.

～

Within hours, we received our first Russian patient. We pampered him and gave him extra tea and a bed in a corner where he would not be taunted by our Germans.

He was shy, this soldier, and grateful that we were treating him. He had a wound to his leg, which I bandaged. I could not help but feel some hostility. I thought, *How many of my men have you killed? How many boys are lying in the street now, dead, because of you?* But I took pity on him. It was my job, after all, to care for my patients.

# 16

## The Final Days

I.

We heard intense noise approaching from the east—tanks and artillery—and finally we saw them with our own eyes. The Russians were crossing over into our city. They had made it as far as the Heerstrasse U-Bahn station, just around the corner from us. The Volkssturm was still holding them back at the train embankments, but it was inevitable that they would be here by the morning.

We were not allowed to go home. Amazingly, the telephones worked, and I called Mutti and told her to come to the Lazarett. It would be safer, I said, at least safer than there in Charlottenburg. But she refused.

The situation at the Lazarett was dire. Soldiers were screaming for their bandages to be removed, for someone to care for them, for someone to say, "It's going to be all right," for someone to hold their hands and say the Lord's Prayer with them. We did what we could.

It was growing dark, and I knew we were to finish soon. No more lights. Who knew what the night would bring? With a sense of dread, we continued to work. Outside there was the noise of war.

❧

We could already hear women screaming. They would scream and scream and then there was a gunshot and no more noise. We were next. We were sure of it, and yet we worked as if it were just any other day.

There was more screaming, this time from the convent just down the street. "Oh no! Not the nuns! Not the nuns!" We were horrified. The screaming went on for a long time. Then it was quiet.

None of us thought we heard a gunshot. We prayed that perhaps they were saved. Who knew?

Late in the night, with only candles to give us light, when the work was finished and the fighting was over, all the nurses, one by one, walked the stairs to our small "party room," the Klossett where we took our cigarette breaks. It was nine or so, and we were all hungry and tired. Schwester Ruth had picked a few tulips earlier that day and had put them in an old milk bottle that served as a vase. She had even arranged a tablecloth of sorts. It was a pillowcase, but it was white, and it made the room feel somehow festive. Someone lit a few candles and we sat, about six of us, feeling calm, almost blissful for the moment, denying what we all believed—that this was our last day alive. We had already heard that in other Lazaretts it had not gone well. Even in hospitals, the nurses were all raped and murdered. Why would our fate be any different?

Someone pulled out a bottle of red wine she had bought with her blood-donation money. We passed around some glasses. God only knows where they came from. We toasted to what we believed would be our last night on earth. "To a better place. Wherever that may be . . ." Someone made a silly comment. It was about the nuns. "Well, at least they finally got some!" And we fell silent. We knew it was in poor taste.

I pulled out the twenty-Reichsmark bill I had just earned for donating blood and held it over the candle's flame. We watched as it fizzled away. What good would that money do any of us now?

⸎

Then the real onslaught came. It was sudden, and within an hour everything was in turmoil. They were shooting from everywhere, tanks were rumbling down the streets, men were shouting.

Most fearsome were the Stalin Organs. Nothing as dreadful had ever been seen in Berlin. *Katyushas* is what the Russians called them.

Russian *katyushas*, the "Stalin Organs," positioned in the streets of Berlin.
"Nothing as dreadful had ever been seen in Berlin." (akg–images/RIA Novosti)

They looked like long bullets that were mounted on the back of trucks. These trucks would drive through our neighborhoods and shoot right into the homes, right at eye level, and, of course, they fired into our Lazarett. The building shook. The entire top floor, the Gymnasium, disappeared. There was now a huge hole in the hallway that separated the severely wounded from those who were awaiting their operations. Everything lay in debris. Plaster and glass everywhere. A few of our soldiers died in that moment, just from the blast, possibly from a heart attack, and one of our nurses was killed.

≈

From that day on, a handwritten sign hung in front of our doorway, telling us where to look first, which direction the shooting might come from. "*Achtung.* The enemy is to your right," or "*Achtung.* Look to your left. Take great care."

The Lazarett filled to double its capacity. The heavy fighting lasted several days, and during this time I worried tremendously about Mutti. I was able to phone her once things had settled down in our neighborhood. She said that there was still fighting in our street but that the Reichskanslei had been secured. She was working hard to help the wounded men in the street.

When the fighting had subsided somewhat, we were allowed to leave the Lazarett again. The Russians had occupied the abandoned homes around us, to use as outposts. We could leave only in groups of twenty or more, and only if we were accompanied by men—either soldiers who were not so badly wounded, perhaps on crutches, or the Sanis.

Our orders were to be back at the Lazarett no later than six o'clock. That was when the Russians would begin to drink. *Not* a good time to be out, and not a good time to be a woman. We would make our plan: We'll walk to the Heerstrasse station, drop off Trudi, then on to the Theodor-Heuss-Platz and drop off Ria, and so on, until we were all home. Then we'd make the same plan for our return.

Outside, we no longer feared bombers, but now there were tanks. And drunk Russians. The only airplanes we saw in the sky were the rickety Russian ones we couldn't help but call "sewing machines." How they even flew, we had no idea. The Russians might be good at ground battle—they had good panzer troops and infantry, and gruesome artillery, and soldiers who were persistent and brave and had endured incredible hardships—but their airplanes were laughable.

One word we heard a lot from the Russians was *Uhri*. In a weird way, it reminded me of my father, Werner, when he was already so far gone after his brain operation and wanted to talk to me about his watch. These Russian soldiers wanted our wristwatches more than anything. Strange. I saw soldiers with as many as seven or eight watches on one arm. What for?

## II.

The yard behind the Lazarett had two big pits. One was the place where we buried our dead. The other was there to collect water in case the building caught fire. During the last battle, the city waterlines broke and we had no running water, so we took water from this pit, boiled it, and then gave it to our soldiers to drink—we had nothing else. And we used it to wash bandages. I sometimes worried there might be a corpse down in there somewhere—a woman, perhaps, who had decided to take her life. These things happened, you know, much more often than you would think.

Our lines were still broken, and the pit water was so foul, I asked Dr. von Lutzky if I could leave to fetch some. I had seen a water pump in a yard just down the street. "No, no. It's far too risky," he said. "They're still shooting out in the streets." But what were we to do? We needed clean bandages and the soldiers were crying out for something to drink. So I ran, anyway, believing that the Red Cross patch on my blouse would protect me.

I was shot at. Red Cross patch or not, I was a target for the Russians. But I had to get that water! I reached the pump and very quickly filled my two buckets. Then, hiding as well as I could behind hedges while the soldiers kept shooting, I ran back to the Lazarett. All of a sudden, to my left, I heard a child's voice from inside a bush. I turned to look. Two boys were standing there with large, frightened eyes. Their pants were way too long, and their jacket sleeves hung below their hands. One of them kept pushing his much-too-large helmet back up.

"Do you know where our captain is?" he asked. "We can't find him. Have you seen him?" His voice had not even changed yet.

I had to ask then, "But how old are you, young man?"

They both replied, "Sixteen!"

It made me laugh, and I said, "No. I haven't seen a captain. But stay safe, the two of you." I wished them well with all my heart, and I made myself forget about them. I had wounded men who needed the water, and I ran on.

Those young, young boys. They always came to us with the worst wounds. Their extremities missing, wounds so bad they'd never heal. They would lie on their cots, waiting for death, and cry for their Muttis. My heart bled for them. They really had no idea what they were doing.

⌘

One night, as the other sisters and I sat in our Zigaretten Klosett, a few of the soldiers who were on night watch came to us.

"You can put that cigarette out. You can rest now. You can do as you choose—sit or leave. It is over. Hitler committed suicide last night. They say, 'He died an honorable death, as a soldier.' We don't need to believe that anymore. We all know that's bunk. He was a coward. An insane coward. And he's now dead."

We simply stared at him. Not one of us put out our cigarettes, but we didn't smoke them either. We simply stared. Our mouths open.

He continued, "Eva Braun is dead, too. Goebbels and his wife killed themselves, and they even killed the children."

Could anyone have written such a strange story? What had become of us?

And what would become of us now?

We were suddenly frightened. We all held each other's hands and we wept. All the nurses, the men too. We had no idea what would come next.

⌘

Things changed dramatically after Hitler's death. At the front door there had always hung a picture of the Führer, the first thing you would see as you entered, and suddenly it was gone. In its place now were all kinds of religious things. A cross. A picture of Mary with the baby Jesus. Flowers. Many, many flowers. It seemed necessary now to go out and find them, pick them, and put them on our altar. Tulips and pansies and the *Flieder* were just beginning to bloom. The aroma of lilacs permeated the entire hospital.

❧

On May 8 an announcement came over the radio. The peace agreement had been signed. All the higher generals, including Dönitz, had met in Reims and signed an agreement to complete the final capitulation. The peace agreement was also signed by representatives of the Oberkommando from the Wehrmacht and representatives for the British, American, and Soviet high command. How things would go forward was not yet clear, but we knew that Germany had surrendered and it was unconditional.

That evening the German radio broadcast was just as it always was. The announcer was his usual controlled, straightforward self. He presented the news as always. Then, on a last note, out of the blue, he said, "So, jetzt können Sie mich mal am Arsch lecken." And with that he signed off. This dry man had for years told lies, and known they were lies, but that was his job. Now the war was over, and as a last hurrah he announced, just as dryly as ever, "Well, thank you and good night. And now you can all kiss my ass."

But it was over. The war was done.

# 17

## IT'S OVER

### I.

Dieter's last letter had asked us to pick up a lens for his telescope at Wolfram, a well-known camera equipment store, and, if we would be so kind, to have a photo enlarged at Porstfoto on the Kaiser-Friedrich-Strasse. It was dated February 27, 1945. Did he know those shops no longer existed?

### II.

Papa? There was no word.

### III.

The streets were now quiet, and that was a welcome change, but they held secrets. Women passed each other wondering, *Has it happened to you?* Other women looked like they were asking for it with their vulgar behavior—hanging on Russian arms, talking and laughing with them.

### IV.

Mutti and I were left to ourselves. Above all else, we wanted out. Berlin was to become a "dead city," anyway.

I still trundled off to the Lazarett until I was let go, while Mutti busied herself, with what, I don't know.

On one of her busier days, I know she did this: She visited Pastor Jentsch from the Swedish Church. The church had been badly damaged, but his spirit was whole. He told Mutti a secret about a man by the name of Raoul Wallenberg, a Swede, who even during the war had managed to provide refugees with passports to leave Germany.[24] Mutti asked if there was still a chance for that, and he told her about a train that Mr. Wallenberg was organizing to help get Swedish citizens out of Germany. Because Mutti had relatives in Sweden, he thought he might be able to get her on it.

Mutti's head must've been spinning. He gave her all the specifics he knew. It would be leaving that night, late. Midnight or so. She should pack only what she would need for two weeks, no more than that. It would be a train of only Scandinavians, traveling first through Finland, then on to Stockholm. He encouraged her. It was such an opportunity. And who knew when something like that would come again?

"What is to become of the people in Berlin, anyway?" Pastor Jentsch was very persuasive. Even in his sermons, he had always been so.

It was decided. Mutti hurried home and in a flurry told me all about it. "Grete. We're going to leave."

I only said, "When?"

And she said, "Tonight."

# Part III

## JOURNEY TO A NEW LIFE
### 1945–1949

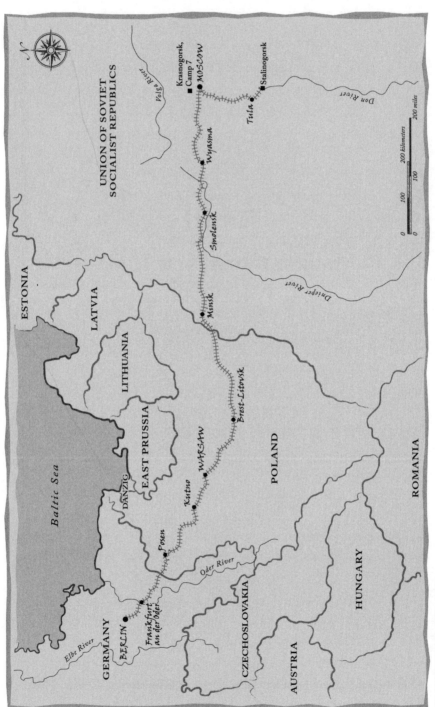

**EASTERN EUROPE, 1938**

## 18

# A Sharp Turn

By early afternoon we were packed. It was only a light suitcase for me. I had nothing much I wanted to bring. Only me and my dreams of freedom in a land with no war. I brought my wool coat, a hat I had knit for myself, a scarf, a bar of soap and a facecloth, a hairbrush, needles for mending, a book, and a photo of Dieter. At the last minute I decided to pack my Red Cross uniform as well, the white blouse with its Red Cross patch. *It might help when crossing the borders,* I thought, although I had no idea if this was true. There was nothing more I needed. I was on my way to a new life, which if all went as promised, would be just two weeks away.

Mutti? She had other ideas. We needed to bring the silver, she decided. All of it. There were forks and large soupspoons, the kind that can hardly fit into your mouth, and knives, twenty-four of each, heavy and all with the initials of her maiden name engraved on the handles: HD for Helga Dahlberg. A set of tiny mocha teaspoons as well, twenty-four of them, ornately enameled with the Swedish colors, blue and yellow. All this she wrapped into a green cloth shoe bag. She then carefully ripped open the bottom of my stepfather Karl's *Seesack*, the bag he had carried with him at sea during the Great War, and hid the shoe bag with the silver, her pearl necklace, and a gold locket she had received as a wedding gift underneath the top flap. This she worked on all day, sewing and resewing it until the seam was undetectable.

"But why are you doing all this, Mutti?" I pleaded. "We'll be in Sweden soon where we'll have a new life. We can always buy new silver once we've arrived." We never spoke of money in our family, but what I did know was that my grandfather—her father—had advised her to send as much money as she could for safekeeping to Sweden when

Hitler first declared war. Many people who had the means did the same—sent their money abroad. With all the horrible memories of the Great Inflation and the Depression only a few years earlier, she said it was one of the few smart things she ever did. I should have appreciated her foresight, but now she just seemed possessive and petty. I continued to plead, already realizing she'd expect me to carry her bag if it got too heavy for her, but she was not to be persuaded. "If we can't have our things, no one will," she insisted, looking incredulous that I didn't understand, and then continued her work.

She didn't want *them*—whoever *they* would be—to have our oil paintings either. So the few that could be bundled and carried for the next two weeks needed to come with us as well. "But where will you put them?" I asked. "How will you carry them?" But she was finished discussing any of it, and the answer was clear. The job was to be mine. Six oil paintings, including one Albrecht Dürer, were carefully wrapped in blankets and tied with twine and those two packages I was to carry, one under each arm. They were heavy and awkward and I was so angry with her. My arms were not even long enough to reach to the bottom. Just try to carry a package like that!

We were to arrive at the Swedish Church on the Kielerstrasse, near the Invaliden U-Bahn station.[25] It was not far from our house, and we were to be there by eleven o'clock that night. We left our home in good time. The night was still and starless. There were no bombs anymore, and no cars or Russian soldiers. We hurried along to the S-Bahn, which would take us to the church. From there we were told we would be transported to the train station from which we would depart for Sweden.

It was summer by now; it should have been warm, but I shivered the whole way. Perhaps it was excitement, but there was sadness and fear, too. We were headed to a completely new life, one I could only imagine. We were leaving so much behind—our entire lives, not least our dear Dieter. And how would Papa Spaeth find us? But Mutti had an answer for that too: "Of course they'll find us!"

We got off the S-Bahn at the proper station and walked to where the church should have been. It was once the very church Dieter and I attended on Sundays, when later we would talk all day about God and all those things that Pastor Jentsch had said. Now the entire block lay in ruins, and when we came to the church, all that was left standing were two bare walls, the interior open to the black night. It must have been a *Sprengbombe* that hit the church, because those bombs would fall to the bottom of the building and destroy everything inside but often leave the walls still standing.

The Russians were not to know about us, Mutti had been told earlier that day by the woman who had helped her at the Swedish embassy. "They may not let you leave," she had warned, and heeding this advice, we managed to stay very still. By eleven o'clock there were about fifty of us in all, all of us suddenly "Swedish," although it turned out many did not know a word of the Swedish language. How can you blame them? They, like everyone, just wanted to get out.

All night we sat. Darkness and dampness, whispering voices and my pounding heart are how I remember this night. And of course the waiting. No transport came, and finally daylight broke. We continued to sit, worried and anxious by now. Some of us had brought sandwiches— bread and cheese—and people ate and moved around a bit. The day passed, and sometime late in the night, transport finally arrived. Was it a lorry? A bus? I cannot remember, but we were brought to the train station in Lichtenberg, on the outskirts of Berlin, where we were told we would need to wait a while longer. I tried to breathe slowly; I tried to stay calm. *Things will be all right very soon,* I kept thinking, hoping to console myself. I wanted so badly to leave Berlin and Germany behind. I wanted no more blackened, broken walls, no more rubble, no more death. But no train came.

❧

It was after midnight when a hefty woman with hard eyes and an accent approached and advised us that we should make sure our papers were in order and readily available. We would be asked to present them upon boarding. She would be our guide for the journey. She said her name was Therese, but her accent said something else. Her German was not fluent—she was probably from the east somewhere. She was not kind; I could not tell whether she was with the Partei, but then I thought, *Of course that cannot be. We are refugees and she is here to help us.* A Partei member would have locked us up. She then told us we would be in Stockholm in no more than two weeks, and that was all I wanted to hear.

"The train will arrive soon and you will know because it's a Swedish train, not a filthy one like those we have here in Germany," Therese informed us.

*Yes, well, now we also have that to live with: filthy trains. It was never so, but of course we have the war to blame,* I thought.

When no train came, we lay on the benches and did what we could to make ourselves comfortable. I fell asleep. So did Mutti.

❧

Early the next morning, on the fifteenth of June, a train finally came. The grimy gray cars with greasy windows were a picture darker than Therese had painted for us. But the train was here, nonetheless, and we wanted now only to find our seats.

Mutti, of course, pushed her way to the front of the crowd and was first to board. She was determined that we would have a sleeping berth and managed to maneuver through every car all the way to the front of the train and then back again.

She found no sleeping cars. She was disappointed but managed to organize two bench seats, one facing the other. They were wooden benches that folded down. A skimpy straw mattress and two thin blankets had been laid out on each of them.

Mutti's bag with its concealed silver and the oil paintings were hoisted by a fellow passenger onto the rack above our heads; I kept my sack at my side. This man would become a friend to me, someone to talk to other than Mutti. He told me he had worked for the Swedish embassy before the war and he spoke Swedish fluently. "God morgon, God morgon," we greeted each other the next day and every day after. Because of a head wound, he could no longer see so well, he told me, and he had been sent home from the front. Which front, I almost asked, but didn't. I didn't want to hear about war anymore. We were on our way to our new home.

Herr Koch was his name, or Knecht, I don't remember exactly. He offered me a cake he had wrapped in his satchel, but I said no. "You are kind, but no." I wanted food, of course, I was hungry as always, but I told myself I would not eat until I knew we were well on our way. Finally, that evening, the train began to roll. I pulled my sack up under my head and was dead asleep before I could even take one last look at the land I was about to leave behind forever.

⁂

The first rays of daylight poked through the windows before I became conscious of where I was, and the idea that I was on my way to freedom filled me with euphoria, the kind I had not felt since I was a student in Jena. We were somewhere east of Berlin by now, it was easy to see. Wide stretches of farmland lay to either side of us, the morning light still painting the fields lavender. Here and there were dense patches of forest, and farmhouses dotted the clearings. All of them, I noticed, were abandoned; all had broken windows. Now and again I'd see a lace curtain flying through an open hole. Where did the people flee to? Were any of them among those I saw flooding the train stations in Berlin, "the refugees from the east"?

A woman and her sister sat just behind Herr Koch, and they had brought a map with them. They were surmising that we must be near Posen. If this was true, we were coming close to the town where I was born, Beuthen, in Silesia. Of course I wanted very much to see what this city looked like and rushed to the window on their side of the car to see.

My heart fell into my stomach. It was no different from everywhere else. Broken walls with no buildings behind them. Vehicles lying askew off in the ditches. I saw no people. Dead streets and everything black and burned.

Therese entered our car with a tray of breakfast food. It was that dreadful Muckefuck we'd had for the last six years, Ersatzkaffee, and dark bread. But she gave us butter and jam made from real gooseberries, which was delicious. I had not tasted gooseberry jam in such a very long time. With our breakfast, we sat in our seats and watched with anticipation where we would be going next. The train took us farther east, through Kutno, then Warsaw—we were now in Poland, according to the train station signs.

Late that evening, Therese came to our car again. She did not come to bring us food this time, but to inform us of a change in route. We would be headed for Leningrad in northern Russia. It was necessary, she said, because there was so much destruction from the war that the train could not go directly. However, "From there we will begin to head west for Finland," she said. "You still have German papers, you know, and Germany is no longer a country. In fact, Moscow is now your capital."

We had lost the war, and it seemed that meant we had lost our identity, too. We would need to get Russian papers, she said, as those were the only ones that would be accepted from now on. The trip to Leningrad would take another five days.

"The passage to Finland will of course cost money as well," Therese continued. Mutti and I were startled. No one had told us anything about money. "*What* money are you talking about?" Mutti interrupted.

"Yes," Therese continued, ignoring my mother. "The passage will cost one thousand Reichsmarks—each," she snapped and glared at Mutti.

"Who on this train has a thousand marks? Who? We cannot do this! This is nonsense. No one has money. We've been in a war!" Mutti said, flustered, and then looked like she was about to cry. I was dumbfounded. We had come this far; we were not about to lose this, our only hope.

"Yes, Frau Spaeth, I understand. But you do have your gold and silver sewn inside that Seesack of yours, I would imagine?"

With that, and the look on Therese's face, Mutti shut up and we merely looked at each other, wondering what to do next. Did she really know about the silver? Or was she just bluffing? Mutti stayed still and we did as the others did: We began to rummage through our belongings, looking for, or pretending to look for, what we could give in barter for our transport.

I quickly decided I wouldn't need my coat. My lovely warm wool coat. *It's summer,* I thought. *And in only a few days we'll be in Sweden. I can live without it.* At the last minute, I gave Therese my hat as well, hoping, I suppose, to be on her good side, and with that the transport for both Mutti and me was paid for. Therese was satisfied. The train rumbled on.

⤶

MINSK. In Cyrillic lettering on a sign at a train station we passed. Someone on the train must have known how to read it, because we knew where we were: deep inside Russia. Herr Koch and I continued to have interesting conversations. He had lived in Sweden for many years, and he told me of his days with his wife, who now was dead—he did not say how, but one never did in those days. He told me of the long bicycle rides they would take through the countryside.

"We would ride and see the sea off in the distance, with a beach that looked to be deserted. We would lean our bicycles up against a fence and walk with our sacks of bread, herring, and a bottle of aquavit or a bottle of wine, and sit in the stillness for hours, listening to the wind whispering through the grasses. It would be dark before we thought to ride home again, and our bicycles were always still there against the fence. No one would have taken them; no one would even have thought of taking them. That's how it was in Sweden."

His stories made me dream about how my life would be soon. Such peaceful days as he described, with no worries, and my grandmother and cousins . . . Oh, I was so excited!

The next station platform held the sign SMOLENSK, and the train stopped here. We did not know why or for how long it would stop. No one dared to venture outside, though. We could miss the train if it were to take off again, and, anyway, everything we could see from our windows looked to be destroyed.

Smolensk. We all knew this name. The battle there was supposed to have been the turning point in the war. "Final victory is only weeks away," the radio propaganda told us back then, again and again, during the first year. Now we saw it with our own eyes, and, like so much of our own country, it too lay in ruin. Just like Berlin, just like Kutno and Posen and Minsk, and like everywhere we'd been. We were witnessing, firsthand, the result of all the fighting and of Hitler's "scorched earth" policy. Ruins, everything deserted and dead.

People from somewhere nearby came up to the train with things they wanted to trade. Women held something wrapped in their long aprons, shriveled carrots, a tomato, a few eggs. We, of course, traded whatever we had. A pair of scissors, stockings, all the things we thought we could do without for the next two weeks.

A woman with her young boy approached us and knocked on my window. She was very pretty but dressed in shabby clothing. There were holes in the elbows of her sweater, and her boy bashfully hid behind her skirt. She could not speak German well, but we could see from her gestures and smiles that she wanted to tell us that her son had a

German father. Perhaps she was hoping we knew where the father was, or maybe she just wanted to trade with us, but we never learned because just then the train began to roll away.

Endless rocking, and endless countryside with endless farmhouses, abandoned. I felt sadness, a deep sadness for this land that now looked so barren. At station after station, as we rolled through, I saw mountains of goods lying in piles as if these things had been simply thrown there, like heaps of garbage. As we passed I could see what the piles were made up of: sewing machines and radios; ironing boards and irons; a china cabinet long missing its china, its doors broken; blankets and down pillows, soggy and useless; eggbeaters, chairs, a broken piano bench. Later, in a village an hour or so farther along, the piano that must have belonged to the earlier bench appeared at the top of a pile. The legs were missing. Rolltop desks, more sewing machines, more radios. Lamps. Many, many lamps, and once a large pile of lightbulbs. Only lightbulbs, nothing else. Many of the Russian soldiers, people had whispered back in Berlin, had never seen lightbulbs before, and for them they seemed to possess some sort of magic. They stole all they could find.

There were bicycles too on these mounds, hundreds of them. All lay rusting away in the sun and the rain and the weather, never to be used again. Mutti surmised it was plunder from our once lovely homes in Berlin.

≈

The train stopped more frequently now. We had been traveling for four days, but it seemed like weeks. It was June, and the heat was unbearable. Some of our people were very sick, and we did what we could to help them. Someone had aspirin that was shared, but that was all the help we could give. I think even someone died, but I cannot be sure of this. My memory isn't clear.

Therese brought us Ersatzkaffee to drink and the dark bread with butter each morning. And in the evenings we were given soup, this too with bread. We were grateful. We were hungry.

We stopped at a station somewhere in a desolate open space for, it seemed, all afternoon one day; we had no idea why. The day was dreadfully hot. No new passengers boarded; of course, no one got off. We never had any idea how long we would stop or when we would leave again, so we stayed in our seats. Some of us stood in the doorways to get some fresh air.

Trains pulled up alongside us from time to time. They were always full of prisoners. These prison trains with their slatted sides and roofs open to the sky were what we in Germany knew to be cattle cars. I could see moving shadows through the slats if I tried, and the shadows were of men sitting in the heat. We tried to speak with them if we could, and we learned they were soldiers, most of them German.

We asked: "Where have you come from?" From the Eastern Fronts. "Where are you going?" They did not know. They were hungry, we heard most often, and they needed water. Some of our passengers still had cakes and chocolates from their Swedish relatives, care packages that had been sent to them through the Swedish embassy, so we did what we could to throw our food over the tops of the cars. They always let us know how grateful they were.

And always I asked, "Have you seen Dieter Dos? Do you know him? He's from Berlin and he fought in Italy. Then he fought in the East. He was to become a lieutenant, and he is my brother. Have you seen him?" Never did one man say yes.

One of these trains pulled up alongside us and came to a full stop. I could hear again the men were German, so I started a conversation with one of them. He whispered yes, they too were all prisoners, and they were very scared. They did not know what was to become of them. Many of the men were wounded and had not had their bandages changed for a long time, he said. Some of their wounds were beginning to fester. My heart beat so fiercely it could have been the noise of an oncoming train. I knew how to change a bandage and clean a wound. I could perhaps save a soldier's leg, but how could I help now? I was afraid to leave the train, and, besides, I had no clean bandages with me. Perhaps it was guilt that filled me; probably it was, the guilt of someone who knew she would help but couldn't.

I talked with another man, whose name I can't remember. He had been an engineer before the war. He had a wife and a young daughter, although he had not seen them in several years. "She would be seven now," he told me, and he had no idea if she or her mother was alive or dead. His home was in Helgoland, on a small island in the North Sea. His people still considered themselves to be Frisians.

Behind him I could hear the moaning of men in pain, and I knew this sound well. It was the moaning of men who were thirsty and men who had lost everything. Men who had no hope left, men who knew they would die. My new friend told me that, yes, indeed, men were dying. It was very hot inside his train. The men were dirty and thirsty; they had not been let out for several days, and it smelled foul of urine and sweat, he said.

"You must understand," he told me, "these are men who once were brave, who believed in their fatherland, who are fathers and sons, who now will likely die here. No one will know. Yesterday, two Russian soldiers came to each of our cars and asked for the dead. The train was still moving, but slowly. When we pointed them out, they were grabbed by feet and arms and thrown out the door into the field. Who were these men? Did we know them? No. Who were their mothers? Their wives? Who would tell their children that they had been brave, that circumstances had deposited their bodies here in this forsaken land where soon enough mud and rain will wash over them, their bodies disappearing beneath next year's grasses?" Then he said, "We have not had anything to drink all day. . ."

I wished I could pass him at least some water through the slats, but I could do nothing. I had no water, and our train suddenly began to move. I wished him luck, and when he was gone, I pressed my hands to my mouth and prayed silently so no one would hear. "Thank you, God, once again, for my good fortune. And thank you that I am not one of them."

﹏

As our journey approached nearly seven days, still on our way north toward Leningrad, the train suddenly took a sharp turn. From the sun we could see we were headed east again. How disturbing! Some of our people began to worry. We all wondered out loud why this was, but Therese was not anywhere to be found. We tried to calm ourselves by assuming what she told us later that evening: We were now on our way to Moscow. Again, she explained it in the same way as before—it was for proper papers, papers none of us had and papers that would ensure our freedom. We had nothing to do about this but to be patient, once again.

The sun became a red streak on an empty horizon, and the land grew purple. There were no lights in this train—a circumstance of war, we believed—and on this evening we were all anxious. Surely we would be arriving *somewhere* soon, somewhere we could get off the train, somewhere we could call our destination. Around midnight—it was dark, very dark, we couldn't see where we were, and by now the train smelled something awful, of human perspiration and worry—suddenly the train came to a stop, our doors were thrown wide, and we were told to get off.

We were at some sort of train station, and several women were there. They wore large headscarves and long aprons, and they spoke Russian at us. "Follow them," Therese told us, pointing. "They will show you where you can sleep."

We followed, Mutti with her sack heavy with silver. She never did acknowledge that she had it, although she did trade her silk stockings at one of our stops for several eggs, which we both ate. They were only half cooked, but we were grateful. I carried my now much lighter suitcase, the suitcase without my winter coat, and the six oil paintings, three under each arm. Through thick, wet mud we made our way, trying our best not to slip. Ahead of me I noticed a young boy who had lost his shoe somewhere. He began to cry. His mother lifted him, and with their bags, she carried him, his bare foot dangling.

It was drizzling, as it had been doing on and off all day. Up ahead, we could barely make out some sort of building, long and narrow. This was where we were led. Inside, it was large and mostly unfurnished. A woodstove was at the far end. One of our men, a quiet one but one who knew a little Russian, asked for water so that we could wash: "We have not bathed in five days. I know the women, too, would appreciate something to clean with. Some soap, perhaps."

Two large tubs filled with water were brought to us along with several bars of black, foul-smelling soap, and happily we washed ourselves. Women and men both, Mutti and I, we all bathed as well as we could. We rubbed each other's backs, we made jokes, we were suddenly elated, happy that something was about to happen. We were off the train at last, and we were clean. With new hope, we made beds from our clothing and laid our bodies down wherever we could find space. I slept a deep sleep, something I had been wishing to do for a very long time.

When I awoke, the sun was brilliant, the fields around us painted in gold. *I'm free, I'm free!* I wanted to dance. I hugged Mutti, who was also unusually lighthearted. Therese came to us then, again with our morning Ersatzkaffee, set the tray down and left. *Strange,* I thought, but then Therese was often strange. Timidly now—we had been in that train car for so long—I stepped out the door. I wanted to feel the new sunshine; I wanted to smell something other than humans. But what I saw before me was the last thing I had envisioned.

# 19

## STAY SMALL

We were inside a sort of compound surrounded by a barbed-wire fence. To one side I could see yet another compound, this one full of people. What divided us from them was a wooden fence, and it was very tall. At each of the four corners of their area was a tall tower constructed of steel. Who were the men, and why were they there, and we here? This was unbelievable.

Somehow I managed to peer over the fence that separated us. What I saw were men, all in German uniforms. *Landser*—German infantrymen—and even some wearing officer's uniforms. I would soon learn they were prisoners of war. We, on the other hand, were merely in a holding camp—a quarantine, we were told, in order to receive our papers.

I learned we were in an area called Krasnogorsk, not far from Moscow, and it was called Camp One.[26] Many of these men had very high ranks, some were generals who still wore their red sashes, and some of them were even rather famous. I heard names the radio news had spoken of in the past, names like Friedrich Paulus and Walther von Seydlitz and others from Freies Deutschland, the Free Germany movement. They had all been detained here. These were men who had fought against Russia once, but in the end they worked against their own people, the Germans, something people didn't talk about much.

What they did was so shameful—they betrayed their own comrades. But what they wanted was the right thing, to stop the senseless fighting, and they thought this was the right way to do it. During a battle in Breslau, some of the men from Freies Deutschland had shouted over loudspeakers, in German, telling the German soldiers where to run, which many of them did, but it was right into the arms of the Soviets. It did not go well for those soldiers. It turned into a mad bloodbath, and this is what was remembered of the men of Freies Deutschland. Of course, it did not go well for these men in the prison camp either. Many were treated very poorly.

The "quarantine camp" in Krasnogorsk was where we would stay while, again, our papers were being put in order. There were new arrivals now, too, most of them also Scandinavians: Finns, Danes, and Norwegians. It was a Sunday, I remember, a week later, when Therese informed us, "It's very difficult, you know. Identity needs to be verified, and with so many dead and so much misinformation . . . well, it will just take time."

Mutti said it must be the Swedish embassy in Moscow that was holding things up, but then Therese informed us we also needed to be checked for lice. This was news. Of course we did not have lice. We were not pigs. Among us were diplomats and ambassadors. One from Thailand, another from Greece, another from Hungary, men who were always addressed as "Your Excellency." We women were dressed well too—well, in comparison—and some even carried stylish handbags. Why would she think we, of all people, had lice? Some of us were becoming skeptical. I tried to stay calm. At least we had left Germany behind.

⟨≈⟩

Our days became routine. We were fed twice a day. Always the food was relatively good, much the same as on the train: bread with butter, jam, sometimes cheese for breakfast. Ersatzkaffee or even tea. In the evening we were given soup made with chicken or some other kind of meat, some bread, and again tea.

During the day there was not much to do. I wanted to know who the men were on the other side of the fence, and I often took my soup bowl at night to a place I found where I could talk to whoever would listen, and many did. It was a good way to pass the time, it seemed, for both of us.

There was a man I had come to befriend. He was, he told me, a German translator for the Russians. We spoke nearly every night, sometimes for hours. Before long we discovered that we might even have some friends in common. There were many soldiers here from Berlin, he told me.

"Oh," I said, "I'm sure I know some of them. So many of my school comrades fought on the Eastern Front, and some of them might even be here." I began to mention names. "Do you know Horst Viedt? He was a lieutenant. Or Franz Doebl? And there was my friend Hans-Wilhelm Hendel, a parachutist who fought in Russia. Have you heard his name spoken?" In turn he gave me names. Some I vaguely knew. Perhaps they had been grammar school friends, but none whom I knew well. And then he mentioned Willi Hohorst. "Oh my! Willi was one of my dearest friends! He sent me a letter once from Breslau. Oh, tell me, is he here?"

"Dear Margarete. I am so sorry. He is here. He was badly wounded, though. I don't know quite what happened to him, but he is not right. Do you know what I mean? He talks in his sleep. He screams sometimes. We try to calm him. We give him warm soup and our bread if we can. His eyes are cold. Something happened. I don't know what."

"Oh, but do bring him here to the fence. Do. Please. Tomorrow, when you come, bring Willi. Tell him, Margarete from Charlottenburg is here and wants to see him. Tell him that."

The next evening—and I had a hard time concentrating all day—I went to my seat at the fence and there was the translator sitting, waiting, along with my dear friend Willi. What a shock it was to see him. He was gone. Gone, all of him. His body looked like bones dressed up in a uniform. His eyes, when they looked at me, were distant and removed.

"Margarete!" Willi saw me, it is true, and he knew me. He threw his arms open, and if we could, we would have held each other a long time.

Tears we could no longer control ran down our faces. We wished to know everything that had happened to each other. How did you manage to hold out? How did you survive? Who do you know who is still alive?

"And what about the street where I lived, Margarete? Tell me about it. Is my house still standing? And do you know how things went for Rosemarie?"

"No, Willi, no. Your street is in ruins. I cannot be sure, but your house probably is, too. I'm sorry. This is the story of most of us, you know." Willi had been my confidant, my friend. Rosemarie was a girl he said he wanted to marry one day. I knew about their private meetings after the Tanzschule—that's how close we were.

The translator, only too happy to have made the introduction, quickly excused himself and left. As soon as he was out of earshot, Willi lowered his eyes.

"You are a prisoner, Margarete. Make no mistake. You are here to work for them, nothing less."

"No, Willi. You're wrong," I said. I shook my head, worried for him that his circumstances were so different from mine. "We are mere refugees, Willi. Raoul Wallenberg sponsored this train, a special train for Germans of Swedish descent.[27] We are all on our way home to Sweden, and that is where I intend now to live. Berlin, as you must know, is no more. In fact, when we left, everyone was saying it is to be a 'dead city.'"

"You are mistaken, dear Margarete. I am sure of this. You are here to work. These people cannot be trusted. They are Russians and we were their enemy. They will tell you one thing and then do the opposite. They will tell you a lie, something you know is a lie, and they will look at you as if they believe every word they are saying is true.

"I have been here nearly five months. I do not know what they intend to do with me. They will not say. I have been through one

Willi Hohorst. "You are a prisoner, Margarete. Make no mistake."

interrogation after another. They think they will find informers. They will find none. We only want something to eat. We want to bathe, and we want to go home. I don't think they'll ever give us this last wish."

When I knew Willi in Berlin, when we were in high school together, he was muscular with thick hair that he would comb neatly to one side. The corners of his mouth were always somehow turned upwards as if his next sentence was poised to make you laugh. He had a strong nose; his arms were full like those of a man ready to take on the world.

What he intended, he once told me, was to become a teacher of German history. He loved the old German sagas, and I always thought he would make a delightful man to listen to, standing at the front of the class. His favorite stories were myths from the Rhine, where he was born. "The Lorelei," about a beautiful woman who sat atop the cliff, combing her long hair. She mesmerized the sailors, causing them to fall in love, and they, not being able to take their eyes off her, would crash into the rocky cliffs. The lines of the poem he had recited for me often:

*"What wouldst thou with me?" Lorelei cried, starting to her feet.*
*"To cast thee into the Rhine, sorceress," said Diether roughly, "where thou*
*hast drowned our prince."*
*"Nay," returned the maid, "I drowned him not. 'Twas his own folly which*
*cost him his life."*

He described her long wet hair streaming over her shoulders, and her haunting songs sung in an otherworldly voice, like that of the wind. This same Willi now sat before me as I gazed into a face that had long disappeared. Willi with his jagged cheekbones and barely a voice inside him, scratching at his ears, his hair, his groin. The sky was turning dark, and he suddenly seemed not with me. He was like an actor in a film with his sentences memorized, looking past me more than at me.

"Don't eat the salt fish," he blurted, out of context and into the void. "And don't eat garbage. Don't do that. Never do!" His eyes became sharp. "Both will kill you. I have seen it too many times. Men go crazy for food. They begin to steal from each other, they lie, they wander in the night, and I have seen them crawling around over the garbage heaps like ghosts in the moonlight.

"They eat anything they can find. Eggshells. Rotten fish scales. Dirt, even. Anything. And then they go crazy and die. Intelligent men, strong men once, smarter than this, reduce themselves to nothing but flies landing on every piece of rot they find. I saw a man chewing on the legs of a pair of trousers once, moaning and convulsing like he was making love to the dirt. The next morning his body lay like a lump at the side of a building, a half-eaten pant leg still in his mouth.

"But you must know something else. They will try to kill you, too. They will watch you die slowly. Of thirst. We get them once a month or so—salt fish. You get so hungry you want to eat anything that is put in front of you, and you get so tired of cabbage soup, so every once in a while they will serve you salt fish.

"Don't eat it! It has been cured in a salt brine. You will never have enough water to wash it down with. And you will die of thirst. This, too, I have seen."

A long pause, and then: "Never let food be your motivator. You will betray your comrades if you do." Then Willi was silent.

The night stars were bright now, and I remember the sky had turned the color of lapis, deep blue, not black. It must have been late, or early, really. The sun never set during those summer nights.

My gratitude to Willi would come in later months. For now, despite his sad condition, I was only happy to see him and know he was still alive.

But I never saw Willi again. The translator informed me through the fence a few days later that Willi had been "called up" in the night and had been shot. It was the fate of many men on his side. They were suspected of talking, suspected of having been a Nazi, suspected of conspiracy, or suspected of nothing, but meant to die anyway.

And that was Willi Hohorst. Maybe he was a spy. Maybe he was an informer. Maybe he wasn't anything. Just a man caught in the wrong place at the wrong time.

❧

While we were here in this place I no longer had a definition for, we would need to work. "It is the way of Communism," Therese told us one day. It was July now, and some of us were to work on the collective farms, some on a construction site. For me it would be out in a field. I was to plant trees, and so was Mutti. We would begin today after our soup, we were told.

Trees, lorries full of them, all pine, stacked one behind the other—along with me, Mutti, another woman about my age who was very shy, and several men—were driven out to an empty field, and here we were to spend our day. The trees were dumped by the side of the road, where all around us was nothing but wide-open fields, and we were left standing with shovels, along with our supervisor, a Russian woman who spoke no German. She seemed less interested in us than in her dirty fingernails, which she looked at, and picked at, nearly all day.

"Dig holes in rows five feet apart. Make them deep enough to plant each tree. This is to be a forest for the next generation. We will have furniture from this wood and it will feed our fires. Now work," she said, and picked some more.

I befriended the shy girl. I don't remember her name, but I remember it was my birthday, July 10. I was twenty-one now, and I told myself it was to be a good day. I showed her how to do it. I said, "We'll plant the trees upside down. Just like this. Watch me." I dug my hole. Thankfully the soil was soft from the weeks of rain we'd had. Muddy, actually, but I didn't mind. Not the dirt, not the work. I was happy at my discovery of how to let them—these people who were keeping me from my new homeland—know who they were dealing with.

I took my first pine tree and planted it pointy side down into the dirt and then proceeded to fill in the hole so that the tree stood straight up, like it was supposed to be there, just like that, all along. My friend giggled from behind her hair, and we both continued on our mission. Together we planted trees, row by row, all with the root balls sticking up high to the sky. What a wonderful birthday it was! Mutti thought it was terribly funny too and wished she had thought of it herself. We returned to our wooden house that evening content and tired.

⁓

Days dragged on into weeks. The heat of July became the heat of August, and we were still waiting for our papers. Some of us had work; others didn't. I was, at the moment, one of the latter. It was the seventh of

August, an otherwise uneventful day. Boredom had long ago set in. Hot as I was, I walked to the latrine for something to do, then decided to sit for a while on a bench and lean my back against the rough wooden wall. Some flies were sitting on a stain next to my hand. I let them sit. I closed my eyes, wanting to dream, to envision my home, how it would be once we were in Sweden. How my room would look and where I would put my books and my photo of Dieter. My dear brother—I still had no idea where he was or if he was alive.

A man sat down next to me then and wanted to talk, interrupting my quiet daydream. By his accent I could tell he was Bavarian, and he seemed anxious to speak. "Have you heard?" he asked, and continued without pausing for an answer. I hoped what he was about to say was something good. Some news about a call for transport. A reason to believe we were about to head for Finland. But no. He said this instead: "The Americans dropped a bomb on Japan yesterday. I heard this from one of the Russian guards. Although he didn't speak German well, he seemed to be quite knowledgeable and wanted me to know all about it. He seemed excited. But not in a good way. He said one bomb destroyed the entire city. One bomb!"

He looked at me intently. I returned his gaze, unable to fathom what I had just heard. Already, war had been shifted so far to the back of my memory that it seemed impossible to still be going on. What this man said could not be true.

I had no words for him. The clouds seemed to darken in that moment against the white sky, the same sky that also looked upon this city in Japan, one I had never heard of, Hiroshima. My head hurt suddenly, something fierce. And I felt sick. I stood up and managed to walk to the edge of the path and vomited.

He and I never spoke again. I don't know who he was or what happened to him. Perhaps he was sent someplace else. But the news he gave me that day I did not repeat. It was too horrible, too terrible to imagine. I wanted nothing more to do with bombs. *When, oh when, will it all end?*

∾

The time for interrogations began. These were frightful times. It happened suddenly, and only in the middle of the night, when all was black and no one could see or hear, when all were asleep. Guards would come to your bed and wake you up, rudely. "Get up. Don't bother with your things; you'll be back before daylight. Now!" they ordered.

We would only know about it the next day, when we noticed an empty bed and would ask, "Where is Peter?" "Where is Stefan?" Those who slept next to Peter or Stefan, or whoever was missing, would report what had happened at night, each of us happy they hadn't come for us. Sometimes Peter or Stefan would be in his bed again, back in fetal sleep the next morning, and we would imagine it had been just a bad dream.

The few Jews who were in our camp had it the worst of all of us. This was true. It was believed that if they survived the Nazis, they must have been spies, informers for the SS. How else did they manage to still be alive? There was a family I remember, a man and his wife and daughter from somewhere in the east. They spoke German well. Their name was Schmidt. Somehow we knew they were Jewish. They were among us Swedes but could not speak a word of Swedish. When guards weren't around, we jokingly called them the Juden-Schmidts. The daughter—I became quite good friends with her—had the name Gisela on her passport, although I knew her only as Rebecca.

I felt so sorry for this family. One day they were gone, just gone, and I would never see "Gisela" again. We all speculated that they had been sent to another camp, or possibly—and this thought frightened us terribly—they had been shot. This family, this quiet, reserved family, I am afraid to say, might have been suspected of conspiring with the Nazis. I think they ended up in the Lubyanka. I cannot say for sure. They were just gone one day, and all their belongings too. No one ever asked about them or mentioned their names again. They were simply gone.

Then it happened to me. I was called in the middle of one night, my turn for an interrogation. I could not imagine what they would want from me. I was just a girl, I had only just turned twenty-one. What did I know? What was I to say? That I had worked as a Red Cross nurse and bandaged German soldiers? Helped to operate on war-wounded men, but they had been German? That I had been in Berlin and seen with my own eyes the brutal treatment our women received from their own kind, the Russian soldiers? Was that what I would be accused of?

My interrogator was a Jewish man. His name was Stern and he spoke fluent German. He was not very tall but he was handsomely dressed in his blue uniform, and on his head was a blue hat. He asked me kindly to sit, which I did. He himself sat and then asked about my past—about my involvement with the Red Cross, about my Abitur, and what my hopes were for the future. Chitchat, really, my date and place of birth, that sort of thing. He asked if I'd seen any Russian workers, the Fremdarbeiter, when I was still in Germany.

"Of course I did, sir," I said. And then, like a fool, I added, "I could always tell they were Russians, because their clothes were always so ragged. I felt sorry for them. But now that I'm here, I see that everyone dresses just like them."

Immediately I knew I'd said too much and felt ashamed, but it seemed not to have fazed him. Instead he folded his hands in front of him and I felt the heat of the bare lightbulb above my head. *What now?* I thought.

"You have been quite friendly with the soldiers in this camp, have you not?"

"Yes. I've met some of them, sir."

"And you know we have generals from Germany here too, do you not?"

"Yes, sir. I do know that."

"Have you been introduced to any of them? Perhaps you would like to meet some?"

Something I had taught myself long ago from my first encounters with the SS: *Do not say yes. Do not say no. Stay small.*

"I have only spoken to a few men on the other side. And I have made one friend." I was alluding to my translator. For a fleeting moment I thought of mentioning Willi and how happy I had been to see him, thinking that by talking about a friend like this, I might endear myself to this man, help him to see me more as a person. But I stopped myself. Suppose Willi actually had done something or said something, and now, because of our friendship, I could be implicated. I said nothing more. *Stay small.*

"But people speak, they talk, you know," the short man with the blue cap continued. Yes, I knew this. And I knew too that "walls have ears." Often we suspected one another and were always careful of what we said and to whom we spoke. A friendly man, someone with cigarettes, sometimes real coffee or chocolate—something no one else ever had— often came to our barracks, just to talk. Of course we suspected him most of all. He was Finnish, but, really, all were suspected, and all were suspicious. So again, I simply said nothing.

"You would like to leave soon, no?"

"Yes, sir. Yes, I would, very much. And my mother, too."

"We know about your mother. And both of you can leave here much sooner than otherwise if you can help us out a bit."

"I would be happy to help," I said, suddenly relaxing, thinking, if all this talk was only to ask me to work more, of course I could do that. *I could even plant trees right side up*, I thought, laughing to myself.

As the interrogation went on, however, it was clear we were not communicating. He thought, he fully believed, that I was a Partei member. He believed that I knew about the concentration camps in the east, the camps where the Jews had been interned.

"I knew nothing of those camps, sir. I only first heard about them toward the very end of the war, and then not again until I came here. I was horrified, actually—and I must tell you, I was never a member of the Partei!"

With this, he stood so fast his chair fell over backwards, his face so close to mine that I could see the outline of his irises. "You lie! You lie! Just like all the rest of you. Of course you were a member of the Partei! All Germans were in the Partei. All of you. You all lie!"

I took such a deep breath that I felt lightheaded. "Sir! I was not! I'm sorry. I am so sorry for the horror of it all—" And again he would not let me finish. His face was red with anger, but I remained unmoving in my chair. *What is to become of me now?* I thought. *Will I be imprisoned for this lie, that I was a Partei member?*

Suddenly he became calm again. He picked up his chair and sat once more, acting again as though we were friends. He reached across the desk for my hands, which were folded in front of me. "We only want some information," he said. "Perhaps you could help us. When you are with the men, the German soldiers, perhaps you could keep your ears open. Perhaps you could listen a bit. You seem to be good at that."

With this, I felt I had an out. "Yes, sir. I can listen. But all I ever hear is what the men wish for once they are home again. Their wives, their lovers, their fiancées. Is this what you are looking for?"

He stared at me. He must have thought he'd never seen such a stupid cow before in his life. We had been talking for more than an hour, and my head was aching. He shut his file and stood up. "Danke, Fräulein," he said in his most polite German, and ushered me to the door. The interrogation was over, and I never saw him again.

Never again did they come to my room at night, but there was a time after that when I felt the others mistrusted me even more than usual. Women looked at me with suspicion. Why had they taken me to the interrogation room? What had I said? What had I agreed to? The same night as my interrogation, a Greek diplomat was taken away as well, and he never returned. They came for his clothes in the morning, and that was the last that was seen of him. Did the others suspect me of implicating him? I don't know. It was all too difficult to understand.

I do remember that a young mother with her baby and its grandmother, an old babushka, arrived some time later. I learned that they were the wife, daughter, and mother of this diplomat from Greece. They spoke Russian well, and the young mother spoke some German too. They were with us for a few weeks, and at one point the babushka decided to wash our windows. I'd never seen anything like this! She filled her mouth with water and then squirted it at the windows. With an old rag she had managed to scrounge up from somewhere, she then wiped the windows clean.

This poor family, too, soon disappeared. I heard them screaming, the mother picked up first, the baby and her grandmother left behind until the following night, when it was their turn. They were all sent to the Lubyanka, we were told, as punishment for conspiring with the SS.

## 20

## SNOW

Five months and we were still here. The nights became longer, the days became cold, and often it would snow, a drizzly snow, sometimes turning to rain. I longed for the coat I had so hastily given away. An eternity had passed, and Sweden now seemed so far away.

An announcement came on the thirteenth of December that we were to line up early, before dawn, the next morning. Our names would be called, and we would be boarding for transport "home," as we now referred to our Scandinavian destinations. At five a.m. we lined up outside with all our belongings, once again daring to hope. There were important-looking Russian men in uniforms, some more distinguished than others, standing around us, and their presence made our new orders seem official. Some of the Russians among us suggested they might be Cheka. I never quite knew what it meant; I thought it was an endearment of sorts. Instead it was the term for the secret police, the NKWD.

After we had stood in line for most of the day, the program was suddenly called off. There was no train, and we were to return to our barracks.

The next day was the same. Again, the important-looking men. Again, no train. Again, disappointment.

The day after that was a Sunday and a week before Christmas. Again, we lined up for roll call at five o'clock in the morning, but this time there was a train waiting. All of us, with the exception of one Chinese couple, were ordered to board. Our Cheka were suddenly no longer so friendly. We were pushed up onto the train with rifle butts, our bags thrown up after us, and we began what we thought would be our final journey. It was winter, of course, and the train had no heat, so we tried to huddle together as best we could.

Dirty wooden benches without mattresses, without blankets this time, lined the sides; only some of us were lucky enough to grab one. Along one side of the car was an iron luggage shelf that ran the length of the car just over the top of our seats. A man was already trying to hoist himself up to use this as his bed. We anticipated a long ride ahead of us, and sleep was the only protection we had in an otherwise miserable situation. The floors were grimy and slick, where men had been spitting on them, it seemed, for years. There were oily blotches on the walls, even on the seats.

Snow began to fall just as we left Krasnogorsk. At first I thought it might stay behind as we traveled on, but it kept coming down, harder and harder as the hours passed. It was bitter cold, and the darkness never seemed to leave. One of the windows in our car was stuck open. It wouldn't budge, neither up nor down. The seat below it remained empty. Snow blew in as the train moved, piling up on the window ledge, then filling the seat. All through the night the snow blew in. By the next morning it reached all the way to the top of the bench.

It was a blizzard such as I had never experienced before in my life. The snow blew so hard and swirled around in complete circles so that it looked like it was snowing *up*, and the wind was so wild, it blurred whatever you were looking at, leaving you without any sense of direction.

The day passed. We were terribly cold and had no food. The wind continued and night descended. Suddenly the train stopped, and we were ordered to get out. *For what?* we wondered, but we did as we were told, the snow still falling in sheets, the wind blowing it up into the black sky. We had no idea what to expect next, so we just stood in the middle of the train tracks. It was a desolate spot. Darkness surrounded by darkness.

It is true. The worst possible things really do come true. We were now told we had to start walking. I only remember this order and that we did it. Then we were ordered to run, and this too we did. Where to and why? We did not know, but my mother fell. Somehow, she lost track of the direction she was going in, stumbled on something, and she was down on the ground, not knowing which way to turn if she got up again. I heard her voice from what seemed like a great distance away, calling my name. "Gretel!" she cried, a name she had used only when I was a small child, and I hated that she said it now.

But I answered, terrified, "Mutti! Where are you?" The wind took my words away so fast I did not know if she heard me or not. Then I heard it again: "Gretel." Her voice was close enough that I thought I could reach her by stretching out my hand and waving it, which I did, frantically, while I still could not see her. I had no idea where she was, yet I kept reaching for her, my arm sweeping through the snow in the air around me, her voice crying out to me, "Help!" Finally I found her. She was lying on the ground, not far from where I stood. Had I not helped her then, she would have been trampled to death, or frozen to death, but dead all the same.

Our run through the storm brought us to a wooden house, much like the barracks we left behind in Krasnogorsk. Women were there who didn't speak German, but they showed us to some beds. It became clear that they were, in fact, giving us their own beds to sleep in. Why, we wondered, but we had no way of communicating, and we were exhausted. Suddenly a woman, one of the first to enter the bedrooms, screamed out in German, "Watch out! These beds have lice!" And that was the end of it. We did not take their beds, as wonderful as it might have been to lie on a mattress again. We managed to pile our bags all around us and made ourselves comfortable as best we could. Mutti and I lay down on the floor and slept.

Morning came, and through the open door I saw what looked to be a gloriously sun-filled day. Still sleepy, I made my way over to the doorway. Outside, the air was so bright I had to squint to see that the snow was as high as my waist in places. Once I could focus, I thought the stars must have fallen during the night and landed just here. Everywhere it looked like diamonds lying on top of the powdery snow.

I could see from where I stood that the distance we had covered the night before was not that great. The train was still there, although the tracks were now buried. The station, and the very spot where Mutti fell, were only a few hundred feet away. I walked down a path, which had been cleared, to the latrine, as it seemed some of the others were doing as well.

From out of the brightness, a woman and her older daughter—she was about my age; I had seen them often together in Krasnogorsk—walked toward me, away from the latrines. "You will not believe what we heard in the latrines!" one of them shouted, breathlessly. "The other women here, they're German, too. They say they've been here for many months. And you will not believe this. They say they are prisoners!"

"Yes," I said, not quite understanding their point. Had we not seen prisoners in Krasnogorsk already?

"They told us they have been working in a matchstick factory for months already, and then they said that we were brought here to do the same."

Now the message was sinking in and I became frantic. "But this is not possible! It's just not possible! We've not done anything. How can we be prisoners? I was a Red Cross nurse! I did no harm to anyone!" Then I started to scream to no one in particular, "Who here has done anybody harm? No one!"

"There are other women here, too," they continued, trying to stay calm. "They have come from coal mines and a collective farm, where they were also forced to work. Many have been treated very badly. 'Rape' was a word we heard more than once." Both women looked directly into my eyes, wanting to make sure I understood. Then, again, "No, no, don't be mistaken. They said they are *prisoners*. And that we are, too. And they looked very scared. Dirty, too, and thin."

The three of us now stood and stared at one another, unable to speak further. It was true, as Willi had warned me: We were, indeed, prisoners.

⇌

Therese was no longer with us. At some point she'd been replaced by another woman, Anna Iwanowna.[28] The respect with which some of the Russian guards in Krasnogorsk used to speak to us was no longer evident. Instead, harsh orders were barked at us, and there were always the NKWD, the dreaded secret police who had so suddenly shown up when we boarded the train in Krasnogorsk. Orders to line up: men here, women over there, children in yet another place. Orders to move. And finally, orders to load onto a waiting lorry, a cattle wagon with metal sides and a roof, but this time with nothing to sit on at all, only a floor covered in straw.

For three days we huddled in this lorry, frightened and cold. Twice each day we received water and bread, but nothing to put on it. A mother had a baby with her, and she had a terrible time with the diapers. They were, of course, impossible to wash. Even if she were to find water, it would most likely be frozen. The lorry began to smell foul. Dirty diapers, stinking bodies. There was a man, a diplomat from an embassy—maybe Herr Jäger was his name—who became a sort of spiritual leader to all of us, and in this time of desperation, he was a godsend. Time and again he reminded us that we were beyond this misery, that we had dignity.

"There are differences only you can make for yourself right now. Remember that. They can take away your food, and leave you without a comfortable bed. They can do all kinds of things, but *you* they cannot take away." I believe he spoke as much to himself as to the rest of us, but oh, how those words helped. Often I would hear his voice, months later, when it was bitter cold and I was just too hungry.

When we arrived at our destination this time, every thread of hope had been left behind and the reality of our situation was clear. We were Russian prisoners, and our fate was now in the hands of God. All around us, barbed wire and watchtowers like those I'd seen in Krasnogorsk. Across an empty, wide-open land that stretched to meet a hazy line separating it from the arctic sky, I could see watchtowers and more watchtowers until they disappeared into the horizon.

The place we were in was called Stalinogorsk, near Tula, along the Don River, and it was a Gulag, which had a sign hanging over the gate written in Cyrillic. It had taken three days to get there, and it just looked like a vast and forsaken desert covered in white. "The middle of nowhere" could not even begin to describe where we were. And yet, I imagined that we must have been close to the home of Count Leo Tolstoy, where he wrote *War and Peace*.

We were ordered to run, once again, I with three oil paintings under each arm—the blankets slipping and frayed—tripping on the frozen mud. I ran, hating my mother once again. Far up ahead, she was, as usual, the first to get to what looked like it would be our spot in a barrack, the place we would now call "home."

Inside this long wooden building were rows of bunk beds, constructed from rough-hewn wooden planks, lined up head to foot on either side down the full length of the room. In the aisle between the two rows of beds was a table with two benches, one placed on either side. An electrical wire stretched the entire length from which hung a number of naked lightbulbs. At the far end were a wood-burning stove and a window. Here was where Mutti decided we would make our beds.

"We should sleep up top. That way we'll have a little extra room and there'll be fresh air since we'll be close to the window. We'll have light, too. And now, with the winter, we'll be a little warmer, right here next to the stove." I was grateful for this, and I hugged her, happy that she could have her wits about her enough to be so practical. But I still had to remark, "Mutti, where, tell me, do you think we'll hang the Dürer?"

Inside a Gulag barrack. (akg–images/RIA Novosti)

She only looked at me and then looked away. I felt bad now. Of course, she was not to blame for where we had landed. She had tried only to make the best out of what little we had. And didn't she think about Dieter too? If he were alive, how would he find us, or know anything about us? And Papa. How would he know what had become of us? People back home would think we were dead, just as we had always thought of anyone who was missing. And perhaps that was to be our fate anyway: that we would die here.

Our bed near the stove and close to the window proved to be a good choice. We had room to store our things, and I was glad for the window. The first night—oh, it felt so good to finally stretch out—I lay down hoping for a good, long sleep, but that was not to be. All night I tossed and shivered. It was cold, even with the stove right next to me. Cold from above—the blankets were terribly thin—and cold from below, because the mattress, too, was thin.

At one point I felt Mutti's arm around my neck. I pushed it away in my sleep and then pushed it again. Over and over I pushed her arm away, but always it returned to the same spot on my neck. Finally I awoke, wanting to shout at her to please keep her arm to herself, and one last time I felt for it with my hand, wanting to give it a good, hard shove back to her side.

What I felt was furry. And it was warm. I opened my eyes wide then and saw that this arm also had teeth. It was a rat!

Should I have felt compassion for this creature that only wanted to keep itself warm, as all of us did? And what better place than in the crook of my neck? I tried, but no. Instead I screamed. I probably woke the entire barrack with my scream, and the rat scurried off to who knows where. Maybe inside someone's boot or under the blanket of some other unsuspecting prisoner. Somewhere else that was warm.

In the morning, after we were all awake, I told everyone about Mutti's arm and the rat. Everyone got a good laugh out of it, although, in truth, the whole idea frightened me. Someone asked, "Aren't you afraid of typhoid? Rats carry typhoid, you know. That ugly thing could have bitten you as easily as sleep with you, and then what? You could be dead!" To make light of it, I decided to name my rat Sergei.

A girl only two years older than I, Susanne Erichsen, lived in my barrack with me, and over time we became close friends. Each morning, Susanne got out of bed early and decided, first thing, to sweep. "Enough of this dreck," she said. "If we can't have a cozy home, at least we can have a clean floor."[29]

Sergei showed up frequently, even in the middle of the day, and with each appearance he became bolder. One morning while it was still dark, the only light coming in from the camp lights outside the window, Susanne told me, "Like this. This is how I would swing the broom if I were to see that old Sergei," and she demonstrated a wide swoosh, accidentally hitting a large hook on the wall. As she did this, she managed to hit Sergei, who happened to be sitting right there! *Whack!* Right on his head! And he fell dead, right at her feet, like an offering. Susanne was shocked, I was shocked, and then we all laughed. Susanne was our heroine for the day.

But only for the day, because Sergei must have been a female, a Sergina. As many as a dozen young rats soon wandered out from the walls, blindly sniffing here, then there. It took all of us now, with brooms and shoes and shovels and anything else we could find, to rid ourselves of those babies. It was a good story to laugh about that night, though, because it was Christmas Eve.

Someone produced candles that evening, and we spread them across our table. A few of us sat on the benches, others sat on the beds, both on the top and on the bottom, and we sang Christmas songs, all the ones we knew and could remember. Songs from Bavaria and places in eastern Germany. Swedish ones and Finnish and Norwegian, all sounding very much the same. It was Christmas, after all. The room began to feel warm, and the windows fogged. Mutti sang that Swedish song we had sung when we danced around the Christmas tree, that first year when we thought the war was nothing. Then she grabbed the hands of the two people next to her, encouraging them to stand up, and the rest of us did the same. Our little candle-lit table became our Christmas tree, and we danced a circle around it, arm in arm, as she tried to teach the words to the others:

> *Nu är det jul igen*
> *och nu är det jul igen*
> *och julen varar väl till påska.*

> *Now it is Yule again,*
> *And now it is Yule again,*
> *And Yule will last until it's Easter.*

Suddenly a whirl of snow blew in, and in the black emptiness of the open doorway stood a man with a rifle at his side. Two leather boots and a Russian voice that shouted, "*Nyet!*" Stop the noise! No singing! With that, our first Russian Christmas was over.

~

The next morning we were issued camp clothing: a padded coat, padded pants, and boots made of felt. We all now looked exactly the same. Gray, like the air that surrounded us. Breakfast was the same as we would receive every morning from now on—a bowl of kasha, or gruel, with some bread that was very black and tasted like cardboard. It had been baked with potatoes, I learned later, which kept it from molding but also made it so hard that you had to be quite creative to figure out how to eat it. Soaking it in the kasha helped.

A lorry picked us up for work. It was very dark still, maybe six or so in the morning. I wore the clothing I had been given and tied my scarf around my neck. My job was to work in the coal mines. This was what I would do from now on for many more months. Sometime later that morning, somewhere in the deep white, the lorry dropped us off, and we still had to trudge through a forest to get to the mines.

It was always cold, I was always cold, my hands, my feet, my face. I pulled the hat I was given—it was called a *chapka*—low onto my forehead and wrapped my thin scarf around my face. Our eyelashes became white with frost and froze shut at the corners. It was too cold to talk. If I tried, it felt as though my mouth would freeze, so I just stayed quiet.

There were moments when someone had to make a toilet stop as we walked to the mines. It was never a good time, always too cold, but because of the poor food, we all had to go often. Whenever this occurred, the guard soldier would stop the entire trek, and we all squatted just there on the side of the path and pissed in unison. It no longer mattered who squatted next to whom, who saw whom, man or woman. These things didn't matter any longer. We just squatted and took care of our business, pulled up our pants, and trudged on.

In the coal mine, my job went like this: There were small open railroad cars that needed to be loaded with coal by the workers down in the mine. I was one of them—one of the workers who climbed a ladder to get below. All of us were women. We would fill the cars with this brown coal—I believe it is called lignite in English[30]—and then call out to the men above to come push the cars along the rails and out of the mine. These cars did not fit the rails well, and often they fell off, sometimes dumping the entire load on the ground. So what did we women do? We picked up the lumps of coal and reloaded the cars, and the process started all over again.

It was always wet down there. My felt boots would have been warm had they stayed dry, but they were always soaked. Everything was wet. And we all had to urinate so often. We could not hold our bladders, I don't know why. The effect of standing in water all day, I suppose, so we just wet ourselves. This just happened. We were wet through and through. Wet from the outside, wet from the inside. And always cold.

Susanne worked alongside me in the mines. We laughed some, told stories about the guards when we thought no one was listening. Our jokes helped to distract us from our miserable situation. Then one day Susanne fell to the ground, unconscious. She had always said she wanted to find a way to get into the clinic, so she wouldn't have to stand in this piss-water any longer. "The clinic is warm, I hear," she had whispered to me one day as we were loading a car. "They have blankets and they feed you food. I mean, real food."

"How do you know this?" I was curious, too. What would it take to be admitted to the clinic?

"Joachim—do you remember? He ran a fever. Only yesterday he returned to work. He was gone for two months. He told me all about it. He said his only regret was that he did not know how to keep the fever high."

And now Susanne had fallen. I thought it was a great job of acting on her part. She really did pull off the look of an unconscious person! Her arms fell limp to her sides as the guards tried to revive her. Never once did she move or open her eyes. And they did indeed take her to the clinic—packed her on a horse wagon, on top of straw, wrapped several blankets around her, and drove her away.

About a week later Anna Iwanowna came to our barrack and, along with a few men who had a horse wagon, loaded Susanne's belongings. Everything, even the sheets from her bed. "She's dead," Anna informed us. "Died of pneumonia."

I was sad, very sad, but somehow I could not believe this. One day Susanne was here; now we were told she was gone. I thought it must be a mistake, but Anna Iwanowna told us it was not. Susanne had died the day before. They took her things, and suddenly it was as if Susanne had never existed.

I am ashamed of this now, but I grabbed her mattress and put it on top of mine, hoping the extra padding would make my bed a bit warmer. This did not last, however. Only a few days later, when a new prisoner was brought to our barrack in the middle of the night, the guards must have lifted me while I slept, taken her mattress back, and placed it on her empty bed for this new man to use. I never felt a thing. I only noticed it was missing when I was cold again the next morning.

Weeks later, when we arrived home hungry after ten hours of work, a woman who looked like a ghost walked into our barrack. I stared but did not believe my eyes. Who was this, this woman who knew exactly where she was going?

"Susanne?" I asked, incredulously.

"Yes. Why do you look at me so stupidly? Of course it's me." And then she noticed her bed was occupied. "Where are my things?" she asked.

"Well, they told us you were dead, Susanne! Your things are all gone! Anna Iwanowna came to get them weeks ago."

There Susanne stood, not a thing left to her name. The stylish handbag she had managed to keep, her sweater with the holes she had so meticulously mended, shoes, even her Russian-issued prison clothing— all of it was gone. Anna Iwanowna had taken them all under the pretext that she was dead. Really what she had done was take advantage of the fact that Susanne was sick. She probably secretly hoped, or simply assumed, she would die, so she took her things and sold them on the black market.

Somehow we managed to find Susanne some clothes and a new bed. Perhaps the guards helped, I cannot remember, but that was Susanne's life now, a woman with nothing left of her German history.

☙

We had three very short cigarette breaks during each day that we worked those long hours in the mines. We were given tobacco but no papers to roll it in. Our latrines, however, had scraps of Russian newspaper with which we could wipe our behinds. This paper was very thin, and when we licked it, it would stick to itself. It made perfect rolling paper for cigarettes. It was a trick we learned from our Russian guards, as they did the same. Always it was dark, and always cold, but the cigarettes tasted so good when we could take the time to smoke, and they helped us to forget our hungry stomachs.

At the end of our working day, we were served a sort of "water soup," as we called it, differentiating it from cabbage or potato soup, and it was brought to us in huge blue vats, the same Gulaschkanonen we knew from the rationing days in Berlin. There was nothing identifiable in this "soup," but it was hot, and it felt good to hold the cup and to warm our frozen hands.

Then the long trek home through the woods in snow and mud. My wet shoes soon froze in the shape of my footsteps, the tips up in the front and the heels up in the back. We called them "rocking horses," Susanne and I, and we laughed if we could do so without calling attention to ourselves.

Once, when all of this was still new and, in a way, somewhat romantic—the crunch of snow beneath my feet, the black sky, the silhouettes of trees all around me—I saw a hut off in the woods. There was light coming from behind a curtain, and I recognized the glitter of a Christmas tree. Just this once, never again, and it was so beautiful! It filled my heart with hope. Yes, it did. One small message standing out there in the free world, a home with a Christmas tree.

When we returned to the Gulag, we were served our food for the evening: the soup, called *kapusta*, and bread. I was always so hungry by then, anything tasted good. I learned to soak my bread in my soup and to eat only a small piece of it at a time, to make the soup last longer. But I was always hungry, even after I ate. There was never enough. Five hundred grams of bread—not much more than one slice—and a bowl of kapusta, that's all. This soup was ladled from the Gulaschkanone into long troughs from which everyone just helped himself. No one gave us spoons, and of course we wouldn't venture to let anyone know we still had Mutti's silver hidden at the bottom of her Seesack, so we fashioned our own somehow. For bowls, we used what we could find, and some people shared; others just ate directly from the trough. Mutti hustled off to the camp kitchen promptly the first day we were there and demanded we receive something to put our soup in. She came back to our barrack with two empty tin cans, one for me and one for her, and these were our soup bowls from then on. When you have no choice, it is extraordinary what you will accept as "yours."

The soup most often was cabbage "à la chef." Cabbage water. It had large leaves of cabbage floating in it, often its hard core as well, and very often the cabbage was already rotten. You could tell: it tasted of mold. Sometimes there were potatoes, but more often only potato peels. In that case we called our soup "potato water." Once in a while a piece of meat appeared, but only those who came first to the trough would get to eat it, so of course we hurried each day, hoping to arrive before anyone else. Sometimes there were globules of fat—that, too, was immediately eaten by those who arrived first.

About once a month we would find fish heads floating in the soup. The first time I saw this, I looked into that trough and could not bring myself to eat it. The fish's mouth with its tiny teeth hanging open, its ugly purple eyes staring back at me. I could not eat it. I never could. The rotten cabbage? I did not mind. Not anymore. I was too hungry. I thought I had known hunger in Berlin, but here in Russia it was so much worse.

I often looked into my tin can of soup and thought of Willi, my friend. How he had said, "They will try to kill you with their food." I didn't believe this was true. They wanted us to work, and this food was all they had to give us. Why would they want to kill us? Where would they put our bodies? But then, true to Willi's warning, one day the salt fish appeared. *Perhaps Willi was right,* I thought. I remembered his words and, as hungry as I was, I refused to eat it. *Let the others die, but not me.*

We had nothing with which to clean ourselves, and with all the dirt, I would have been so happy just to give my nose a good cleaning, but handkerchiefs, of course, did not exist. My hands were dirty, my fingernails were dirty, my face—always dirty. Once a week we each received a small bowl of water. I would place mine behind the stove to warm it a bit, and by morning it was at least lukewarm. With this I would wash first my face and armpits and between my legs, as well as I could, and I would try to wash my hair too, but of course I had no shampoo. Then the underwear and stockings got a dousing in this same water, and everything was hung on hooks and bedposts to dry, looking just as dirty as it had when it first went into the water.

Once a guard was kind enough to offer me an extra bowl of water. I was thrilled; I was going to use it to wash my hair. It had become long, and it was thick then, and I wanted to really scrub it well. I did notice little white specks floating on the surface, but I dunked my head into the bowl anyway. Before I could even shake my hair loose, my scalp began to itch. Terribly. That guard had played a trick on me. The water had lice in it. Nothing was a gift, I learned. This was something I would have to remember.

At least I never menstruated in the camp. Not for the entire time I was there. No woman did. It was a gift from God, this. What would we have done to wash? What would we have used as napkins? But women still became pregnant. Avoiding pregnancy was not, apparently, a gift God had granted.[31]

Some men from the Russian high commission came to our camp one day and asked why we were so filthy. "Well, because we don't have any soap!" we told them. We discovered then that soap had indeed been apportioned to our camp, but Anna Iwanowna Ladowitsch, our leader, had stolen it, as she had stolen so many other things, to sell on the black market. Why did she do this? Because she had nothing, just as we had nothing. She was just as much in need as we were. I suppose I would have done the same.

We had a sauna, a Russian-style one, called a *banya*. Sometimes there were birch branches we were supposed to use to beat our skin, "to increase circulation," we were told. Once a month we were to go into the banya. I thought it was so we could bake ourselves clean. The Russian guards watched over our clothes while we all went in naked; no one really cared anymore. We were all so thin, anyway, and there was nothing interesting to look at. Sometimes they then baked our clothes to get rid of lice, which by now were a constant worry, but most often they didn't. And it was only when our clothes became too ragged to wear that they would be burned and we'd be given new clothes.

## 21

# THE SEASONS CHANGED

SPRING

It was now the year 1946, and as the months progressed, hope dwindled to despair. Herr Jäger managed to do what he could to keep everyone's spirits alive. "Exercise," he would say. "Every morning. Do it. If it's cold, do it. If it's snowing, do it. We must keep our wits about us. Stretch. Do a few jumping jacks and sit-ups and touch your toes."

Although we worked until we were exhausted, and his constant optimism often irritated me, a few stretches in the morning did help. It made me feel human again, as if I still had some power over myself. I think Herr Jäger was right. Prisoners in other camps did die, some from diseases of filth, like tetanus and cholera, others because they just went crazy. Our little group, for the most part, kept ourselves together.

I saw some of it, though, even in our camp. It was nearly always old men who would go. Those who lost hope. I saw them scurry to the compost pile behind the kitchen quarters after our evening meal. They would dig through the rot, hoping to find something, anything, more to eat. And there never was anything. What was left had gone into our soup, and that we ate greedily. And what we tried to save for later would almost always be stolen, either by rats or other prisoners, the kitchen staff, or even the guards. I did it too—steal food—whenever I could.

But these old men, they'd become thinner and thinner, their eyes would disappear, and soon you could see they went mad. Spitting when they talked, fear taking over all that was left of them. Then you'd see the guards carry them off, or you'd see the belongings taken from their barrack and you would know, this man had died.

We used them, too, these men. If one died—this was much easier in winter—we'd hide the body underneath the bottom bunk, slide a pile of belongings in front of him so the guards wouldn't notice, and when they came to our barrack at sunrise for a head count for food, we'd prop that man up on his bed. Make him look like just another one of us, ready for his morning soup. His lifeless body would increase the head count, and with that we hoped we might all get just a bit more to eat. Even after his death, he was still working, this time for us, his fellow prisoners.

❧

One morning I woke up to the sun, and I realized how long she had been gone. And then, as if to make up for her long absence, she blinded us with her light. Everything responded. Carpets of wildflowers spread in all directions. My eyes hurt to look at it all.

My job was "reorganized" to a new one. I had become so sick in the coal mines. Often it was intestinal—nausea and cramps—but more worrisome was a cough I had developed.

It was spring, and I was moved to the potato fields to work, and because Mutti was my mother, she was moved as well. Oh, but that was glorious! In the fields and in the dirt, out on a farm, how I enjoyed the sun and the sense of freedom—on top of the land and not under it anymore. Mutti took on a new look of health and even seemed to have a new spring to her step. All day we pulled up potatoes and threw them into waiting horse carts. When I could, I would eat one, dirt and all. But, of course, I seldom could. There was always a guard standing there, making sure we continued to work. We did, however, all of us, fill our trousers with potatoes, regularly, and we saw the guards do the same. We all tied our trousers shut at the bottom. Perhaps we stuffed them into our shoes. This detail I cannot recall exactly. We would walk home then, raw potatoes bumping around our ankles, all of us only so happy to know we would have a little extra to eat that night. Sometimes, too, now that we walked home on these country roads, Mutti and I would pick chamomile and dandelion leaves and eat them along the way.

᠁

I walked into the barrack one day and found Mutti standing at our bunk, exasperated. "She stole my riding breeches! My beautiful gabardine riding breeches! I had been saving them. I wanted so dearly to trade them for eggs or for milk from the kulaks."

"Don't tell me it was Anna Iwanowna!" I exclaimed. We had begun to suspect her of everything now. Missing clothing, missing stockings we had hung from the line after washing, cigarettes. And you could not talk with her; she was unreasonable. Not someone you could ever confide in. After that, Anna Iwanowna did not show up for nearly a week. There was no one we could ask, "Have you seen my breeches? Do you know who could have taken them?"

It had begun with silk stockings, a pair Mutti had managed to save. These she had taken out of her bag and laid on the bed, wanting to simply "rearrange things." There was not much left that she owned, but the breeches she had kept for that one special trade. The silver and the art, though, were still things that would "under *no* circumstances" be traded. This Mutti insisted upon. "Not ever!" I left the issue alone, because arguing was of no use. *But why the paintings? Here?* I could not understand. But there they stayed, wrapped and hidden under her bed, along with the bag of silver. I still don't know how this was possible, but they were never discovered, the whole time we were there, not by anyone.

Anna Iwanowna walked in then, just as everything had been laid out in orderly piles, and asked Mutti what she was doing. Mutti replied, "Looking for something," but, of course, Anna Iwanowna was not interested in the answer. She was much more interested in Mutti's possessions. "And that's when she must have seen the breeches," Mutti said. "Because all I had to do was turn around, go to the latrine, or the soup line, and the next moment they were gone."

We hated Anna Iwanowna. We feared her. We wanted only for her not to be around. It was not much later that we learned she had been taken away to the Lubyanka, that filthy, gloomy stone prison in Moscow from which no one returned. A terrible fate, but she deserved it all the same.

⇌

Around our camp was a village. It was not clear to me that people lived around our Gulag until we'd been there for some time. People would come to the fence, wanting to trade, sometimes eggs or whatever they had in exchange for some of the things we had. Silk stockings were the first to go. These women had never before seen them. It always seemed to be the same women who came, all wearing long aprons and headscarves. In time I learned who they were. They were known as the kulaks, the poor ones of Russia, and they lived around the camps, making a living from servicing us.[32] We called them the "half frees," people from the outside, but all the same people who could not leave. They were there because they had to be there. There was nowhere else they were allowed to go, and our camp was their only livelihood.

A young kulak boy befriended me at one point. He was perhaps fifteen. A bit of fuzz had begun to grow on his lip. *He's going to be handsome soon,* I thought. Each day we met at the fence; each day he would have something new to bring me, perhaps an egg or some carrots, and I tried to bring him something of mine—a cigarette, my bread, something. Mostly we exchanged looks and a silent desire for life to be somehow different. I felt more sorry for him than I did for myself. You see, we always believed we would leave here one day. For us, there was somehow still hope. For him, that was not so. He would grow older here, marry a girl from his village, another kulak, and die here, too. So it would be.

## SUMMER

Summer came, and nothing changed except that we grew thinner and sicker and a number of our people died. I was moved back into the coal mines to work.

New arrivals came to our camp, and more and more they were Slavs—Poles and Russians. We could not trust them. They did not get along with each other, either; their history was so dark. When they had their little "wars" with one another—and this would go on for weeks—the Poles claimed to be German and tried to buddy up with us and would claim to be from Westphalia. They were people who had worked once in the German industrial sector and could even speak some German. But then, when they became friendly with the Russians again, suddenly they were big-time Poles, the ones who won the war against us, their German enemies. These were people I always made a huge detour around. In truth, they must have had it very, very bad in this camp. They did not know if they were loved or hated, or, if they were ever released, if they would be murdered once they returned to their own country.

The Russian prisoners hated us Germans equally. They spit into our soup when we weren't looking, and they stole whatever they could from us. Often your bread would disappear right from your very own lap. The worst of them were the Wolga Deutsch—Germans who had lived in Russia for generations. They would snitch on us, make up stories, do whatever they could to sell us away to the guards, just to gain their own freedom. Perhaps they were jealous, because there was a sense that they would be here for a very long time, while we still hoped one day we would be returned to our homes.

## AUTUMN

My cough became worse; sometimes there was blood. Some nights I lay shivering in my bed with a fever, thinking it would be better just to die. The thought of another cold, dark winter in this place made me wish I were dead. *How long now will we be here, dear God? How much more can we take?* I had nothing left. I had given away my coat, my scarf was now in rags, and I had no mittens to keep me warm, only the fingerless gloves I'd received from the Russians. And I had to work so hard every day. Mutti scolded me, "Nimm dich mal zusammen!" But orders to "pull myself together" didn't help. I longed for home; I dreamed of our fatherland. Always in these dreams I saw spring flowers and smelled the summer air. Marigolds, I don't know why, reminded me of home. We had some growing in the camp, here and there, during the summer months, and I would get so homesick, thinking how they were growing in Germany too, but those flowers lived in freedom.

## WINTER

Our second Christmas in this desolate land, and no one back home knew where we were. This thought haunted me. No one knew whether we were alive or dead. Papa Spaeth would be so worried, and what about Dieter? Candles, however, turned up—who knew from where? I suspected Herr Jäger had organized them from one of the kulaks. We set them upon our little table, and someone, it must have been Susanne, pulled a bottle of vodka out from under her bed. "Don't worry where I got this. I got it, that's all," she said. She gave a shrug and a giggle as we passed it around. The vodka helped me out of my sullenness, but I was so ill, and we had nothing else.

But we did have stories, that was true, and someone began to tell one. A story of home. Someone else began to sing a song, and we all learned the words to it. Even our guard seemed much less interested

Gulag barracks in the snow. "No one knew whether we were alive or dead." (akg–images/RIA Novosti)

in making things difficult for us. He was still young and quite amused by our Christmas mood. We sang, and eventually he joined in. Others came from other barracks, and soon our little room was full. People were on the beds, on the floor; we put our arms around each other, and tears were on everyone's face. It seemed we all missed *someplace* different from where we were, even the guards. They sang then, too, in Russian, and strange as it was, the songs sounded so familiar. It was Christmas, after all, and we wanted so badly to celebrate something.

Guards, prisoners, Scandinavians, Germans, Slavs, suddenly we were all the same. That evening—I will never forget it—lasted until morning. "Slap-happy," I think you say in English. "Punch-drunk." When nothing was funny but it still made you laugh. Some of us danced, even with the guards, and when one of us opened his mouth to speak again, we all fell over laughing; he never even got the story out. The Russians laughed, too, and they couldn't even understand our language!

~

I spat up blood sometimes, my cough was so bad, and I wanted only what I'd been craving off and on through all this misery, for Death to come take me. Mutti was lost in her own thoughts most of the time, and I would sometimes catch her staring into the distance, an unutterable sadness in her face. She would work in the cold fields, come back to the barrack, arrange her bed so it was comfortable, and close her eyes. Rarely did she talk with me, or with anyone else, for that matter. Somehow, she kept her suffering to herself.

I got up from my bed one night, hand to my mouth, feeling completely forsaken by the universe. I took off my undershirt and pulled on my Russian-issued coat. Then I walked outside. The night was black as coal, nothing but a sliver of the moon and the distant stars in the sky. The winter wind stabbed at me, but even this didn't stop me. I shuffled toward the latrine, with its frozen-piss floors, in my bare feet. I was finished. Whether I died there in the stench of that shithouse or in my cold, hard bed, it no longer mattered. There I stood, for a long, long time. I held my thin coat open for the winter to take me. The wind whipped around my throat. I begged God to have me now. I stood against the latrine wall, with my coat wide, until I must have fallen asleep. Was that a man walking through that halo of lamplight? I did not know, nor did I care. Let him look. It was a dead woman he was looking at anyway.

# 22

## You Still Have Hope

### 1947

When I regained consciousness, it was daylight, and I was looking into two eyes the color of dark honey. It was a kind-looking face. A deep worry line ran the length of the man's forehead, under a mop of sandy-colored hair. He wasn't German. Just beyond his head was a stark ceiling with two rows of lightbulbs, bare and bright, and I couldn't understand where I was. This man had large hands, and one of them gently brushed my hair back from my face.

"You must rest. You are very sick, Margarete. You nearly died last night. Do you remember it?"

I did remember a man walking through the camp light, the wind slicing my skin, and the familiar smell of the latrine, but I did not remember this. How did I get here? The lights and the ceiling were not familiar. I noticed for the first time that I was bundled, like a swaddled infant, inside several blankets. My head lay on a pillow, and the air smelled antiseptic, a fragrance I knew well.

"The guards brought you here late in the night. It was this morning, actually. I had just arrived for my shift at four when the horse wagon rolled in with a woman on it. She wore only a thin coat, and her feet were bare. She looked to be dead. I was, at first, afraid I would not be able to revive her. Now do you remember?"

Oh, the disappointment to know where I was! I began to weep. I had hoped for Death, I had prayed for it, and now here I was, once again in this pigsty, this shithole of a place.

"Oh, sir, please!" I reached for his hand as well as I could. As soon as I moved, I realized how weak I was, and I began to cough again.

"Oh, please. I'm finished with this life. Why wasn't I left where I was? I was happy there. What more do you want from me?" I turned my face toward the wall and let the tears come. I didn't care what he thought. Would he see this strong German woman—this woman whom Herr Jäger so often used as an example of strength, this woman who could plant trees upside down—would he see her like this now, broken? A woman who wanted only to die?

"Grete," he said. He knew my name. "I too am a prisoner here. I know how you feel. My home is in Latvia. But I am a doctor; I am useful to them. You, they will work until they have no more use for you. When your people become too sick or too old, they will let you go, and they will replace you with others to carry on the work. For me? I believe I may never see my family again. It's even possible they will keep me here until death. You still have hope. You will be released one day, I do believe that. But now, first, you must regain your strength. You must heal."

I think he was forty, although he may have been much younger. It was difficult to tell. I too probably looked older than I was. By now we all looked rather "fat." Years of poor food, and not enough of it, made everything in the body swell up and dulled our eyes.

He spoke German with an accent, but only slight. His voice was soothing. I learned his name was Janis and then a long last name I have forgotten. It sounded somewhat Scandinavian, ending in something like -sons, or -sens. But I called him Dr. Janis from then on.

I had tuberculosis, I learned, and Dr. Janis gave me penicillin for it. It was given to anyone who was sick. And he had me lie out in the sun under a blanket. He said it was to get vitamin D. He told me he had let the guards know where I was, and he also said he talked to my Mutti. Mutti! Where was she? Was she concerned? I never once thought of her. I was simply too sick.

I stayed in this *Revier* as we called it—the camp clinic—for several weeks. Janis came to me each day, and each day he brought me food.

There was soup that first morning, cooked with real chicken. There was even chicken fat floating on the surface and a few bits of meat in it. "Eat," he said to me always, and all the while he stroked my hair. I felt so weak. My hands were gray and swollen, my eyelids felt heavy, my belly so hungry. He brought me bread with butter, and he brought me tea. The tea had a strong aroma, different from what I knew at home. It was dark, but there was always a little milk and some sugar in it. It was, I believe, this cup of tea each day and Dr. Janis's gentle hands that slowly brought back my will to live.

He sat with me and we talked, when we could, for long hours. He told me that his parents still spoke a North German dialect, Baltisch-Deutsch. He told me too about his homeland in the beautiful area of Wenden in the north of his country. He said his family was Protestant, not Catholic as many Latvians were.

Then he told me, "I still believe in a God." He seemed to struggle with his thoughts for a moment. "I believe in a God, I do. But not this one. This one has allowed my eyes to see what I should never have seen." To this I could only nod. *Yes. If there even is a God here, he has been hiding for a very long time.*

One day Dr. Janis came to me and said he could not keep me in that lovely warm Revier any longer. I needed to go back to work. "But don't lose hope again, dear Grete. Don't do that." He was a kind man. "I wish the best for you," he said, and he had genuine tears in his dark-honey eyes.

Things did not go well for me. I was simply too weak to work so soon, and again I was sent to the Revier only a week later. This time I learned I had malaria. It was only March. How could I have malaria? There were no mosquitoes, but I ran a very high fever, every day the same fever, and I was weak. My legs were swollen, my ankles so big I could not put them into my felt boots. My feet hurt; I could not walk. My eyes hurt; it was difficult to see. Again Dr. Janis was gentle with me. Again he sat with me.

When I felt somewhat better, I told him about my brother and how much I missed the German landscape with its gentle forests and rolling farmlands, its farmhouses with their thatched roofs, a sky so different from here, an overcast one, but one I had known since I was a child. How much I wanted to go home. He said he understood. He touched my face often when he spoke, but he was a gentleman, and often, too, his eyes welled up with tears. "I wish I could change things for you, Grete. I truly wish that. If I could, I would help you." Then, after a pause, in a voice no louder than a whisper, he said, "Maybe I can." But then he said no more.

꧂

Many new prisoners arrived. Many of them now were Russians, not so many Germans or Poles, trainload after trainload. One train came when I was still in the Revier, and it was full of doctors who had been taken as prisoners from Eastern Europe. Some were Polish, others Ukrainian, and others from the Balkans. Some could speak German quite well, and I was already feeling much better, so I tried to speak with them. I asked where they were from. One told me he was sent here as a doctor. He had come from Moscow, but he was Wolga Deutsch, a German.

"And what do you think they gave us for work?" he continued. "A shitpile of syringes to sort through! For that I was taken prisoner. As a doctor! We stand over piles of goods, stolen from the lands the Russians now occupy, mostly from Germany, and we are ordered to sort through them. Bandages, all wet and useless; medicines with no labels and surely gone bad by now; surgical masks and hats; medicine chests, empty of course; and *Gibs-Material*—the plaster we use to make casts. That too is useless, as it has become wet and hard, something merely to throw away. But of course the Russians won't hear of it, so we just put it into a pile labeled 'For Broken Bones.' Do you want to know the truth? We made up the labels. Who would care? 'For Diphtheria,' 'For Cholera,'

'For Tetanus,' we wrote. None of the items would ever be used anyway, but we did have some fun sorting through this rot." He gave me a quiet smile that we both understood.

A week later I was released again from the Revier. Back to the barracks. Back to work. I did what I could to remain hopeful, as Dr. Janis had encouraged me to do, but even joking with Mutti and my friends, Susanne and the others, no longer helped.

❧

Anna Iwanowna busied herself in our barracks more often than before. Apparently there was a train, she said, that would leave soon, taking refugees back to Germany. *Who is she kidding? After all this time, working here as slaves? And we are still considered refugees?*

"The camp is to be cleared out for others," she huffed at us in her thick voice. It was the fourteenth of March—I remember because war was expected to break out. This is what she told us. We needed to be released in order to make room for incoming prisoners. From what war, I did not know. Russia, I assumed, was about to make war with America, but I had no idea whether this was true or not, and neither did anyone else. But the fourteenth of March came and went with no transport trains to take anyone anywhere.

More trainloads of prisoners arrived, and they were always loaded with Russians. More and more we heard only Russian being spoken, and the people who were delivered to us seemed much more like countryfolk, no longer ambassadors and doctors like those who had come before. There were men as well as women, and children too. The women were dressed like those we saw along the train tracks when we first came—babushkas with headscarves.

We did not speak to one another. What should we say? Hadn't the news of these dreadful Gulags reached them? Should we tell them that we were happy to give them our beds, because perhaps that meant we would soon be leaving? No, no. We said nothing. We only renewed a hope that had long been buried. Spring was here. The snow was turning to mud, and soon little white flowers would appear along the dirt paths again.

There were a few other German girls I met at this time. They were all about my age. They lived in another barrack that had mostly women prisoners from East Prussia. One was the girl who, with her mother, had heard the news that we were to become prisoners that first snowy morning when I walked to the latrine. Brigitte Martins was her name. I remember it well, because we remained friends long after our time together in the Gulag. Then there was another girl who was from the island of Rügen in the Baltic Sea. She had long thick braids like the ones I wore when I was young. How I remember her name, I don't know, but I liked the way it rolled off my tongue, so I always called her by her full name: Felicitas Jahn.

The day I came back from the Revier, the second time, Felicitas Jahn pulled me to the side and whispered the latest gossip: Anna Iwanowna had been sent to the Lubyanka. We would never see her again. Sorry I was not, but to be sent *there?* The place that tortured its prisoners, the place you could never leave? For a fleeting moment I wondered if she was wearing Mutti's riding breeches when she was captured, but then I realized what a terrible thought that was. The Lubyanka was a fate I would not wish on even her.

A new leader had been assigned to us. I had already met her when she was brought on tour through the Revier. Katarina was her name. Felicitas Jahn told me she was even worse than Anna Iwanowna. "Katarina die Grosse," Catherine the Great, was her name when she was out of earshot. "She wants everything! Everything!" my friend said, and then did her best impersonation: "If you want to eat, yes, you can eat. I can get cheese and I can get butter. I can even write you a day off from work. But first your pullover!"

A month went by and it was April when Katarina came to our barrack in the early morning. She had "good news" to announce. Mutti whispered in my ear, "What? That we are now also allowed to give her our underpants?" Even in my weakness, I managed to answer with a giggle. No matter how dreadful things were, Mutti always seemed to maintain a sense of humor. I did appreciate this about her.

"Every worker who has worked on the collective farms is to be released," she barked, standing "at attention" with her heels together and arms rigid at her sides.

Her announcement, of course, turned out not to be true. I was one of those who had been working on the collective farm, but by the middle of May at least a hundred of us, including Mutti, Brigitte Martins, and Felicitas Jahn, were still there. June came. July. There were no more transport trains arriving. And we continued to work.

❧

"Tenner" was a word we learned from the first Russian arrivals. It meant a ten-year prison sentence, which many of them soon discovered they had. But now some even had sentences of twenty-five years. I did not learn why, but I was frightened of these people. I did not want to become too friendly with any of them. To worry I could be sentenced just like them? Oh God, no! No, no, that was just not going to be.

Then one morning I could not get out of my bed. The sun outside was already baking, and as soon as I stood, I had to retch and then retch some more. I was running a fever, I could tell, my head was hot and my legs felt weak. Once again I was taken to the Revier.

Dr. Janis once again was gracious and warm. Again he took the time to find me during the day; he would arrive with his milk tea. He was kinder to me than he needed to be. Perhaps he was falling in love, but we both knew he still had a wife at home in Latvia, and a daughter. I was grateful, and I was kind in return.

He worked to bring my fever down; he fed me; he sat with me for long hours while he put compresses on my forehead. I told him more stories about my brother Dieter and how I had worked for the Red Cross in Berlin. How I had bandaged so many wounded soldiers and how I had hoped to become a doctor one day. I then even told him something I never said to anyone, but I felt I could trust him, this man from Latvia.

I told him how frightening it had been those last days when the Russians marched into Berlin and how terrified we women were, how many of us had been raped and even murdered. After one of these conversations, I told him the German saying we had said so often when one of our Landser went off to the front. It was something we nurses also said to each other at the day's end. It was, in a way, a sort of prayer, like *I hope I'll see you tomorrow*, but, really, we knew nothing was certain. "We would squeeze our thumbs, like this," and I showed him how, pressing each thumb tight with my fingers, "and then we would say, 'I wish you all the luck of the soldier.' It was to mean everything." He smiled softly when I told him this, and I knew he understood.

～

The summer was beginning to wane as hopelessness crept deeper into my veins. No trains came, no trains ever came anymore, and soon another winter would descend upon us. One evening I sat on a rock I had claimed for my own when I needed just to sit and cry. So many people had been released already. Over and over we heard names called up, names of prisoners whose turn it was to leave. Never me, never Mutti, and I felt so desperate. Dieter was long gone. So much time had passed and we knew nothing of his whereabouts. Sweden was now nothing but a lost dream, and surely Papa Spaeth would have made a new life for himself by now.

A man walked over to where I sat on my rock and took a seat next to me. I could feel the warmth of his body, but I did not look up. I was ashamed of my tears. Who was I to cry? We were all in the same mess.

I was no one special. I turned and saw two honey-brown eyes gazing at me. Quietly he pulled a handkerchief out of his pocket—a rare item, something I had not seen since I left Germany—and he wiped my tears from my cheeks.

The things that mattered most were the things we felt inside: hope, trust, compassion. In this moment, I can say, I knew all three. Janis waited before he said anything more. And then, hardly moving his mouth, he whispered, "I have a way to help you. Don't speak right now. Don't even look surprised, but take this," and he took my hand in both of his. He was pressing a piece of paper into my palm. "It's for you and your Mutti." He squeezed my hand shut. Then we both went on sitting in silence. My heart pounded. I could only imagine what he had done.

It was a medical script he had written, indicating we were too sick to remain in the camp and giving us orders to be returned to Germany. We would be taken on an invalid transport, he informed me, when he could whisper again and we knew no one would hear. He said, perhaps that would mean it would be better than the cattle cars we had seen taking the other prisoners away. Perhaps there would even be real beds, and good food, too. "I have permission to send prisoners home once every year. It's for those who are too sick and those who are too old to work anymore. This is how I was able to write this script for you."

"You are a dear friend, Janis," I said, addressing him for the first time with the familiar *du*, no longer *Sie*. This was a true act of friendship, and it was clearly time to end the formality. "How were you able to do this? We're not even that sick. I only have this silly intestinal ailment. And Mutti? She's mostly grumpy, that's all. There are others who need it so much more desperately than we," I said quietly, turning my lips to his ear. Wouldn't he be in grave danger if the wrong ears were to hear? And then, even more quietly, I added, "Janis. I have nothing with which to repay you."

"Dear Margarete, if there is anything I can live to feel proud of, it would be to help you get home. Me? I will remain here until I am no longer useful. You? You have a whole life yet ahead of you. One day you'll fall in love, you'll be married and have children. This is what I hope for you and what would make me happy—to know what had become of you."

I could not even open my mouth, let alone know what to say, but from the sigh that came from deep within me, I let him know he had done a very good thing.

I told no one. I couldn't. Then I told Mutti.

❧

It was true. It was the first of September. The air still felt like a furnace when Katarina announced, "There will be an invalid train in the morning. It has been ordered." We mustered up hope once again.

We were anxious. It was almost too good to be true, this idea—a train—but we prepared ourselves nonetheless. Mutti and I packed what little we still owned, then waited. All morning and all day we waited. Still no train. That we were not sent out to work made it appear as though we might actually be going home, or at least somewhere other than here. New prisoners had arrived; their lorries now stood empty in the afternoon light. Our beds were given away. All good signs. "Perhaps tomorrow . . . It could very well be tomorrow," Mutti and I whispered to one another, and we made ourselves look busy.

I decided I needed to visit my "hairdresser." Something special had to be made of this day, and it was all I could think to do to lessen my anxiety. This hairdresser was a large tub behind the kitchen that one of the cooks sometimes let me use. It was dark in that yard, no lights, and it smelled foul—a place most prisoners would not go, but a place, too, where there were no guards. Here I would come sometimes, after I had eaten and the sun was beginning to hide behind the clouds that always hung so low on the horizon, when I wanted to bathe, just to wash my face and hands. On this night I found my cook standing in the yard with a cigarette, and begged again for my tub. "It may be the last time I come to pester you," I said, and he laughed. He motioned the back of his hand in the direction of the stinking yard, pulled the butt of his cigarette from his mouth with three fingers, and turned back to the kitchen.

I hid in the shadows, and shortly thereafter he came, carrying a large tub of cold water. He said something in Russian I did not understand, but his face broke out in a toothy grin. I thought he was wishing me well—*Go. Enjoy.* Perhaps this. Then he simply turned and went back to his duties. The tub full, the darkness hiding anything that may have been floating in it, I held my breath and quickly put my head into the water. I made sure to drench all my hair, and I swished it around, wishing all the Gulag filth to dissolve away one last time. After my "shampoo," I did my best to shake it loose and then tied it up in a knot, wet as it was.

⁓

Back at the barracks, it was dark already, and everyone was in a festive mood. I think we all believed *something* was about to happen. Someone— one of the guards?—produced an instrument, like a mandolin but with only three strings. The Russians call it a balalaika. We began to sing. We sang German songs, and then Russian ones. One of the guards got silly and got up to show us his *kasotsky* dance, even holding himself with one hand on the ground as the opposite leg kicked up in the air. We tried it too, and fell, of course.

Janis appeared late in the evening after his work shift was over. The mood had become more sedate. The music was more melancholic and our voices were more hushed. He stood beside me. We talked some. He talked with the others, Brigitte and Felicitas Jahn, and then he took my hand and we danced. He pulled me close. Others too were dancing in this way. We moved to the outer circle. I could smell his aroma. It reminded me of the Revier, but then something else too, something like autumn. We—the two of us, as well as all the others in our barrack—danced into the early hours of the morning. The guards on this night were part of us. There was no Katarina, no heavy boots, and with the last dance, when it was already becoming light out, Janis kissed me.

It was a gentle kiss, and we held each other a long time. He whispered then, softly into my ear, "I wish you all the luck of the soldier. And I will squeeze my thumbs for you until you are all the way home." My throat had a lump in it so big I could not speak. I knew we would never see each other again, and this thought made me terribly sad.

## 23

# THE WIDE-OPEN NOTHINGNESS

Late the next afternoon we stood at the entrance to the camp with our suitcases—at the gate with the sign in Cyrillic over it. I never learned what the letters stood for. It was Mutti and me and a handful of others who had been told the same—that they'd be going home. Some of these others had danced with us the night before.

Finally a lorry pulled up and we were motioned to get in; some guards pushed us to make more room. Standing tight, one body against another, we drove off. That was it. It was nothing like I thought it would be. I had no tears. I just went along as everyone did. Our fate was still at the mercy of our captors, and we all knew this.

We arrived at yet one more camp. Here we saw people we recognized: some Finns and a couple from Switzerland. We hugged and laughed. None of us had any idea what was to come next, but for today, life seemed to hold some promise.

Mutti and I were quartered in a tent with seventy or more other women, and this was where we were to sleep—for how long we did not know. We were each given a cot and a blanket, and there we sat and waited. I remember there was a rip in the roof above my cot, and I hoped it wouldn't rain. Many of us were sick; some even died during the two weeks that we were here. For me, the days became eternity, each day longer than the one before it. There was no work, so with the long days and nothing to do, it was easy to become anxious. *Is it true, or are we just waiting for another disappointment, another labor site to work at?*

Then it came. A call to line up. It was four a.m. Moscow time, and the sky was the twilight gray of night, but a train was waiting. "Na transporta, na transporta!" a guard was shouting in Russian. Whether it was an invalid train or just a regular train, I never quite knew, but we ran, because we were being told to board.

❧

It was a sweltering day, the way it can be on the steppe of Siberia, where the sun refuses to set. Our train moved, then it didn't move. It moved, then it didn't. Sometimes it was necessary for it to move backwards in order to switch tracks, and this maneuver often took hours. Back and forth, and men on both sides yelling Russian words I did not understand.

We had been told it would be about four days to Moscow, but five passed before we saw the station that someone recognized. Moscow! Oh, how I remembered those months when we languished in Krasnogorsk, not far from here, believing in lies, thinking it was the Swedish embassy that was keeping us there!

We passed Smolensk, and of course we remembered that city, the one that was so terribly devastated in the war, and we passed so many of the villages we recognized from before, too. Then suddenly the train stopped and we were ordered to get off. All of us, sick or not, wounded or not, we all needed to get off. And once we were all on the platform, the train reversed and slowly took off, back in the direction we came from, leaving us alone on the platform in the sun, somewhere in the wide-open nothingness of Russia.[33] "A new train will arrive soon," we had been told. Our train, apparently, was going back for more prisoners.

The wind blew heat into our faces, and there was nothing to eat, not even water, and we were terribly thirsty. The entire day we sat while fear crept through our veins. *What is to become of us now?* No train, no leader, no guards even, and in a desolate land we did not know.

As night descended, many spread their belongings out on the platform and lay down to sleep. Mutti and I? We couldn't. So we sat on top of our bags, holding each other's hands. We stayed silent with our thoughts of home.

Another day and nothing. Nothing but flat plains in sight, the wind blowing, a few flies, ants, and dust.

❧

Finally, off in the distance, we could hear the rattling sound of a slow-moving train. At first we thought we were fooling ourselves, but the sound was unmistakable. Yes, it was a train coming, but we could not see it yet. Closer it came, then we heard its whistle.

Looking like a toy on the horizon, then like a gigantic beast, it pulled into the station, all as if in slow motion. When it stopped, nothing happened for a long, long time. Slowly, maneuvers took place, back and forth, and then a conductor mysteriously emerged from the engineer's car and announced what I intuitively already knew: It was going back to the Gulag. We were all so desperately hungry, so many of us were sick, and a good number of our group decided they would rather return to the Gulag than die here in this desolate land. For Mutti and me it was not even a question: We would rather die than return, and so we prepared to sleep on the platform yet one more night.

Still no water, still no food, but we were in the open and no longer in the Gulag. *If I must die here, at least I'll know I died under the stars, and I died a German woman, a free German woman, no longer a prisoner.* I was thinking this as I fell into a deep sleep.

I awoke before sunlight the following day to Mutti shaking my shoulder. "Wake up, Grete, wake up. A train has arrived."

Yes, there was a train. And it was pointed toward Germany.

❧

I jumped up from the stone floor I had been sleeping on. I looked around the station platform. Everything was in movement. A train was indeed standing in front of us with its doors open. A conductor was waving his hand and calling out in Russian, ordering us to board. I rubbed my eyes awake and felt the growling in my stomach. After four days without food or water, I felt I might fall over with weakness. Of course, Mutti too felt terribly weak, but there she stood with her Seesack over her shoulder, and there were the paintings leaning up against a post, ready for me to carry. Then I noticed it: My suitcase was gone, stolen while I slept. *Well, that too now.*

The train conductor was looking at me intently, and Mutti was pulling on my sleeve to hurry along. With or without my suitcase, my only thought was, *Skoro domoi*, that Russian term I had learned to say—We're going home! Carrying both bundles of oil paintings, still wrapped in their original blankets, I stepped up onto the train platform, Mutti right behind me. My first surprise came as I looked up: It was a German train. I could see this. The signs for the washroom and for the locks on the doors were written in German. It was an older train, but noticeably cleaner than what we had been traveling in. There were seats with leather upholstery, some of it torn, but I saw the floors had been washed, no black spots where men had spit.

We settled into a bench seat, packed tight as the train was quite full, and I turned to look out the window to see what I was leaving behind. From where I was sitting, I could see a wagon was being loaded with produce: onions, potatoes, cabbage, I don't know what else. And then, with a jolt, the train began to move in the direction of Germany.

I tried not to think about food. I just leaned my head back and watched the gray sky and the flat horizon pass slowly by. Everything seemed as if in a fog. *Is this a dream?* I kept thinking. *Or was that a dream, the life we left behind?*

❦

It was the twenty-second of September. Suddenly I thought of my father, the man who died when I was young. He would have had his fifty-second birthday soon. I missed him terribly, suddenly, wondering how he would feel, knowing what had become of us. And what had become of his country—how gruesomely right he had been about the Communists, although, in truth, it ended up being the Nazis who were "the undoing of German industry." What an understatement that had been!

For another four days the train lumbered onward through various checkpoints, and on the twenty-fifth of September, around four or five o'clock in the afternoon, the train finally rolled into Frankfurt an der Oder.

We had entered Germany. My heart skipped a beat. Germany! And Frankfurt an der Oder. How long had it been since Dieter had been here? And Dieter? Would we see him again? Would it be soon?

I was shaken out of my reverie by a command shouted in my mother tongue: "Raus! Alle raus!" We were to get off the train. Although all we saw was the interior of a train station and we could not leave, it was the very first sight of Germany since that fateful July of 1945, and my heart felt like it could burst through my rib cage. No one around me spoke— everyone seemed shell-shocked. We just moved to where we were told to move and stood, obediently, awaiting our next orders.

We were soon shuffled off to a hall, a holding station of sorts, and were told we would need to wait there for our release papers. Once again we sat and waited all afternoon and into the night. Sometime around two or three o'clock in the morning, shivering and sleepy, we were discharged to an interim "release camp." It was just outside the station, and because it was dark, my first vision of German land was difficult to make out. This camp was full of other refugees from God knows where, and we were shown to some cots, all lined up, row upon row and side by side, where we gladly lay down to sleep.

The next day, for the first time in forever, we were able to bathe. We were shown a large room that held a number of open showers and rows of sinks and latrines. There was still no soap, but to stand under a shower, and to feel the water running over my back, to put my face up into the warm stream and feel it soak my hair, to know I could stand here for as long as I wanted and no one would come to order me to move along—oh, it was heavenly!

Each of us was handed new clothing by the Red Cross. It was used, probably donated, and by early morning we were ushered to the check line in order to finally be released. What if we were, for some unthinkable reason, refused? We all stood there holding our breath, anxious to know what would come next.

Suddenly we realized something we had not thought about in all this time we were gone. We were in Germany again, and surely we would need to identify ourselves, the way it used to be. Nervously Mutti and I pulled out the Ahnenpässe, the old passports we had to carry with us that certified our non-Jewish genealogy. *O Gott,* I heard Mutti say under her breath. *O Gott.* A cousin, or someone else, had been in a marriage that was not clear. Was she Jewish or was she not Jewish? And that page in her Ahnenpass had never been stamped CERTIFIED. I saw

Helga's Ahnenpass.

The ragged line across the middle of the page indicates where Helga tore out the bottom half.

the fear in Mutti's eyes. It was not possible, not even conceivable, that she would let us be sent back to the Gulag for having the wrong papers. Not now, of all times, when we could already see our German soil.

Mutti and I both took our places at the rear, fearful, watching to see what was going on around us. Then I noticed what Mutti was doing. Slowly and meticulously, so that there would be no evidence, she tore out the second page of her Ahnenpass, the page that included the name of a woman I did not know, the page with no official stamp on it. When she had cleanly detached it from her book, she quietly stuffed it into her mouth. And she ate it.

All of our names had been recorded on index cards—this seemed so odd, having just returned from a country where our existence was measured only by roll call—and systematically, as each person approached, the card was pulled up and that person was free to move to the next line in order to wait some more. As Mutti and I approached the desk, we realized that none of the papers we were prepared to show, our Ahnenpässe, even mattered. The woman behind the desk, a Russian, found our index cards, shoved a piece of paper at us, and motioned us to sign it. In broken German, and with misspelled words, the statement said something like "I hereby swear, upon oath, never to speak about the time I visited Russia." Below this was some sort of threat, like "Doing so will be immediate cause for imprisonment."

We signed. Of course we signed. This would be the last thing I cared to talk about. Then we were motioned to move on to the next desk, where we were given certificates with our prison numbers on them, stamped, saying that we had been officially released from imprisonment.

"From the High Command of the Red Army, Dos, Margarete Werner, is released from punishment and is free to return to her place of origin, Berlin." My prison number was 61948 and was written clearly at the bottom of the form. Did this mean I was the 61,948th prisoner? I don't know. I think so. The woman had quite a bit of trouble with Mutti's name. She tried three times to spell and respell the name Helga in Cyrillic. Funny, we thought later, it must not be a common Russian name, but then what about Olga?

Gladly we signed all the papers. We were only so happy to be coming home. We were then loaded into a waiting freight truck along with many other prisoners and were driven a few kilometers away. It was to the German release camp, Gronenfelde.[34] Much later I would learn this was a momentous day for Gronenfelde, the twenty-sixth of September. One hundred and twenty thousand German prisoners had been released from Russian Gulags just the day before, and I believe there could have been an equal number of us there that day.

Here we were met by the German Red Cross, all women, and tears of pride and exhaustion welled from my eyes. *This,* I thought, *is what I would be doing now, too, had I remained in Germany. I would now be standing here, helping these very refugees returning from their ordeal in*

Gronenfelde near Frankfurt an der Oder. Former prisoners of war returning home.
(Bundesarchiv Bild 183-S78949)

*Russia.* The women were all in their uniforms, the same one I had been so proud to wear, although the swastika was no longer a visible patch on their blouses. We were each handed enough provisions to last for three days—bread, a little butter and cheese, and a small bit of sausage. I had seen onions and even a few tomatoes, but they were long gone by the time we came to the front of the line.

We were able to sit at tables then and write letters and telegrams. I wrote to my brother: "Dear Dieter. We are home! We are home. Where are you, my brother? How was it, the end for you? How did you get home?" *Oh do tell me you're safe,* but this last line I could not write.

❧

I was in conversation with some of the other released prisoners at that writing table, and it was here that I learned for the first time what had become of our country while we were in the Gulag: Germany had been cut into quarters. Some of it was in French hands now, some in American, some in British, but much of it had gone to the Russians.

The same fate was meted out to our capital, Berlin. It had not become, as we had been told at the war's end, "a dead city." It was quite alive, in fact, but it too was quartered, Russia owning all of what was in the east, including what was once the Reichstag and the now very damaged Brandenburg Gate. I wondered how it would be in Berlin now with the Russians as administrators. And what of the eastern sector where the Opera House was, and the many museums? But then, was there even an Opera House? Were there even museums? Or was everything still in ruins? Charlottenburg, we came to understand, was apparently in British hands. If this were true, we felt grateful. At least the British would treat us in a gentlemanly manner. This is what we believed.

The day dragged on into night, and Mutti and I slept in our seats. Suddenly we were awakened to shouting. It was four o'clock in the morning. "Up, up, up!" There would be a train soon that would bring us into Berlin. Quickly we grabbed our things and ran to line up for it. Three hours later, we still stood and nothing had come to pass. Mutti muttered, "So this is what we have to thank our victors for? That our trains, too, are impossibly late?" But I had no desire to complain. We were about to be free.

～

Schlesischer Bahnhof.[35] It was large, one of the largest in Berlin. It stood in near total ruin, but the trains seemed to be running, even if not quite on time. We were finally in Berlin, and for the first time in more than two years I laid eyes on my city, the one I had left believing it would be for good.

Timidly the two of us walked out into the daylight. It was morning, and people were rushing around. Were they rushing to work? I had no idea. Everything felt so new to me. The fear of bombs falling from the sky was no longer there. The rubble, much of it, had been swept away, but half walls and half buildings still loomed like beheaded monoliths all around us. People, I noticed, were dressed nicely, much better than we had been used to.

I sheepishly approached an older gentleman, a man walking with a cane. I asked if he knew if there was an office or a station for returning refugees so that we could get information—about S-Bahn cards and finding work and, well, about our house. He only eyed me up and down, wrinkled his nose, and, under his breath, I believe I heard the word *pfui*. A word you use only for shit or pigs.

I stood in my tracks and stared after the retreating man, completely bewildered. *Well, this is Berlin, after all. We never had a reputation for having good manners,* I told myself. But, at the very least, humor was something Berliners nearly always offered one another, even if it was done in a rude manner. This "pfui" was not even that—it was pure disgust—and as I looked around at all the rushing people and saw that no one seemed even to notice us, I realized how very alone we were, and how much we both stank. Our clothes, given to us by the Red Cross, were hand-me-downs and didn't even fit properly, and we had not had a real bath in more than two years.

I again gathered up my courage. This was not the time for self-pity, and I approached another person, this time a woman. I tried to explain our predicament—that we had just returned from Russia, from the prison camps there, and we only needed a little help, some information. She too seemed less than willing to listen. She only said, "Ja, ja, everyone has a story," and with that she walked off in the opposite direction from the one she had been going in. I understand this now. Millions of Germans had to flee the east. Millions more came to West Germany from Poland and Czechoslovakia—sixteen million in all, I believe— and then there was us, the returning prisoners. No one wanted to know.

Alone, we managed to find our way to the S-Bahn, which was noticeably clean. Somehow we were able to board, and we took it to Charlottenburg. I don't know how we paid our fare. Perhaps we didn't; perhaps we sneaked on, as I am sure we had no money.

It was an indescribable moment, when we saw our station up ahead: the Sophie-Charlotte-Platz, just near the Windscheidstrasse, the very same station I had waited at for so many years, each morning before school. The walls of the station were broken, but the bricks that once lay in piles were now neatly moved to the side to give automobiles (though I saw none) room. The street was swept clean. Still, everywhere I saw walls standing singly and with no purpose, a bathtub still hanging from two pipes, a stairwell that led to emptiness.

I felt I was inside a dream. Closer and closer we came, yet our walk from the station could not go fast enough; it seemed to take place inside a slow-motion filmstrip, as if the air itself were thick gum. Everything was so familiar and yet so not. Then I noticed it, something new: slips of paper, fluttering in the breeze, stuffed here and there between the bricks of walls and door frames, even those door frames where doors no longer were. I walked over and pulled on one, curious to see what these papers were. This is what I read: "Dear Wolfgang, we are at Tante Luise's." And I read the next one: "Papa, if you are to return, call on Heidemarie. We have gone to Hamburg." All around me, the same was true. At every door, slips of hope: "We are here," "We have left the country for America," "We are there," "We have not found our brother/our father/our son. Please send information to such-and-such address." I became filled with my own hope—a vision that we might also see such a note at our own door. I could not speak, and Mutti, I know, shared these same thoughts. *Oh Dieter, Dieter. Say you have been here and have left us some news.*

Our home on the Windscheidstrasse was exactly as I remembered it—three floors, the fourth and fifth still missing. The tavern across the street was indeed open again, and there were even tables out in the garden. We arrived at our doorstep. There was only the door frame, no door, and, worse, I saw it had no slip of paper. It would be the first of our many homecoming disappointments.

We entered the main floor and carried our bags up the two flights of stairs, the same ones that Mutti and I had so meticulously strewn with chairs and iceboxes in our effort to save her from drunken Russian soldiers. The door to our apartment felt strange. There was a new lock on it. Perhaps, we thought, the manager wanted to make sure the little we had left behind was kept safe. We stood on the landing a long time, staring at that door, wondering what to do next. Suddenly it opened, as if by itself, and a strange woman appeared, blocking the entryway I knew so well. I spotted our *Garderobe* and umbrella stand just behind her.

"What can I do for you?" she asked, a scowl on her face and her fists set firmly on her bony hips.

"This is our home. Who are you?" Mutti said, bewildered, not sure to whom she was speaking, and careful this time not to mention that we were returning prisoners.

"I'm afraid that's no longer true. This is now our home. *Schade*"—too bad—and with that she slammed the door shut. For a minute we had been able to peek inside our house, view the Persian rug we once owned and, off in the parlor, the marble-topped table at which we used to sit for our evening meals. Now we could only stand with our mouths agape, staring at the door.

There was nothing to do but find the Schulzes. From what we remembered, they lived, after having been bombed out and having lost their kitty, just one flight below us. When we found her, Frau Schulz greeted us with warmth and, it seemed, pity. "My God! I thought you were dead!" she exclaimed again and again. Hugs and tears, and from some deep place inside her, an air of reserve.

I had remembered Frau Schulz as a plump woman. Her stocky body was once made of two halves, the top an overly large and soft bosom, and the bottom, two *Krautstampfer*—what we called the legs of women who stomped around in a tub full of cabbage and brine to make our beloved sauerkraut. Those had been the legs of Frau Schulz. And her bosom—at all times covered by an apron with tiny roses and green leaves—was used as a brace for cutting her bread. It would be a large round of brown-crusted bread, and she would use her serrated knife to cut each slice clean through, pushing the last bit of crust against the knife with her thumb. Each slice of her bread was cut as perfectly as the one before.

Now she stood in her doorway looking as thin as everyone else in Berlin. Even her full, rose-printed apron couldn't conceal the boniness of her hips, and her bosom was empty. Frau Schulz took our bags and our coats and led us back to the kitchen she now shared with two other families.

She was sorry, she said, about our Wohnung. There was nothing she could have done. With the new administrative government, this was how it was. Homes were needed to house the many, many wandering people who had lost their homes in the bombings and all the refugees coming from the east. Each family, she explained, was allotted only one room; kitchens and bathrooms were to be communal. All homes, in all of Germany, in fact, even homes that weren't destroyed and still housed the original families, had strangers living with them.

Four families, we learned, were already occupying our home. There was, quite possibly, Frau Schulz tentatively implied, no more room for us, even though it technically *was* our home. Again she said there was nothing she could have done. "We all thought you were dead!" Over and over she said this, shaking her head, as if even now her eyes were deceiving her. Apparently no one else in our family had returned either, and as much as this posed a question, neither Mutti nor I dared ask it.

"*Na ja.* But do come in," and with that we entered her own communal kitchen. "Sit. Make yourselves comfortable. Let me make some tea." I looked around, trying to orient myself to the fact that this, this home of hers, and the one up a flight of stairs with four new families in it, was in fact the free world. The wallpaper, once with a floral pattern, had torn long ago. The wall beneath it was smeared. A small shelf had been attached to the wall above my head, and it held a few plates and a jar half full of sugar. Herr Schulz, she said as she filled the teakettle, was missing, and without looking up: "He is probably dead.

"I keep my hopes up, though. One has to. Just the other day, Frau Berne said her husband had returned. After walking all the way from an internment camp in Italy. The last she had heard from him, he had written her from the front . . ." And then she stopped. I knew she was trying her best not to cry. "Ach, this is the fate of so many of us. Of course we must go on. And now you are here! There is, truly, always hope!"

Frau Schulz handed us each a cup of tea and sat down with us. She told us then about the terrible starvation still going on even though the war was over. "There is no food to be found anywhere, nothing to buy, not even to barter for, not anything. Scrounging in cellars and potato fields for food scraps and rummaging through the forests in hopes of finding mushrooms and firewood. This has been our life."

She told us how it was when the city was split: One lived here, the other there, friends suddenly became enemies, and people in different sectors were not allowed to visit one another. "It sounds no different from where we were!" Mutti laughed. "Just another prison camp!"

"Exactly!" Frau Schulz exclaimed. "Suddenly we need papers to travel to the eastern side of our own city. My Mutti lives there, and it is nearly impossible to visit her. Sometimes I do, but not often.

"The British and the Americans, well, they are quite reasonable. Amusing, even. It is difficult to look at them, at times, and see such healthy young men when all of ours are so thin. They laugh and tell jokes often, which I never can understand, and they try out their German with us. And the Americans are always eating something they call chewing gum. But on the other side of Berlin, those streets that go east to Malchow, Friedrichsfelde, even to the Opera House, have roadblocks with armed Russian guards who will order you to stop and will allow you to go no further. They want us to have special papers to travel there, and of course these are impossible to obtain. Then, let me tell you about the rest of Germany! My God, just try to go to Frankfurt or Kassel! Impossible!"

She paused for a long moment, and the silence became the reason to hear what we were so desperately waiting for. The question we had been holding inside all the while we were in Russia, and the question that followed us all the way home. She said she knew the answer and was so sorry to be the first one to say this: Dieter was dead.

"I heard this, Helga, from your cousin, when she came some months back to see if we had heard anything from you. *Ach Gott*, I'm so sorry. We all have so much sorrow . . ." Frau Schulz stopped. What else was there to say?

I could not think for myself; I only looked to Mutti. She sat still in her chair. Nothing moved, only large, large tears spilling from her eyes. Her face looked so sad, it was as if nothing in the world would ever bring her happiness again. "O Gott," Mutti whispered into her hands, her body convulsing with sobs. It was the purest sadness I had ever seen.

## 24

# MUTTI WAS STOIC

Suddenly the truth of all my fears was now a fact. No home, no brother, and my city torn into pieces. I left Frau Schulz's kitchen to go outdoors. Mutti and she could finish the stories without me. *Dieter, my Dieter, you are gone.* Out on the broken curb, the same one where we both used to sit for hours as children, throwing stones into the rain gutter, I now sat with my head in my hands, and I wept. They were bitter tears. *What now? What now?* Nothing felt a part of me. My body was boneless. I cried until I was empty.

When I returned to her kitchen, Frau Schulz and Mutti were still in quiet conversation. She had nothing much in the way of food to offer, she said, but she could make room for us in her home. About my stepfather she knew only that he'd been taken prisoner by the Americans, but where he was she did not know. I was sure that realization would hit Mutti very soon, but we did not dwell on it. "Your Papa is safe," she always said while we were in the Gulag, and I was not about to bring up any other possibilities. Not now.

"Stay here with me. And stay as long as you need," Frau Schulz said, looking over to me, seeing my tear-streaked face. "Aber selbstverständlich," she added. No question. Of course we could stay with her. She said she would help us get in touch with the Red Cross, and "things will work out, you'll see." It was not a solution. I knew this. It was just another step in the direction we were going. She showed us the only other room in her home. It was a hallway of sorts, long and dark, but she pushed some mattresses up against a wall and told us to make ourselves comfortable. "Tomorrow we'll go together to the British Red Cross station. I'll take you. I know exactly where it is. But first, tonight, we'll have something very special to eat." Her smile was large. At least we knew we had one friend.

Frau Schulz had managed to acquire six tins of fish, and she told us she had been deliberating on them for so long: How many to open? Should it be one every day? Or all of them at once? "Eat until I'm full? No, no. That would just never do! I would have to eat fish conserves an entire month long! So. I've saved them here on my shelf, and I know now why I did that. I kept them so that they could be shared with you!"

Over our dinner of six tins of delicious herring smothered in mustard sauce, we heard how things had gone in Berlin. Not well. Frau Schulz told us of the returning children from the *Kinderlandverschickung*— those who had been sent off to the east to stay safe during the war. Many had landed in concentration camps and stayed there for years, as there were no homes left available to them.

"This went on for all those years. For some, it was their entire school life, six years, some eight. Many of them seem never to have learned to write or read. And now they come back to us, their families are dead, their homes are gone . . . and they are still so young! Sixteen! It's a travesty." But then Frau Schulz shook her head and said, "Na ja." What we all learned to say—*Oh well*.

❧

The Red Cross was not friendly. In fact, no one in Berlin was friendly. No one cared; no one wanted to hear our story. We could move back into our home, we learned, but we would need to share it with the four other families already living there. And yet, to even do that, we needed our birth certificates. Both Mutti and I had been born in what was now East Germany, and all those papers, if we ever had them, were either burned or buried underneath rubble, but in no case available.

"No birth certificate? Well, then, you'll need a residence identification card," we were told. But of course we weren't residents, we were refugees!

So, no residence identification card. Oh, such a runaround, and all the while we still had our diarrhea that never quit. Poor food, stress, dirt, the Gulag—I don't know. Maybe even hunger caused it, but we just had diarrhea. I cannot remember how it all went or how we finally received permission to move back into our own home. I only remember how difficult it was when each office that was supposed to help us turned out to be at a different location in the city. How could we get to them without money and always needing a toilet?

We finally managed to reenter our home, however unwelcome we were. In fact, we were scolded—a woman quite yelled at us to get out of *her* house! These were *her* plates, she said, and *her* chair and *her* cutting board, when, really, most of it had been ours. But who cared anymore? Why such a fuss? We needed a bed, a place to come home to. *Take the plates, take the chairs,* and we settled into a mutual distance. We learned to tolerate each other, but we never spoke.

Mutti and I were relegated to the back porch. It had been a laundry room for us once, where we used to wash and mend and iron our clothing. We noticed that much of what we had left in this home had somehow disappeared. A wooden stool, for example—I remember it was green and it had always fit so nicely under the washbasin. The stool was one thing, but what mattered most were the memories that were stolen. Never again would I be able to look out of our parlor window the way I did once; never again would I walk down the long corridor from the kitchen to the front room, happily singing and tiptoeing over the Persian runner in the hallway; never again would I sink into the oversized bath I knew as a child. All this was now shared, occupied, or gone.

Mutti did somehow scrounge together some of our belongings, the things "they" no longer wanted. My violin, for example; Dieter's bookshelf; the book of Grimm's fairy tales that Mutti had bound in leather and gold leaf. Dieter loved Goethe, Rainer Maria Rilke, Schiller, as did I. We had this in common, our love of literature. I took these books, the ones we used to share, and organized them carefully on a little shelf. I told him, as I still spoke to him often, *This is for you. Finally now, you have your very own shelf, dear brother, with all your books arranged so nicely. Just until you come home.* My violin sat there where Mutti had put it, and I took it into my arms and cradled it against my chest. *Oh, dear Dieter. I want to tell you something. It made me so mad. Mutti wanted to throw out your curtains! That was out of the question, I told her. You'll see, dear brother, I will have everything nice for you when you finally come back to me ...*

&#10149;

After those tears in Frau Schultz's kitchen, my mother was stoic and she was Mutti. Once we were "home," she decided she should immediately go out to find what might be left of our hidden things, those that had been stashed in the military bunker on the outskirts of Berlin—mostly our Persian rugs. They were authentic Persian rugs, hand woven, and we had original oil paintings stored in that bunker as well. That she would be upset when she returned empty-handed that day, we should have guessed before she even left.

"Of course the first thing that was robbed when the Allies marched into Berlin was the military bunkers. Of course!" she said, shaking her head and clasping her hands in exasperation. "Why would I have believed otherwise?"

"But we still have the Dürer. Shouldn't we be so happy about that?" I said, not without sarcasm. Her answer was merely a disgusted look, which let me know she was not about to give up, and that my comment was out of place.

The next day, again hopeful, she went off to the Berlin Symphony Hall to reclaim our grand piano. Mutti, who had already experienced one terrible war in her life, had shrewdly acquired permission to store our piano in the basement of the symphony hall, where all the pianos for the Berlin Philharmonic were packed away for safekeeping. Perhaps

Dieter and Margarete at the piano in Swinemünde, about ages five and six.

she received permission because she was an officer's wife. I no longer remember the details.

She told us she arrived at the symphony hall, and yes, all of Berlin's precious instruments had been carefully wrapped and hidden in the basement, the Russian admissions guard assured her. Mutti was prepared for anything—to hand over her identity papers, anything. She was determined to be successful this time and told the woman behind the desk, politely but firmly, she was there to reclaim a piano that had been stored away for six years.

"But which piano is it?" the woman wanted to know, as she handed back Mutti's identity papers, barely having glanced at them. It was clear she was not in the least interested in helping.

"I know my piano! I've been playing it since I was twelve. I know every scratch. I probably put each one of them there myself. I would even recognize the patina on the pedals," Mutti said.

"All right, then. I'll show you into the basement. There are only a few pianos left; I suppose you'll know if yours is one of them," the woman said, and they walked together down the hall.

"Right away I recognized it! Right away!" Mutti told me over our tea that night. "It was there. The wing lay on top of the piano, somewhat skewed, but I thought, *What could I expect after all those bombs?*

"Now, this is how the rest of our conversation went: 'Yes, Madam. It's true. That may be your piano, but the legs are missing.' Well, of course the legs were missing; all the legs of all the pianos were missing. I suppose it's what they did with everything, the Russians. They unscrewed them or sawed them off and sent them all back to Russia, just as they did with all the radios and bicycles we saw piled up at the train stations.

"So I said, 'It's quite all right. I'll take it as it is. It's my piano and I can play it without legs just as easily as with. I'll just set it onto chairs, four of them, and it will play just fine.'

"Do you know what she answered? 'Oh, but no, Madam. You can't take a piano without its legs. Without its legs, it's no longer your piano!' That's what she said!"

This is the story Mutti told, half laughing, half crying over her cup of tea because, again, she returned empty-handed.

⊸≋⊷

Germany was still under severe rations imposed by the Allies, and we were given only four potatoes per day per person—not enough to get well on. Later this became better, but it seemed they wanted to starve us out, the entire country. That's what it felt like. Don't misunderstand me—things did improve, but not right away. While we were on these meager rations, the only thing we could do to help ourselves was barter on the black market. That's how we sometimes had extra bread, and that's how Frau Schulz had come by those cans of mustard herrings.

My cough got worse, the diarrhea never let up, and Mutti often felt terribly weak. Both of us were weak. We tried so hard to make our lives work, but we were undernourished, and, with the poor rations, it seemed every scratch and bug bite turned into a pus-filled infection. We were physically depleted, but even worse, we were finished. Nothing was left. Dieter was dead, Papa Spaeth was somewhere else, and all we wanted now was to leave Germany. For good.

Mutti came upon the idea of staying with our relatives in Neu Ölsburg, a small town near Hannover. She found out from the British Red Cross that we could quite easily obtain travel documents for the British-occupied sector of Germany. They would only be temporary passes, but we could travel if we showed a need. "Surely our poor health would speak in our favor, wouldn't you think?" Mutti asked one evening. Our relatives had a home still, a house that had not been bombed and some land where they could grow food. The prospect made me feel better—to be somewhere where people actually might care who we were, and care about Dieter and my broken heart and Mutti's sorrow. Somewhere to rest.

Suddenly an interzone pass felt like the greatest gift on earth. With the passes and the few items we might need—sweaters, a coat, some aspirin—we took a train to Neu Ölsburg to stay with my Tante Erna and my Onkel Axel, Mutti's brother. I cannot recall how we knew where the home was or even how we knew it was still standing, or that they would receive us when we arrived. All I remember is we arrived on their doorstep, jittery with hunger. We simply stood at the door for a long moment, staring at the knocker, our suitcases at our feet, and we both took a deep breath.

Tante Erna answered the door immediately when we knocked. She was thin, and her dress hung loosely from her bony shoulders. Her young son, my cousin Axel, who could not have been older than seven, ran to the door and promptly hid himself behind her legs. His large brown eyes peered around her skirt, and suddenly he let out a loud scream. Then he ran, shouting through the house, "There are ghosts at the door! There are ghosts at the door!" I suppose it was our clothes, the rags we wore, or it was our faces, or our sunken eyes, with our swollen legs, bruised and scabbed, I cannot tell you, but what else could a child have thought?

Tante Erna kindly welcomed these two "ghosts" into her home.

"*Aber* Helga! Margarete! Where, oh where, have you come from? We all thought you were dead! No one knew a thing about you. My God, come in!" Tante Erna shed tears of delight while she held the two of us in her thin arms. "Come, come, I'll take your things," and we were warmly shown into the parlor to sit. "My, but you look terrible! How thin your faces. Your eyes! And your fingers look like chicken feet! Oh my. What's become of you?"

We told her our story; she told us hers. We had been in the Gulag in Russia since the summer of 1945. She housed refugees from the east. And now we were fatigued and hungry, and yet so happy to be somewhere where we could rest. We discovered that we were not the first relatives to have come to this idea. Tante Erna and Onkel Axel were our only relatives still living fairly well, and the many other relatives who had to flee the east at the end of the war had come here, too, to take refuge. And then there was the mandatory housing of strangers that they needed to comply with. There were, in all, thirty-four others! "But don't worry. Somehow we'll manage," Tante Erna said. "We are some of the lucky ones. We still have a garden. We have fruit trees, potatoes, and a few cabbage plants. We manage."

They were "some of the lucky ones," too, in that they also had a small plot of land on the outskirts of town, the way it was in Germany, where they grew oats and more potatoes. The children were sent out each day to watch over this plot to make sure no one stole what was there, Tante Erna explained. With the oats and the peelings from the potatoes, the chickens and the rabbits were fed, and from time to time there were even eggs to eat.

At first there were only four potatoes per person per day, but later we were also rationed forty grams of meat per person, although only once a week. You may think this is something, but you must realize, forty grams is about as much meat as only one bite of a sausage. This we received once a week. Yes, we were still very hungry.

Mutti and I could not get well. I coughed, her joints hurt. What I recall most about that time is this: both of us lying for hours each day, sunning ourselves in the garden in the back of the house, and sleeping. We were given comfortable chairs, long ones—lounge chairs—and we wrapped ourselves inside several blankets and slept. For many hours, we slept.

Our interzone pass was to expire soon, and we needed to return to Berlin. It was time for me to piece my life together, and I began to dream about finishing my university studies, but I never gave up my dream of leaving Germany. I was quite finished with all of it, and I still had the sliver of hope that I might one day reach Sweden.

On a blustery winter day, Mutti and I made our way back to Berlin. Again we moved into our "washroom." Mutti took the pearl necklace she had hidden among the silver she had carried through Russia and brought it to the black market. It was all she had left. There she traded it for a large sack of potatoes. We were ecstatic to have them. When she returned home, she put the sack into the washbasin in our new little Wohnung. We would cook them the next day and make a soup out of them, we decided.

I remember that day so well. I awoke, excited to begin to cook. In the night—there was no heat in our home—the potatoes had frozen solid, and when they thawed they were nothing but glassy, watery mush. Where our knives cut, it was soft and turned black immediately. It was a familiar look I saw in Mutti's eyes. Terror. Panic. The shortage of everything. Our hunger.

During the war, we had somehow learned to soak frozen potatoes in vinegar water to revive them. But we had no vinegar, so we just stood there at the sink, the two of us, and stared at those shriveled, brown, glassy globules of mush, and said nothing. And that is what came of Mutti's last bargaining chip, the pearl necklace my Papa Werner had given her.

## 25

# HOW I CAME TO KIEL

1948

Kiel, in the very north of Germany, near the Danish border, has a university long known for its medical studies. It is one of Germany's oldest universities, built in the early seventeenth century. I was going to pursue my dream again and believed, with my Red Cross training and my experience as a medical assistant during the war, I would be accepted to study medicine without much difficulty.

There was a problem, though. I did not have papers to stay in West Germany, and Kiel is in the West. I had papers only for Berlin, and only once did I receive papers for a short travel abroad—the one we took to Neu Ölsburg.[36]

One day, while speaking with an old school friend, a crazy idea began to blossom in my brain. He was the boy I used to swim with at the Reichsportfeld. He gave me red roses once for my birthday. I didn't thank him. I was arrogant and young, and I was thinking of other things . . .

Karl had found me after sending notes and making telephone calls and leaving messages with Frau Schulz every few months all that time I was in the Gulag. When we first saw each other, it was as though not a day had passed, but of course so many had! He had fought in Africa, he told me, and had been badly wounded and lost his left eye. He too had been in a prison camp, but a French one. It was a terrible existence, he said. "The French were not nice. They thought it was funny to laugh at us and watch us grovel for the bits of food they would sometimes throw over the fence. But I escaped." I asked no more. I did not want to hear about suffering. We had all suffered, and now those of us who survived must try to make the best of what life had left to give us.

Karl Sommerfeld. "He stood proud when he talked, always flashing a bright smile."

Karl was once a tall, handsome man. He stood proud when he talked, always flashing a bright smile. He did not smile like that now, and he looked beaten down. He was a man I could have been attracted to once, but not anymore.

I told him of my desire to go to Kiel. "I want to study again. I want to make a life for myself and become a doctor," I told him. I suddenly felt very proud of myself and also very adult. I had never quite uttered that declaration, just that clearly, before. We were sitting at his small table in a kitchen he shared with a man and his wife, his "co-occupants." They were very nice and very, very quiet. They left us to ourselves when I came to visit. They probably thought we had been lovers once, though we never were.

"I know how to get you to Kiel," Karl whispered, not wanting his "neighbors" to hear. "Let's go out for a walk. I'll tell you more about it there." We managed to duck out the door without being noticed. "It's dangerous, but I've done it a few times already," Karl said as soon as we were out on the street. He told me he too wanted to leave for the West. "You, with your Gulag history, I think the Americans, or the British, will have sympathy for you. They may even give you amnesty, and with amnesty you'll be able to move around anywhere you like, dear Grete." He turned to me then and held my shoulders in both his hands. "It will be dangerous, but you can do it."

I didn't really mind this word "dangerous." Had I not already experienced dangerous? Many, many times before? How bad could it be? "Well, tell me, then, Karl. How do we do it?"

"We have to travel through Thüringen. We can go by train. Thüringen, as you know, is Russian. We stay on the train all the way through Thüringen. As soon as the train hits Niedersachsen, we jump off. It is British. From there, for about fifty meters, there is a wide strip of land known as No-Man's-Land. That's when we run. I've done it before."

"Karl! What if we get caught? I've heard terrible things happen if the Russians catch you running across their borders. I've heard women get raped, people get shot, or even worse, they are sent to the Gulag! I'll never go back to the Gulag!"

"Yes, yes. Grete. You must not think of these things. You must think of what you want to have and then work to get it. It's not easy, but I've done it now a number of times. I go to Hamburg, or to Köln, buy merchandise I believe people will want, and then I return to Berlin, and I sell it here for five times what I paid for it on the black market. Here where American cigarettes are worth more than our own currency. This traveling and black marketeering is how I'm saving to make my final escape one day too."

"When do we go?"

"Soon. It should be when there is significant activity going on. I'd say this coming Tuesday, if you'll be ready. I know I can get you into British territory. From there, we will take a train to Hamburg. You'll have to get to Kiel on your own, but that will be easy."

⌒≫⌒

Tuesday came. I prayed to Dieter and told him where I was going. I said goodbye to Mutti. It was quick; I didn't want tears. I didn't tell her my plans; she would have been frightened. I only told her I had found work, I would telephone her in a few weeks, and I was gone, out the door.

Karl and I took the train that traveled through Thüringen, taking us through the East Zone—all the land that surrounded Berlin and was now Russian. This was so strange. We traveled several hundred kilometers with nowhere to sit. The seats had all been given up, as was polite, to those with handicaps and to old people. Some passengers, young men, even climbed to sit up on top of the cars, as there really was no room inside.

Karl knew exactly what to do. "We need to run almost as soon as we arrive, Grete. This will be frightening. But don't worry. We run at noon when the Russians are having their lunch up in their guard towers. They won't be paying so much attention to anyone trying to run across the land. It's much safer than running at night. Always, you read in the news, you hear it on the radio, another 'escapee' was shot. This won't happen to us. The fools always try to run at night."

I wore my Red Cross dress—I really had nothing else. I had my papers that said I was a citizen of the British sector of Berlin, a few Reichsmarks, and a scarf and gloves, both of which had been mended many times.

The train slowed to a stop in Niedersachsen. Karl poked his head out the window and said, "Look. Over there. Do you see the watchtowers? Those are the Russians. Now, as soon as the train stops again, and I squeeze your hand, we make our way carefully to the edge of the forest without being noticed. We must not look suspicious; we must look as though we have somewhere to go. Don't draw attention to yourself. On the other side will be the No-Man's-Land. I'll squeeze your hand once again, and this time it will mean we run."

No sooner had our feet hit the platform than Karl grabbed my hand and gave it a squeeze. My breath came short. I looked furtively around and I followed him quietly, staring straight ahead to get through the trees that stood just up ahead. Branches crackling underfoot, my bag over my shoulder, quickly we crossed the forest to the land that was barren, and I felt his squeeze once more. This one was very hard. All I could think was *Run! Run! Now! Fast as you can, run!* Each minute was too long, each step not fast enough. I never looked back. I never even looked at the ground we were running on. I simply looked at Karl's back, his broad shoulders, and I trusted God.

A bullet zinged past my head. Then another. Apparently at least one of the guards was not quite so busy eating his lunch. I didn't even look up then. I didn't want to see my enemy—I was afraid I'd lose hope or lose my focus, or both. I was afraid I'd stumble or he'd shoot me, this Russian with the gun. We ran and ran. Karl ran, and I was behind him.

The distance was probably only fifty meters, as he had said, but it could have been fifty kilometers. The moments took so long, it was as if they lasted all day. There was no barbed wire yet around No-Man's-Land—that would come later. On this day it was just land, empty land, with watchtowers and Russians with guns.

When finally Karl stopped running, I knew we had crossed to the other side. We were in the West, and we were safe inside the British Zone. Such a frightening day, just when all that fright and all the danger was supposed to have been behind us. It was terrifying, but I was in West Germany, and I was going to Kiel.

⚘

After a heartfelt goodbye, Karl and I parted, each to move on to our futures. I left for Kiel, he for the black market.

My arrival in Kiel was very late at night, and, my God, it was cold! It was the middle of April and I had only a thin coat, a thin scarf, a thin pair of gloves, and no hat. I stayed in some refugee barracks I somehow found, and there was no heat. By four in the morning I could not take it any longer, so I got up and walked alone through the dark streets to the university. I thought I could just as easily freeze at the university as in the barracks.

I found the school easily. Somehow I arrived at a gate to the university, which had a small gatehouse, and inside it a watchman. I was shivering something terrible by this time, and I asked if I couldn't come in to warm myself. He opened the door with a smile and welcomed me in. Perhaps he was bored and wanted some company. "Sure, sure. Come in! Come warm yourself." He placed a small stool in front of a little stove he kept lit with bits of wood, and I was able to warm my hands. Together we waited until nine o'clock, when the university opened. I walked, then, the long walk up to the main entrance. I was nervous, and I had no idea how things would go.

First I had to fill out papers. Oh, there were so many papers. Who was I, where was I born, what was my party affiliation—all that. I

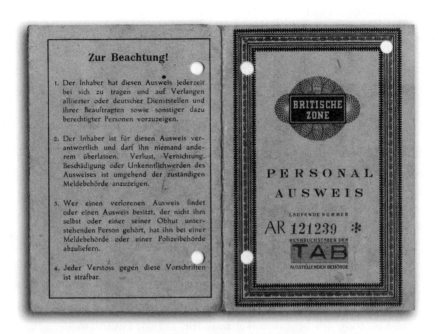

Margarete's British pass. "Somehow I fell into the classification for British amnesty."

suppose they were still fishing for the Nazis, but the Nazis surely were long gone. They had either been found and prosecuted or, if they were still living among us, they were lying. No one claimed to have been a Nazi anymore. Who would write "Nazi Partei" on these papers?

I did acknowledge that I had been in the Hitler Youth. Of course I had been, as everyone had. I wasn't going to lie. Having been in the Hitler Youth, in the end, was what saved me. Somehow I fell into the classification for British amnesty, and I was never questioned again. I was eventually given a British pass that allowed me to stay in the West for good.

❧

The Anatomy professor was already at his desk this morning. He was on the second floor in an office that looked like an Anatomy professor's

269

office. There was even a full-scale human skeleton in the corner, facing out the window. The professor's name was Barckmann, and I promptly and politely introduced myself with a curtsy: "Margarete Dos. I would like to study here, sir, and I was told you are the professor who can give me the permission."

He asked me to sit. He had a graying beard and his suit was worn at the edges of his sleeves, but he had dignity, I could see this. His eyes twinkled. "*Nun sag mal, Fräulein,*" he began. "Tell me what brings you here."

"Sir. I am well versed in all the medical practicalities," I began. I wanted to impress him. I could not bear the possibility of him writing *Not Accepted.* I needed this placement. Where else could I go? "I can bandage a wound, I have stood in the operating room while amputations were performed, I can administer morphine, and—oh, sir, please accept me! I'll study. I'll be brave. I'll pass the exams. I want to become a doctor. Please. Tell me what you need from me."

"My dear," he said, "tell me how you came here."

"Well, sir. I would have been here long ago, but you see, I was in Russia until now. I have been in Siberia and was only recently released."

His eyes widened, and he looked at the Red Cross insignia on my dress, noticing it for the first time. He raised his eyebrows then, and with an amazed look, he barely whispered, "*Women* were in Russia?"

"Yes. Yes, sir. We were all women. Mostly from Prussia. We all thought we were going to Sweden, you see, but it was a hoax. We were swindled and ended up working in the coal mines—"

He took my hand warmly into his. "Say no more. I believe you. I just have never heard of such a thing. This was a terrible fate for you. You've suffered so much. *Mach dir keine Sorgen.* Have no worries. I will make sure you'll be taken care of."

He then told me of his own sorrows. He himself was a refugee from Königsberg, a city that, like so many of the others—Dresden and Hamburg—was decimated by British and American bombs.[37]

But Königsberg warranted a special prayer, and he told me all about it. Once the bombing was over and most of that beautiful city lay in ruin, the Russians marched in. It was a terror for the people who were left behind. Nearly everyone who could fled. Years later, after the war, Stalin still wanted his revenge for Germany's betrayal of Russia. The war was over, but even then he wanted to "ethnically cleanse" Königsberg of all the remaining Germans and tried to murder whoever was left. This was the Königsberg that Professor Barckmann had come from.

"We ran, my mother and I. We simply ran with just our shoes on. No bags, nothing. It was late summer 1944. We hid in the forests and ran at night. I stole eggs from farmers' henhouses when I could. If the Russians were to find us, it would have been certain death. We ran more than eight hundred kilometers. It took several weeks, but we finally arrived in Hamburg. There, it was not much easier for us. We were from the East, you know. No one wanted to help us. One man, an old man, threw garbage at my mother's face."

The professor then walked around to his desk drawer and pulled out a form. With a fountain pen, he put a long strike down the page and signed the bottom. Then he handed me a *Studienbuch*, the book that would contain all my future grades, and on the cover he wrote in large letters, just after my name, the course of study I was accepted to: *Medizin*. "Please, have no more worries," he said as he handed me my book. "I will make sure you're cared for. I can even help you with an apartment. I will make life as easy for you as I can. Now go. Study!" he ordered, waving the back of his hand toward the door. He sat and became a professor once again.

≈

It is possible to go to bed and awake to a new day, one that has changed its color forever. It was Monday, and the day before, Sunday, June 20, 1948, the Deutsch Mark was introduced. It was done on a Sunday so that the occupying forces—the British, the French, and the Americans—would have nothing to say about it, because their offices were officially closed. It would be the *Währungsreform*, the Currency Reform.

Every German would receive forty new Deutsch Marks, and we could trade in our old Reichsmarks, one for one. We were three years out from our former Führer's death.

Everyone was happy with the forty Marks we received. It was not enough to start anything with, barely enough to eat for a week—and then only if you were very resourceful—so it may sound unimportant, but it was not. We all felt we could finally breathe again. New businesses sprang up everywhere. In the streets you saw new signs—HOUSE PAINTING SERVICES, LETTERPRESS SERVICES, anything. Universities were filled to capacity. In the summer of 1948, an enormous weight had been removed from our shoulders.

⚭

Kiel had been my home now for several months. Professor Barckmann had been too kind. He had found housing for me. It was only a room in the attic of a house where several other families lived. But it was my own room with a small table and chair just beneath a round window that looked out upon the street. I was impatient for school to begin again in September, and Mutti was still stuck in Berlin.

For her, more than ever, Germany had taken on a face she no longer wanted to see. The feeling was that things could not help but change, but they were changing much too slowly, and she wanted out. Of course I said I wanted to go too. Sweden was the most logical destination, so Mutti tried her luck at the Swedish embassy, even at the Swedish Red Cross—anything to get us out. But Sweden didn't want refugees any more than any other country did, and to be accepted, we had to prove our work-worthiness. Mutti hoped our Kriegsdienst experience would be enough.

A letter arrived from Mutti. It seemed Berlin was no different from Kiel. "The city is up in cranes. Everywhere there is construction. The churches were first. Much of the old stained glass has been put back. The only thing Berliners won't do is see the Kaiser-Wilhelm steeple replaced. It will stay as a remembrance of that terrible time, that strange time we just passed through." She went on to talk about the new businesses that were opening, and how some of our neighbors had gotten permission to leave.

"I hope to get our visas for Sweden soon," she wrote.

⤳

Several months went by, then Mutti's letters, three of them, came all on one day. She was so excited to tell me about Papa. She had finally heard from him. He was safe. He was in Göttingen, where he had decided to study medicine. This man who had once been an engineer wanted something new. Medicine. And now we would both become doctors. His story was a difficult one, not unlike our own, and, like us, he had managed to survive.

When he returned to Berlin, he saw we were gone. This would not have surprised him. Everyone was gone. He hoped, he said, we were safe somewhere. He had contacted our relatives in Sweden, and from them he learned we had left Germany. They knew we had supposedly boarded a Raoul Wallenberg train, but they also told him we never arrived. That we had been taken as prisoners to somewhere in Russia was something they all hoped; certainly they did not want to believe we were dead. So Papa went on hoping and praying we would return one day. The Russians, of course, never even acknowledged they took us. To them, we were dead, lost, or otherwise unimportant. It did not matter to them what the story was. We were Germans, and we were gone, no need for explanations. And Papa needed to make a new life for himself. The German navy no longer existed, so he decided to study medicine.

## 26

# THE MAN WHO HAD BEEN TO CANADA

1949

His hair was blond, but only in places. Mostly he was bald, with just a strip of hair running around the bottom of his head. His shoulders spread wide, and the nails on his fingers were broad. The tooth in the front of his smile was chipped. Just a little bit. *He's too old to be going to university*, I thought, but didn't we all have our stories these days?

He smiled at me that day. In fact, he had smiled at me often. If I turned around, he was looking at me. He had a pretty smile, even with his chipped tooth. His hands took their time to gesture, and he had a habit of running his long fingers along the top of his head, smoothing the few hairs that were still there. I finally returned his attention that day and asked him how Anatomy was going for him. Mostly I felt sorry for him. He was so old, at least thirty-five.

To my surprise, he was an easygoing man and a gentleman. He offered to hold my books for me while we walked across the campus. He asked me how I had held out during the war. Where was I from? Did I have a brother or father who died? To this, my only answer was what everyone said, "We all have our stories. Mine are no different from anyone else's—things were difficult. And I'm here." And so he smiled some more. He smelled good, too, something I had not remembered since the early days before the war, when I was young and Mutti and Papa had elegant guests come for dinner. I was intrigued by this man. Who was he? And why did he make me laugh so easily?

His name was Jürgen. He was a charmer, and he smiled often. When the time was right, when the sun was sinking, when the birds had stopped chirping for the night and we were still walking, he took

274

my hand in his and he told me how lovely I looked. Sometimes he'd put his arm around my waist. But he always was a gentleman. He waited for me after class. He'd be there when I rounded the corner. Jürgen even picked some spring flowers for me once and said, "They were just waiting for you at the side of the road. Calling your name." They were white, I remember, and I thought it might mean something. They were the same flowers I saw when summer arrived in Russia.

I still thought he was old. I still felt sorry for him. But we all had our stories, and every one of them revolved around mystery. He asked me if I would be so kind as to accompany him to his favorite tavern. He'd like to share a bottle of wine with me, this tall man with the chipped tooth, but he leaned into me ever so gently when he asked, and just that made me say yes.

The tavern was dark. A fire burned in a fireplace, the atmosphere was one of warmth and candlelight. The tavern waiter seemed to know Jürgen, or at least they were familiar enough with each other to say *du*. "Very lovely to make your acquaintance, Margarete," he said, giving a slight bow with his head, and he led us to a corner table with a bench that wrapped around two sides of it with red cushions and small embroidered pillows to cozy into. I remember deer horns decorated the walls. I could have sat here for a very long time, and Jürgen was so entertaining.

Of course I would want to know where he was during the war. I hoped he would leave the bad parts out, though, and to my surprise he did. He made it all sound so simple, so easy, so *exciting*. He had been a pilot in the war. He had flown a Messerschmitt, and it was dumb luck, as he put it. He could as easily be dead as alive. The other man, a Brit, did not survive. It had been a battle of wills: The first one to retreat would probably lose, and Jürgen said he was the one who "stuck to his guns." It happened during the first air battle of the war, the Battle of Britain, as it is now known.

The outcome that had been reported to his parents was that he had been killed in action. Witnesses on the ground said they saw two

Jürgen Möller. "He had flown a *Messerschmitt.*"

planes crash, midair, a Brit and a German, the Brit flying a Spitfire, the German—Jürgen, of course—in his Messerschmitt. One man parachuted and landed in the cold water of the Channel. He was soon rescued by the Allies who were waiting in ships below. The wrong part of the story was that it was the Brit who jumped and Jürgen who was dead. Instead, Jürgen was taken prisoner and sent away for seven years. His parents eventually learned the truth, but it was one I could hardly believe myself.

"The British are proper men, I have to say. I was taken to London— along with all the other German POWs who had been fished out of the sea—to be brought before a court, where I was sentenced to a prisoner-of-war camp. They needed to determine what to do with us, where to put us while they had us.

"There we were marched through the streets. It was a sunny day. It must have been a weekend, because many people came out to watch, or they just took time off from work. They lined the streets, men and women, so that they could have a good look at us. I was number 162. That means

I was the 162nd prisoner, and I had a sign on my chest announcing this. We were spit at, as can be expected. Booed at, sneered at. Vile things were said, some of which I understood, much of which I merely ignored. I was an officer first and foremost, and I kept that at the front of my mind. Of course they would sneer. They were English, we were the enemies.

"My comrades and I had known we were about to appear before a judge, and so we asked if we couldn't please shave first. And perhaps receive a set of clean clothes. We were so dirty. The British, with all proper manners, obliged promptly. We were each given shaving implements, soap, and clean blades. A clean towel and a white shirt each, and fresh trousers. I am proud to say, it was clean officers the British were sneering at."

I then told Jürgen about my own experiences with the British. How it was for me in Berlin and now here in Kiel. And yes, they had been ruthless during the war. I spoke with the knowledge of a woman who had been there on the ground when it happened. They bombed civilian neighborhoods and destroyed our beautiful cities, and it all seemed so useless and for no good reason. But they were also men of honor. I too had to admit this. They provided food to us when the war was finally done.

"I was sent to Canada then," Jürgen said.

"*What?* Who went to Canada? I've never heard of such a thing!"

"No, no. Don't misunderstand. I went as a prisoner. I was sent to a prison camp in Montreal."

Although Montreal sounded romantic, my blood chilled at the sound of those two words: "prison" and "camp." No matter what life would bring, what beauty still lay ahead, I would never outlive the feelings that come with those words.

"I was there for seven years."

Jürgen kept speaking, but I suddenly felt too sick to listen. *Seven years. I would never have survived that. Seven years! Oh God!*

And when my ears tuned back in, I heard the most unbelievable things:

"We were given an officer's paycheck, just like we would have in Germany . . ."

"We ate very well. We cooked elaborate dinners with meats drenched in sauces made with dill and mustard . . ."

"We had access to the library . . ."

"I attended one of their best universities, McGill . . ."

*Spinnt er?* I kept saying to myself. Is he spinning stories? How could this be true? The past had such a different reality for him than it had for me. And yet, we all had our stories, he his, I mine, and he poured another wine.

Then, this man kissed me.

I was light-headed. He smiled, and I smiled back.

"Margarete," he said from another place, one more intimate. "Margarete . . . you have a lovely name."

I was feeling something like love, and he was looking straight at me. He held my hair in his hand, something a man didn't usually do, and he pulled me close. "Margarete. Would you kiss me again?"

I had not felt this, this feeling, in such a long time. He was there, his eyes large and bright, and his grin with the chipped tooth. I let him kiss me. We were sitting at a corner table, where other couples must have sat; the tavern keeper left us alone. The kiss felt soft and easy, and in that moment I felt trust, a feeling I had long ago lost faith in.

"Do you know how many languages you can learn in seven years?" Jürgen asked suddenly.

"No, I don't."

"Seven. I learned seven."

"No you didn't. What languages?" His story was so fascinating, but some things were too big. I mean, who lives the war years doing things like this?

"Swedish." He then said, "*Svensk flicka,*" calling me a Swedish girl, and I giggled.

Oh, this man could make me laugh! This man who spoke English well, the man with large fingernails and warm hands. With what I'm sure was a strong German accent, he called me a beautiful woman in Arabic and Czech and Italian. Then he said it in one more language, and this one took me by surprise: Russian.

"Oh, Jürgen, tell me anything. Tell me about sauces made with mustard. Tell me about your dress shirts and ties and library books. But don't tell me about the Russians. Not their language or any of it . . ."

Right about now Jürgen's face was much closer to mine. We had slipped our bodies closer, his eyes, such a rich blue, never left mine, and his voice soothed me. I noticed his top button was in the wrong buttonhole, but I dismissed it as just a silly thing to notice and thought only of the man he'd been, so young, and to have fallen from an airplane!

He walked me home that night, as a gentleman, and then asked if he could see me again. Could we see a film together, perhaps, the next time?

⟶

Jürgen and I went together to see that film he had promised, one we'd been hearing about, even though, with our limited money, it was an extravagance. The film, *Die Mörder Sind Unter Uns* (The Murderers Are Among Us), upset us both terribly. It made me feel a shame I had never experienced before. It was a love story, and a very popular film, but there was a scene—one that haunted the main character, and it certainly haunted me—in which women, old men, and children, hundreds of them, were purposely shot. It was an SS officer who gave the orders for the murders. I couldn't believe this. I asked Jürgen if he, as a military man, had known any of this to be true. He said he did now.

When he was in Canada, the Canadians had shown him and his comrades photos of piles of decaying skeletal bodies and mass graves, but they hadn't believed them. "Germans would never do such a thing" was what they said, and then dismissed the entire thing as just a bunch of enemy propaganda. "We never gave it another thought," Jürgen continued. "Such a thing was impossible. Things like that would never happen in Germany!"

*Erschüttert.* There is no proper English translation for that word. "Shaken to the core" might come close. I was so unnerved by this film, it made me feel sick. The two of us walked home without conversation. I think Jürgen was *erschüttert* too. I had never seen him so quiet before. We didn't even kiss good night. *After all that,* I thought. To have lived with that tyrant, to have survived starvation and destruction and persecution and want, and now to be handed this. It was an insult: I was suddenly one of the guilty ones, and, more than ever, I was determined to leave Germany.

It was September. I was to start my third semester at the university. One day a phone call came from Mutti. She was in Sweden! With the help of our relatives Johan and Emma and Gurli, she had arrived, and I too was about to realize a dream I'd had since the first time she and I left Berlin.

Mutti had found work as a housemaid. This didn't last long, but it gave her the papers to leave Germany and immigrate to Stockholm. She never complained about her job, but oh, how I knew it bothered her. She who had employed maids all her life! Who had worn silk dresses and long pearl necklaces and pinned her hair up with an ivory comb. She was now forty-eight, but she did not complain. She had work, and it was her salvation. She was away from Germany and we could begin new.

The day came when I held my immigration papers in my hand as well, October 26, 1949. Never more than on this day and this night did I know I was standing in the middle of history—my own history, for once. I was sad to leave Jürgen, "the older gentleman," as Professor Barckmann referred to him. And yet.

"Jürgen, I'll find work for you. I will, and when I do, you'll come!"

He only smiled as if he'd been expecting this proposal all along. "After all," he said, "why did I go to all the trouble to learn Swedish?"

"We'll have a good life together in Sweden. I have no doubt. Trust me. Somehow I'll find a way for you to come, Jürgen." I had tears in my eyes, but they weren't tears of sadness, and then we both did something we hadn't intended—we both burst into laughter. We laughed so hard, all our fears and trepidations about the future fell away with the wind. I had a future ahead of me suddenly, and I saw only what was bright and what was good, and surely, I thought, Jürgen would be a part of that future too.

The time for my departure came. Jürgen visited me that last evening, that Sunday night, and his kisses had never meant so much. Three times it happened. Three times he asked for a kiss. I kissed his lips and he kissed me back. But this time was different . . .

Jürgen brought me to the ship that would take me to Stockholm the next morning. It was a brisk, clear day. The ship was a large pleasure ship, and for a moment we remembered the refugees who had boarded a ship just like this one only five years ago. The thousands of refugees who had not made it because they were killed when the ship was bombed and sunk. What a different world that was! What a different time!

It was with tears and gladness and many, many embraces that I embarked. I had just one suitcase. One suitcase, and my freedom, and I could not help but wonder whether Mutti had remembered to take those paintings with her to Sweden. The ones I carried through Brest and Smolensk and Moscow.

Jürgen stood on the pier and I saw genuine sadness in his eyes as he waved a handkerchief at me. It would not be long. I knew this. A new feeling was growing in me: We would be together, Jürgen and I. It was to be a new life, and a good life, and we would have it together.

❧

Sweden was so blue! The sky was bright, the sidewalks so clean. People weren't friendly, but they weren't unkind either. They had their own soft way of smiling and then walking on. Of course, they didn't want to know about a German girl who had been there in the midst of it all. No one wanted to know about me. But I was here! In Sweden!

Mutti was at the pier to greet me, and she too looked Swedish! She had cut her hair short; her skirt was short, to the knees. She had on a white shirt and smart shoes. She was beaming. She was in Sweden and she had a job, and I was here too.

"Onkel Johan has organized an apartment for us," she told me immediately in an excited voice. "It's not large. Very small, actually. There's only one room, but to the side is a small cooking area. I have bought an electric teapot, a few blankets, and an electric fan. And I found a paper screen that can serve as our dressing room. You'll see! It's such a sweet little Wohnung. Can I call it that? Of course! It's ours! Our home. It has a small sofa, where I will sleep, and a bed, where you can sleep. And on Monday, in a week, you are to go to the Karolinska Institute. Uncle Johan, the dear, organized an interview for you there."

I couldn't remember when I had seen Mutti so happy and so enthusiastic, so *full* of life. Perhaps it was in Swinemünde, the last time she smiled like this. She looked young—her cheeks glowed, and she had even gained weight. Her hair was dark and shiny again. Her eyes were no longer full of dread. She had been to Göttingen, where Papa Spaeth was living in a small room in a house with a family. They had spent a week together, and he wanted her to be sure to tell me how happy he was about my decision to study medicine. They decided Karl would finish his studies and I should pursue mine. He would stay in Göttingen until he was a doctor, and then join us in Sweden.

The first thing I did was contact Brigitte Martins, my friend from the Gulag. She was not difficult to find. She was in Stockholm, working where I hoped to work, at the Karolinska Institute. "Hugs and tears" can't begin to describe the joy of seeing each other that first day. When once you've experienced the absence of food, of kindness, of soap and clothes and toothpaste, and you reunite in a place so blue and bountiful, there are no words for this. She told me that she and most of the others had been released from the Gulag shortly after I was. She too hoped to become a doctor, to build a brand new life.

⤸

After a week Jürgen's first letter arrived. How easy it is to forget! How quickly I had left Germany behind! He was sad, he said. He missed me. I missed him too. Somewhat.

> *I am so sorry I've not written sooner. I should be ashamed of myself. That's what my Mutti told me. I have such a lovely girlfriend and I don't even know how to write to her. I am ashamed.*
>
> *I have gained some weight, though! You won't even recognize me! I can really say, without pushing out my stomach, my ribs hardly show anymore. Yesterday I ate eel for the first time. It was smoked. I bought it at the pier. And I had some whipped cream! Oh, that was good!*
>
> *If you remember that little reindeer we were looking at? The one on the tapestry in the tavern in Kiel? Do you remember? Do you remember, too, how I said, "I believe he's crying because he can't find his beloved?" That's me, now, crying for you.*
>
> *I miss you terribly.*
>
> *Your man, Jürgen*

I had no doubt he would come. But first I had to find work, which I did at the Karolinska Institute, as a lab assistant. I'm sure Brigitte had something to do with that. Uncle Johan too. The stars were working in my favor. My boss was such a friendly fellow, and he liked the two of us so well. He often brought us Swedish cakes with raisins in them that his wife had baked. He said his mission was to "make us fat," like him.

Brigitte and I talked all the while we worked. It was as if we had not lost a single day. If it wasn't funny, we'd laugh anyway. We were together and we had freedom and it was 1949, a world away from where we'd been. We felt as if, together, we could own the world.

In my thoughts there was Jürgen, too, of course. Sometimes he seemed far away, sometimes very close, but always he was back in Kiel and I was here in Stockholm. Sometimes we visited one another, and I still loved him. I think he loved me back.

# Coda

## SWEDEN
## 1952

# 27

# THE LAKE

It was the summer, and times were easy. I had work, I had made some
money, and I had friends. It was a warm, sunny day when Brigitte invited
a whole group of us who worked at the Karolinska Institute for a long
weekend at her family's hut, a *stüga*, on a lake not far from Stockholm.
Would I like to come for a long weekend, she asked me one Tuesday
afternoon as we were taking our tea break. She would invite our whole
clique. There were quite a few of us by now. There was Dagmar and
Inga, Anny and Kerstin, and we would have so much fun, she said. Her
Papa, her *fader*, had given her the keys and said, "Enjoy yourselves, you
young ones!" Of course, we all said yes.

A *stüga* in Tumba, Sweden.

Kerstin Jurke was a woman who could make you laugh at everything. Everything! I mean, all we had to do was go for Swedish Brötchen in the market and already we were laughing. I don't know at what. The goofy blue hat the ferryman wore with the ribbons on it? The boy who picked pansies and threw them into the water? Was that the funny thing she told us about? Oh, she could make us laugh.

So we went, six of us. We packed our food, fish, plenty of it, bread, cheese, and of course bottles of wine. Plenty of wine. The stüga was just there on the lakeshore. It had a small back door with a screen that slammed over and over because it had no latch. We had a small rowboat, and loons on the lake called all night. A full moon showed itself to us twice—once in the sky, once on the water.

On our first night, we were rather melancholic as we exchanged stories about the war. Of course we talked about the war. Even now, so many years later, the wounds still ached and we had to talk to say *something* about where we were when it all happened. Because I was from Berlin, the others were particularly interested in how I had managed. Sure, I wanted to tell them, but too much had happened, too much was still too raw. I said only, "We got along. Like everyone got along."

Then Kerstin Jurke took out some newspaper clippings she had cut from the *Dagens Nyheter,* the daily newspaper in Stockholm, and asked if I had seen them. Kerstin was the one who made us laugh at everything, but this wasn't funny.

I stared at them in shock. They were photos that must have been taken from above, maybe by some American or British bomber. It must have been '44 or '45.

"That? That is my city! That is what they did to us! Look! Do you see those ruins? Do you see where there is nowhere for anyone to go? Can you see that? That's me down there! Yes, that's where we lived! Inside those ruins!" And I wept. Oh, how I wept tears I hadn't known since I lived those terrible years, and Kerstin held me and said, "I'm sorry, I'm so sorry."

And, in that moment, she became my best friend.

⥰

I had crocheted myself a swimsuit that I hoped to wear once Jürgen came for his visit. It was quite sexy, a two-piece suit, nothing like what I used to wear or Mutti used to wear at the Wannsee. It was light orange, almost a pink color, which at that time was a color only prostitutes wore. Quite scandalous, and Mutti knew nothing about it.

I strutted around one evening, all full of wine, modeling my suit for the girls. I wanted their approval. Would it work? Would it make him love me more?

"Do you know what you look like when you talk about him?"

"I'll tell you what you look like. You look crazy! Like you haven't got your feet on the ground anymore!"

"I'd say she's in love." That came from Kerstin.

She then kneeled before me and made the sign of the cross, only in a Swedish, Protestant sort of way. I think she did it backwards. And we laughed all night.

⥰

Each morning we sat at the shore with our coffees and watched as the sun came red over the edge of the lake. Then we would swim, Kerstin and I, as it yellowed over our heads. We swam in silence except for the sound of our arms as they stroked through the green lake. We swam across the bay, and when we made it to the other shore, we sat on the sand, still and pensive, and when the time was right, we'd slip back into the water. Sometimes not a word would have been said, and we would swim back home to the stüga for another coffee, this time with a little schnapps in it.

Kerstin and I came out of the water on one of those mornings after our swim across the lake. It was a lovely morning. No bugs yet. No heat. Only pleasant air and a perfect sunrise. I came out onto the shore in my new suit, the sexy thing I had spent months crocheting, and as I rose up from the dark lake, my swimsuit bottom stretched down to the sand. The wool that I had used apparently didn't like water, and suddenly I had swim pants half a meter long! Oh, how we laughed over that! And my bottom was right there for all the world to see.

"*O ja!* That is *exactly* what he'll like, that man of yours! *O ja!*" Brigitte took great pains to make fun of that new man of mine, Jürgen, the "old one," the one who couldn't button his shirt right. She brought me a towel, a large one to cover myself with, and we all sat and had our second breakfast of the day. Which lasted until dinner. Which lasted into the night. We sat at the lakeshore and gossiped until the sun sank to the water's edge, while the loons sang their sad, sad song.

Kerstin and I became filled with quietness as we watched the moon's reflection stretch across the lake. We told the others of our swim that morning, how it had been so beautiful, so red and soft, and the shore on the other side, how it was full of birch trees standing in perfect alignment, no houses, and a wide strip of beige sand. How we had sat there for a long time and said very little. It must have been clear to the others how much our friendship meant to each other.

During the war, Kerstin had not seen what I had seen, but she felt what I had felt. This I could tell. She had empathy. She was a woman who understood. She had lived through those years, and she knew there was trouble, but she never judged us because we were German. She was a true friend.

Brigitte started to talk about the Gulag. Not the bad stuff. No, no. We never talked about the bad stuff. It was about Christmas, and how we had celebrated with the Russian guards and how they said nothing when we sang and how we had all danced together. How much fun my mother had been that night, singing "Nu är det Jul Igen" in Swedish to all the other people there. And the Latvian doctor, Janis. Oh, Janis. My eyes welled up to think of him. I was sure he was still there.

Kerstin, my dear friend who had never been to the Gulag, who had never experienced the war the way we had, asked Brigitte and me, "Did you two look into each other's eyes sometimes? Sometimes when it was so difficult? Did you look and see? Did you know you'd be here one day together?"

Brigitte and I looked at each other across the room, her eyes so gray, and I thought, *Yes, you did save me. You were there. You saw it all. You experienced it too, and now we are here, you and I.*

Across from us sat Kerstin, like an angel, smiling as if she had known all along we would have been saved, no matter what. She smiled a smile that was not of this world, and at that moment I remembered my angel. The one who appeared to me in the street in Berlin when I believed no one else was alive. The one whose wing brushed my arm so softly, who whispered this to me: *You shall have a child.*

It had been my secret, a secret promise I had carried with me ever since, and now I knew it would come true. I told the others then. I said, "I'm going to have a child." I blurted it out, because I had no idea how else to say it.

Of course, all the other girls simply stared at me, not knowing what to answer and expecting me to say something else.

So I did. This time, I knew what it would be. I had been thinking of it for days. I said, "I hope she'll be a girl. Because if she is, her name shall be Kerstin."

Briefe an mein
geliebtes Fränzel,
während der Belagerung von Berlin.

Berlin, 15. April 1945.

# Letters to My Beloved Franzel

## During the Siege of Berlin

*19 April 1945*

*My dearest Peter,*

*It's been only a few days since I last spoke with you on the telephone. Was it to be the last time? My memory of that conversation is so sweet. I'm so sorry, though, that I wasn't able to see you in person. My dear Peter, we will now be completely separated until we see each other once again. The mail is no longer being delivered; telephone service no longer works. We can't give up, though, not yet. And we must trust in God and believe in Fate. Maybe it will still turn out well. Maybe we will yet outlive this dreadful end. It's so inconceivable that the enemy has been able to come this deep into the very heart of our country.*

*The military fronts do seem to be holding them back. Last Saturday and Sunday, there was such an upsetting rumor traveling around Berlin. Supposedly, the Americans had already penetrated beyond Brandenburg. In fact, they were to have arrived in Treuenbriezen and Beelitz. Indeed their airborne troops did land in Wittenberge.*

*So, every day, we wait, anticipating their arrival in Berlin. Even though the insult of losing the war has been so unthinkable and so shameful, most of us are breathing easier with this thought in mind: the bombings and the senseless murders will finally cease.*

*The American soldier is of course a much more humane person than the Russian. Of the two evils, this would be the better one. Suddenly, on Sunday morning, the huge Eastern Offensive began fighting all over again. Patients who had taken the weekend to go home to eastern Berlin (Strausberg and Grünau) heard, from early on in the morning, a constant, endless thundering of gunfire.*

*There are five nurses and one head nurse. There is much to do, and we are constantly running around. This morning, my job was to bathe all the patients once again. They are all coming directly from the front. Some of them never even came through the HVP,[38] because they simply couldn't find it, and just walked through the city until they saw the first S-Bahn. We used to joke, saying, "Do you know when the war will be over? When you can take the S-Bahn to the front." Back then we laughed about it. Today it is a horrible reality.*

*All through the night we hear bomb sirens. At eight, Ivan shows up and then retreats toward eastern Berlin or into the eastern suburbs; then he is replaced by Tomy in the west.[39] As soon as Tomy flies off, Ivan returns. So until about three or four in the morning they hold us hostage. At six I need to get up again. One could just as easily fall over from fatigue. What's more, we have no electricity. At first, the lights were only turned off for one to two hours each day. But yesterday we had only one hour with lights because we were supposed to make "thick air," as bomber formations were approaching. At night, during the bomb alarms, we sat in the dark. It's difficult, you know, when you have to run in such a hurry into the basement with all your luggage and then try to do so in the dark. We must run extra fast now because the front is so near that, by the time we hear the sirens, the bombers are already right on top of us.*

*How will all this end? How will the war finally turn out? How is life to be for all of us Berliners? Himmler is to become the city commander of Berlin.[40] Berlin is supposed to be protected until the very end. There are so many women and children still here. We can't get out. But then, where would we go? The enemy has surrounded us. Who will arrive here first? Will there be more destruction and more ruin? Tomorrow, the 20th of April, when the enemy wants to occupy Berlin, another huge burden will fall upon us. If only it were finally over!*

*One can only ride the train with a special permit, but soon even those will become hard to come by. Businesses are closing because they cannot get work papers for their employees. Besides, without exception, there are no materials with which to carry on any sort of business. Furthermore, with all these power outages, many businesses and factories fail anyway. What is astonishing, though, is the human will, which, regardless of the fight, continues to hold its head high.*

*Our Lazarett is about to burst at the seams. There is a constant stream of men arriving. Either they walk in alone or are in a group transported by truck. Every bed is full. They have ghastly wounds.*

*Often they bring us disturbing news. Except from my beloved Dieter there is no news. We have not heard a thing from him since February. A patient who fought in Gross-Born told me that the military school there was full, and that the military training had been moved to Neustettin and Kolberg. Maybe he was transferred for his training. He wrote us that he was returning to Pilsen to continue his studies, but, in any case, we should have heard from him by now. Oh, my dear little brother—nothing shall have happened to you! I cannot bear the thought, that he may not be alive anymore. He is so much younger than I, and should his life already be extinguished?! No!*

*For today, dear Peter, I send you all my most loving thoughts and oh, so much Soldier's Luck! I think about you so very often, and I am looking forward to the time that I will be able to give this book to you as proof. That will be such a beautiful day! On that day the brightest, warmest sun will shine in my heart. That is when my sweetest dreams will come true.*

*With love,*
*Your Grete*


*20 April 1945*

*My dearest Peter,*

*The dearest man in the whole world!*

*Only you hold me close enough that I have the strength to believe that if I play the game right, I will survive the fight and will come out of this alive.*

*The Russians are gaining ground with tremendous force. In Erkner, one can already see the gun barrels of their tanks and the same is happening in Lichtenrade. The wife of one of our patients from Lichtenrade called us today in hysterics. She intends to flee the city immediately. This afternoon there was a huge bomb attack right at the city limits of Berlin. Is the American still supposed to arrive before the Russian does? I hardly believe it anymore.*

*I have a lot to do now.*

*In my thoughts I'll kiss you with all I have,*

*Your Grete*

*21 April 1945*

*My dearest Peter!*

*Once again twelve hours have passed. Yesterday, yet again there were great advances in the northern and southern perimeters of Berlin. The Russian is supposedly already in Bernau. Last night bombs fell even before the alarms sounded. I was in our apartment trying to repack my suitcase by the light of a streetlamp. Out of a sheer panic, I buried my head inside the suitcase, between my clothes.*

*We have no lights anymore. The S-Bahn is operating on steam. You can only ride it with special identification papers. It leaves every hour. But hardly anyone is able to acquire these papers, so we simply walk. All of us nurses are, for the most part, sequestered. I am still living at home, though. Papa is leaving us soon. He is probably going to be ordered to a command post elsewhere.*

*Now the only thing we have to believe in is a lucky star. Yesterday I prayed to the dear lord with such ardent fervor to please take me to you. Whether dead or alive, he shall reunite us!*

*I send you my love and my sweetest kisses,*

*Your Grete*

10 May 1945

*My dearest man!*

*Today, first a deep breath. You poor, poor man, you'll likely be so worried when you learn what has happened to us, although we really have managed to survive rather well. No Russian has caused any of us any harm—so far!—even though so many have suffered such evil, unthinkable horrors. The women are all being handled in unspeakable ways, and Russians are looting everywhere. Supposedly they were issued orders making it against the law, and they would be punished if they were caught. But they've been celebrating victory and peace for a week now, and they are always drunk. And still our Lazarett has been—knock on wood—left alone. We are also nearly the only Lazarett without lights. None of the nurses have been harmed. In fact, there has hardly been a Russian here at all.*

*The civilians, on the other hand, are faring rather poorly. They are all desperately hungry. The food rations are very small—so small, in fact, they are like those that our previous regime used to give the Jews.*

*We are allowed to be in the streets from two a.m. to ten p.m.*

*These Russians have a few loose marbles rolling around in their heads. As a woman, one must try to behave as inconspicuously as possible in order to avoid being taken by one of them. Last night we constantly heard the terrified screams for help from women as they were being raped. But one cannot help them. The Russians are all drunk. What can one do?*

*Even so, we are all breathing easier—we have peace. No bombs, no more fighting! We have survived the worst. We have our "beloved" SS to thank for the way the enemy is now treating us. We, of course, knew nothing of all this. Our Landser keep telling us the SS did the same thing to them. Oh well, that's how it is.*

*It's summer; it's May. It's warm outside—we have peace. Soon you will be home and we will be able to decide how it shall go from here. Will you take me with you to a place that is better than here?*

*Perhaps you will write soon. The troops supposedly have been organized for the march home from Denmark. You should be home soon. I really don't feel afraid for you, because I have such a strong sense that things went well for you. Oh, my dear Peter! There will be so much to talk about! But then, when you return, we will belong to each other forever and we will never again part. Do you know that this hope, this belief, is the only thing that holds me and keeps me going? Soon, dear Peter, soon! Then too, I will be your wife, and I will never leave you. And you will never have to go to war again. We will begin to rebuild our lives. We will be happy and from our love we will draw the strength to exist and to overcome the difficulty and severity of all the fighting. That will be so lovely, Franzel! Tonight I will, once again, think about you for a long time. And you will surely think of me just before you fall asleep. Do you know that I am alive and that I am well? I'll tell you all about it in the night tonight!*

*My darling Peter, the next time I'll tell you about all that we have survived. It was a lot. Difficult, extremely difficult.*

*Recently we were renamed the Reserve Lazarett, then the War and Field Lazarett, and finally we became the HVP. We have many soldiers here who have severe wounds. There are so many dead ones, so many who are bleeding to death. But the rest of us have survived—physically, morally, and spiritually.*

*Now I will kiss you deeply and with all my love,*

*Your Grete*

*12 May 1945*

*My dearest Peter!*

*I think of you so very often! If only that first letter from you would arrive already! I have the feeling that you're still alive and that, soon, we'll be together. I can hardly wait for you to be with me, and we will never leave each other, ever again.*

*Everything is so sad and so difficult. If only that man were with me now—the one who is my friend, my companion (and more)—to help me, because just that is what helps the most—companionship. I wait for you with such hope in my heart. You are the only one I love this dearly. Only you can help me. So often, at night, I dream that you are with me. I wish that I could lock myself within your arms and cry, cry, cry—until everything has been washed away, and then you'll lead me off to that place where we can begin to rebuild our lives once more.*

*I do realize that we women, although we can certainly be tough, are really quite helpless in this world when we are left alone. God planned it this way—that a man and a woman are meant to complement one another so that each of us will be the half that completes the whole.*

*Oh, how sweet it would be if you were only with me now! Sometime soon, before my birthday, surely I'll receive some news from you. On the 25th of May,[41] I will be thinking about you so much that nothing would please me more than knowing you are alive and that you will come home to me soon. If only the mail would run again so that I could write to you!*

*25 May 1945*

*My sweet man!*

*Today, surely you are thinking of me, just as I am thinking of you so very much. My dear Peter, how are you? Will you survive this day? I believe so. I have the feeling that all will work out. Of course you'll survive today. But where are you? Are you on your way home? Did you end up in a prison camp? Are you already home? My love, how I long for you! Soon it will get to the point that nothing will interest me anymore. One day, surely you will come home, stand before me, look into my eyes and give me a tender kiss. Oh how wonderful that will be! Then you will have to say to me: Now you'll stay with me forever.*

*I want only one thing and that is to be with you, even if we are to end up in the poorest dilapidated old hut. I dream of having a family one day. I dream of having many children.*

*Well, in that regard, my patients in the Lazarett are mere children. We have to handle them as if they are small infants, especially when they have such horrible wounds. But I must tell you: they all love me very much and always ask for me. It is me they ask for to change their dressings because they say I have the gentlest hands. That always makes me so happy.*

*30 May 1945*

*Dearest Peter!*

*The last few weeks have been almost too much to bear. There is tremendous physical and emotional stress. Our bad food is cooked with the water from the pit in the yard that could easily be the very water in which a woman has taken her life. At first we only had one bowl of soup and two pieces of bread every day. It is a bit better now, because now we receive 500 grams of bread each day. The bread is fresh but we are missing something to put on it. Canned goods are sometimes available but only enough to put on one slice of bread. As of two days ago, we started to receive rations of lard.*

*There is a constant draft in the hallways, because all the walls and windows are broken. With this and the poor nutrition, nearly everyone is sick. Almost everyone has stomach problems. Others have sore throats and many have angina. For four weeks now, I have had stomach problems myself until I was finally not even able to get out of bed, running a fever of 102 degrees. I ran this high fever for nearly three days. Today, for the first time, it's down to 98.6 degrees once again. I've decided to stay in bed one more day in order to rest thoroughly.*

*These times are so dreadful for us. We live from one fear to the next. And we hear nothing positive. There is still no mail service. There are several organizations that do stop by from time to time. But I must say, people have become so vulgar and despicable, really. I don't know if it's only the scum of mankind that survives a war, or if it is that everyone suddenly believes they must degrade themselves to their lowest level. Women sit around squabbling and gossiping about the most vulgar things.*

*Our Lazarett has become the Civilian Hospital (the hospital on Heerstrasse). Every Wednesday and Saturday night we put on a variety show. But you can no longer say that things have "double entendres," rather they are, at best, a "single entendre." Mutti says the sort of behavior is so typical of postwar psychosis. At every corner and in every bar you can see women hanging around with Russian soldiers.*

*There is also all the cleanup work to do. All the piles of rubble that have been lying in the streets from the bombings need to be hauled off and then dumped into the craters of bombed-out houses. Every civilian is required to do this work. The PGs[42] are required to work even harder—all day long, from early in the morning until late at night. For everyone else, the work hours are only from two p.m. until four p.m. It happens too that you could simply be pulled aside and forced to do the work until you are told that you are finished.*

*Cars and Sankas[43] were of course taken away from us immediately. Fire trucks are being used to transport the patients to us. The PGs have been ordered to vacate their homes. They are to be made available for the returning Jews. All the larger factories such as Borsig and AEG are being dismantled and all their machines, tools, and miscellaneous materials are being sent off to Russia. All engineers and all those with vocational skills are being sent to Russia to work for three years (without their wives or families, of course). It's compulsory. They are being used to rebuild that country. Berlin is to become a dead city.*

*The U-Bahn, buses, and streetcars are slowly coming back into service. Only the S-Bahn is to be taken out of commission altogether. None of this really matters anymore! We lost the war and gave an unconditional surrender. They should have decided to do this a year ago. It would have spared the loss of so much blood and so much of our will to live. Maybe, too, it would not have been such a humiliating end.*

*But I refuse to agonize over the past. Today, all you hear is how everyone is suddenly the greatest Nazi-hater there ever was.*

*To tell the truth, the Nazis left us in such a disgrace. They always spoke so grandiosely of their new weapons and our eventual history-making turnaround. From the very beginning, we always said, if one has the audacity to start a war, one must know when the moment has come that one must give up and have the courage to surrender, and to know when one has been defeated.*

*And to think that, only days before the Russians arrived in Berlin, we were still hearing such stupid lectures from our NS officers: That we, the civilians, would be to blame if Berlin were to fall, because we did not do our duty well enough in our cleanup work. That we have the fat, lazy bourgeois to thank for the fact that the American has penetrated so deeply into Germany. And they, out of fear of losing their laughable little houses, were the first to wave their little white flags in surrender.*

*The army was thoroughly screened by hard-core National Socialists to find those who never yielded at the front, but they also screened for those who showed any sort of cowardice, and they would be shot. The same would happen to any soldier who even attempted to spread bad news. And so it went, on and on. It's shameful how offensive these insults are. The idea that not one soldier ever just once stood up and tore the skin off one their faces! All of our Landser have already sacrificed their own lives, but these Nazi nationalists haven't suffered a thing yet. And then—something I could not even have imagined possible—only days before the Russians arrived, our own NS commanding officer simply disappeared. He was the first one to flee. So this is how our entire regime fell. We were happy of course that he was gone. He was such a nasty fellow.*

*Now I want to tell you exactly how it happened:*

*The enemy kept advancing on Berlin. From the north and from the east, they had already penetrated the city. From the tower of the Lazarett we were able to see where the battles were taking place. The government, of course, always dismissed us civilians as being stupid, so they never told us, and we never knew, where the enemy was. They were still talking about a victory, even right up until the very end. Rumors were going around that the Russians had been driven back in the north, and so on. High-ranking NS officers spread the news that the Russians and the Americans were at odds with one another, and that the Americans were going to join the Germans in an attack against the Russians, and, if that were the case, they would stay at the Elbe River in order to free our army from the Russians. "We just have to hold out a bit longer," they said. "The end of war on the western front is near." But no end came— only Nazi slogans.*

*We already had battles going on in Zehlendorf, Lichterfelde, and Dahlem. Russians had arrived in Spandau and Siemensstadt. That was on the 24th of April. That morning I couldn't get to the Lazarett until quite late because of the constant artillery fire and the danger of strafing from low-flying aircraft. I had to take the East-West Axis, which was fully jammed with trucks bringing in the troops. I had to be careful and at times even run for cover.*

*Our patients who were not quite as severely wounded and those who were ambulatory hid either in the trenches in the garden or in the cellar, to protect themselves from the constant deluge of low-flying bombers. The station supervisors and the Sanis also hid in the garden trenches. Only we nurses couldn't afford such luxury because the work still needed to be done. We had hundreds of new admissions. In some cases, the beds were doubled up, while their former occupants were hiding in the cellar.*

*When at times the noise was too unbearable and the bombs were dropping right close by, we too ran for shelter. Most of the time, though, it was somewhat calmer. We only really fled to the stairwells when it was most dire, as we waited until the very last moment to run.*

*But I don't want to give myself too much praise for having had senseless courage. I only know that I feel 100 percent sure that nothing will happen to me. Besides none of this was nearly as bad as the American carpet bombings. Those bombs used to fall straight through to the cellar. If you were caught in one of those, you could only hope to die quickly. There was nowhere you could be safe from them. How terrible the fears in those cellars were back then. I always panicked so dreadfully when they fell. But, even then, God protected us.*

*What we have now is small in comparison. Russian bombs fell, there were small tremors, and a few windowpanes broke—nothing more. A grenade blew a hole into a wall. It would be really tough luck at this point if you were to receive the blessing of one of those attacks. But everything does have a very personal and very local impression. I mean, you could run down the street and, in three minutes' time, know nothing of what's going on here. You could take refuge behind a garden wall or hide in some basement and feel assured "Nothing will happen to me here."*

*On that 24th of April, we worked until late into the night, because we kept receiving more admissions. We had no lights. So, out of necessity, we muddled through, using candles. At night, around ten, the first wounded soldiers arrived from Spandau. One of them told us that the Russians would surely be here tomorrow, as they had been successful in breaking through the lines there.*

*As it was late, I decided to stay at the Lazarett. Mutti still phoned me that night. The next morning our head nurse gave a very beautiful devotional prayer. We all knew what we were up against. One of our nurses came to us with the news that Russians had been seen at the Reichssportfeld. The Reichssportfeld is ten minutes away from us.*

*I asked for permission to run home quickly to bring Mutti my two pieces of bread and two boxes of sausage that I had received for donating blood. The head nurse gave me permission. I ran home as if I were being chased by a pack of mongrel dogs. Everywhere I ran I saw artillery stationed along the roads in preparation for battle, because the Russians had been expected since 4:00 that morning. With heavy hearts, Mutti and I parted. At first she wanted to come with me, but then decided to stay home, which proved to be the better decision.*

*At the Lazarett, only the most ghastly wounds were attended to; bandages were replaced. Everything had such a strange atmosphere. At times grim humor erupted, followed only by a flood of tears as soon as we became aware of our wretched situation. Then we'd hold each other's hands as if we'd never let them go, and we promised each other never to abandon one another.*

*I phoned your relatives once more and spoke with Frau Steffens.[44] I wonder how she has managed to survive? As soon as I am well enough, I will go out to visit her.*

*In the tea kitchen at my station, we hurriedly distributed the remainder of our contraband. The Landser received cigars and cigarettes. Whatever one had was distributed. We nurses permitted ourselves the last few lovely puffs of our last cigarettes. Understandably, we weren't allowed to smoke openly in front of* our patients, but now that didn't matter anyway. It could be that we were just acting like children during our last moments of calm before the storm.

Again, new arrivals came to our hospital. Just as we began to open their bandages, frightful shooting began right outside our walls. The Landser dashed off, and our short-lived peace was gone. The shooting became more frantic. Debris and the smell of gunpowder were all around us. Everyone flitted down the stairwells to the basement.

Russian tanks broke through the panzer barriers at Heerstrasse and shot into our Lazarett as they rolled by on the one side that, unfortunately, was the side that did not have the Red Cross sign on it. And, of all places, they shot right into the auditorium and into the station where the most severely wounded soldiers lay. Sadly, one of our nurses was killed.

Soldiers with whole-body casts and soldiers who were in such tremendous pain that they would not allow us to touch them now stood in the stairway in mortal terror, barefoot, with their tiny nightshirts, deathly fear on their faces, and couldn't go any further. The picture is impossible to describe. In the bunkers, in the mattress storage rooms, in the hallways, in the cellar, between the beds—everywhere there were wounded and severely wounded soldiers, taking cover.

The artillery fired; the house shook. Instinctively we shrugged our heads down into our shoulders. The wounded men screamed for us not to leave them alone. When the shooting began, everyone ran off. Those in such pain who could not even move ran!

We had nothing to drink or to eat. It wasn't even funny anymore to say, "Just bite your teeth together."

"Of course, we have nothing. They are fighting outside, you know, and the little bit of water we have is for cooking and for those who are much needier than you."

*We waited for the backup infantry. Everything we did was in preparation to surrender the Lazarett to the Russians. We were considered neutral territory. Over and over again, it was pressed upon us that no soldier was to enter the Lazarett with weapons. Every wounded soldier was to surrender all weapons and ammunition. We knew, above all, in those Lazaretts where they found weapons, the staff was badly abused or driven off to who knows where.*

*All around us, the civilian homes are filled with wounded soldiers. Our building is considered a neutral Lazarett building. The soldiers understood—and it was respected—that no one shall use this Lazarett building as an outpost.*

*In time, we noticed that the later artillery, meaning the direction of the shooting, was being directed to the left or to the right of the Lazarett. Now, only the occasional stray bullet hit us directly. But really, that was plenty!*

*Yesterday we were still called the Reserve Lazarett, but we were in part already a War Lazarett as well. Today we are called the Field Lazarett as well as the HVP. Constantly they bring men with the most horrible wounds: torn-off limbs, or limbs that are only attached by a thin thread of skin. They come completely covered in blood. The soldiers that fought nearby in the Heerstrasse are mostly just young Hitler Youth draftees. They fight like wild lions, and they received the most dreadful wounds. Not infrequently, we have to just leave them, unoperated and unbandaged—I mean not even a new bandage on their wounds—we leave them to lie there, because they really only have a few hours of life left. Because they are such poor young boys, just children really, I felt so very sorry for them. Often they cry for their Muttis. Now I understand why they only allow the Sanis to work at the HVP. Women just could never withstand such horror.*

*Seven hundred patients is our maximum capacity, even in the direst of circumstances. We are now accommodating seventeen hundred. Even if they end up in civilian homes elsewhere in the neighborhood, we still need to tend to them and provide for them. Our bandages and medicines ran out, and especially our food supplies, and above all—water.*

*Through the night of the 25th and 26th of April, I was appointed as the watch person. The evening syringes were prepared. Some of the patients were asleep. But, in truth, the night was rather unquiet. There was the occasional shooting outside, but what remained within these walls was the terror from the previous day. Some of the patients began hallucinating, fantasizing all sorts of things. The little ones cried because of their pain, many called for their Muttis. The severely wounded men who were lying on the hallway floors cried to us to please not leave them alone.*

*If I sat for a few minutes with one of them, from another corner came another pitiful voice calling, "Schwester!"*

*There were two of us working my floor. That is, we were in charge of this floor as well as the patient-laden entryway and the surrounding floors that contained soldiers lying on mattresses without sheets or on the gurneys they arrived on. They stayed lying on their gurneys because the OP[45] was right next to the bunker.*

*At one point I heard the heart-wrenching cry of a soldier screaming, "Sister!" It came from the long corridor just behind the OP. I recognized him from earlier, a beautiful boy, strong, maybe twenty-five years old. He was freezing and had only one blanket. I was puzzled about this. He had been lying here since morning. He knew he was going to die. I talked to him, or, better said, I tried to give him hope. He was from the Sudetenland. I gave him morphine to lighten his pain.*

*I wondered about him having only one blanket, even though he was so cold. I looked at the neighboring gurney and saw also just one blanket. Then at a third and saw that all he had was a jacket to cover his face. I felt for his pulse. There was nothing. His hand fell heavy upon his stomach. I removed the jacket from his face. I found it to be so irreverent that a dying man had to take care of himself like this. Actually, I have to say, I didn't really think at all. Mostly I felt an overwhelming compassion for these men.*

*I then removed the blanket: dead. His face was horribly disfigured. I removed the next man's blanket: dead. The same picture! Another man, just to his left, was waving his hands spastically in the air. I went to him and took his hands in mine, and told him to try to lie very still. He peered at me with two large dark and insane-looking eyes, sunk deep into his sockets. Although his face was by now terribly gaunt, and his eyes looked so terribly confused, I recognized him immediately. He had been one of our old patients on Station III; his name was Kückelmann.*

*I was so incredibly shocked to see him. I still remembered this Kückelmann from before he had his meningitis, when all he had was an inflammation to the knee joint, then later he got tuberculosis. He had been a German literature major, about twenty-two years old, and a very handsome and intelligent young man. Later he was moved to the first floor, the floor that bedded only the most infectious and most severely wounded patients. I had not seen him since his meningitis.*

*Now, of all times, in this most sinister of nights, he was the one man I had to encounter. I was irrationally frightened. I tried to compose myself and made every effort to speak to him with compassion and kindness, and to this he responded. He even remembered that I was Schwester Margarete from Station III, and he remembered the conversation we had had back then. It was about Homo sapiens, which we had discussed at length.*

*But then I just couldn't take it any longer. Through our broken windows I could see the flares of the artillery. The building shook. At times the shooting seemed farther away; at other times it was nearby again. Debris flew in from all directions . . . I simply could not take it any longer. I'm not a coward—not by any means. But the impressions of this night of horror just took every last bit of courage from me and threw me right to the floor.*

I went to visit the patient with the gunshot wound to the stomach and stayed with him a few minutes. I stroked his face gently and ran my hands through his hair, caressed his hands softly and told him he surely will recover—he could trust me in this—but he needed to try now to find some sleep. I noticed that he began to relax. I then left him and went to sit with the other Schwester in my ward and told her about what I had just experienced. Still, many of the patients on our floor called for me, but I could not bring myself to go to them anymore. I was finished. Truthfully, I was really just horribly frightened.

Later I went down into the bunker. I was so exhausted I could have fallen over just as I stood there. We were all so fatigued from sleep deprivation that at times we would even fall asleep in the middle of doing our work. We wanted to take turns going into the bunker to sleep, but nothing came of this idea.

Outside at the police station, all night long and nearly every hour, there was a police watchman who, with only seven men to help him, held back the enemy from the Heerstrasse train station. The colonel had abandoned his station. His soldiers, of course, did as well. The police watchman tried desperately to call for reinforcements to relieve them via telephone.

It was nightfall and relatively quiet. But our Landser said that the Russians would make their assault at around four or five the next morning. As the morning approached we began to fear that the soldiers at the train station had been unsuccessful in holding out against the enemy through the night.

We sat in our bunker. Suddenly the Schwester who had been tending to the patients who were in the stairwell came running to inform us, "The Russians are here!" She had heard their cries out in the streets, "Urrä-urrä!"[46]

As if we were statues made of stone, bound together solidly by our fear, not one of us moved. We wanted to tend to those who had recently been operated on, as all of them were lying right at the *entrance to the hospital. But not one of us had the courage to move. None of us knew whether the Russians wouldn't simply shoot us. Then, not even the most courageous willpower could save us.*

*We woke a doctor who was sleeping next door to us in the OP bunker. Through the crack between the curtains we could see a horse-drawn wagon full of soldiers drive by. They were Russians!!! Our nerves were electrified down to the very last cell. Within one instant we had become reconciled to our fate. Now, whatever will come, will come.*

*We crept to the front entrance . . . there was a Red Cross wagon with wounded soldiers and a few Sanis who were to be dropped off with us. It was already daylight. We began to fix the patients' beds and take their temperatures.*

*I ran into the doctor who had been sleeping in the OP and asked him what was to become of the patients who were lying in the hallway. The one in particular had been lying there a long time with a bullet wound to his stomach. He told me to give him as much morphine as I wanted to. And in fact, he added, I could do so with all the patients. "They are hopeless cases anyway," he said. I would simply be making their last hours a bit easier.*

*As it was beginning to be daylight outside, I walked along the corridor and gave my first morphine to a sixteen-year-old who had a wound to his head; and he had been shot in the lung, one arm had been shot off so badly that it just hung by a scrap of skin, and he had a wounded leg. Oh, how deeply I felt his misery! There were more wounded soldiers lying there, but for now they have escaped my memory. I gave half the ampoule of morphine to the one with the stomach wound, and he soon began to sleep. He kept saying to me, "Schwester, today I must die." Of course I knew he would die.*

*We had moved him to the front of the hospital the night before, because at the time he didn't appear to be that close to death. How good it was, though, that he was lying among the dead now. How good it was, too, that none of the dying soldiers knew that they were lying among the dead ones, because that was all they had left to look forward to anyway—their own death.*

*But when this soldier announced to me it was his time to die, this very same man whom I had tried to convince that he would live, it struck me at the deepest place inside my soul.*

*I asked where his home was, while fighting my own tears back. He was such a good-looking man, and strong, and his love for life still shone bright in his face. I finally ran off to cry. The tears became convulsive sobs.*

*Someone very kindly prepared a bed for me. I wept with the most heart-wrenching sobs. Over and over, I saw in my mind the man with the stomach wound, then the eyes of Kückelmann, and finally that little sixteen-year-old boy. Everything that had been stored inside of me let loose and left through the flood of those tears. I felt so ashamed of myself. But I could do no more.*

*This was the most difficult experience I have ever gone through! I cannot describe it any better than this. So much of this is something I will never be able to tell anyone else and have him really understand, because no one is I. And then, it doesn't even matter anymore, because we have already lived through the worst of it. Things will never be that bad again.*

*Often our destiny is perceived so much differently in our memories. And I am only writing these things down because I want to actually tell them to you one day as I have remembered them— some day when there is a time for that. But even as a mere memory, I must write it into my diary so that it will never be forgotten.*

*The man with the stomach wound died soon. He had inadvertently been brought to the sterile OP where they really only "butchered around." Then he lost his place in the lineup and ended up between the most severely wounded and the hopeless cases. We finally pulled him out of the line. The next morning he received his operation in the OP, but it was too late. There had already been too much internal bleeding.*

*That men of war must die in this way! That they all look so bloodied and shot to pieces before their death! I had never thought about it before. Whenever we, in the past, had seen a corpse, it was tidied up and beautifully laid to rest inside white sheets and adorned with flowers—one hardly noticed they were dead. But war casualties! How gruesome! No corpse can make an impression on me anymore. And still I walk up to everyone who is dying among us and approach him with a tender heart. I try to be reserved around the surrounding patients. They should not be so aware of it when men are dying.*

*Often, when a soldier dies, I think he will go to that place where we all will follow one day. Why, then, do we have fear about this? Today, death seems so far away, and yet it is so very near. Right here, next to this patient is where Death is standing. He becomes aware of Him, and he already becomes a calmer person. Then, not long thereafter, he leaves us. Now, just a useless piece of flesh is all that is left, something that could perhaps have some biological value, but a soul will never enter it again.*

*What is Death? What is this Life? Death is the survival of the soul. You can understand this logically: we are created from that which is dead; Death lives within our Soul; and in the third phase, this Soul then leaves the body and lives on with God.*

*Oh, but how much I love to be with my patients! A little one always called so sweetly whenever he saw me in the mornings, "Schwester Margarete!" I just had to go sit with him. He was still such a delicate young boy. He was very sick, but despite the poor conditions here, he was able to heal and was actually released after only fourteen days.*

*He complained so much about his pain, but I really didn't have much time. Yet always, whenever I walked past him, he called for me. After a while I actually lost my patience with him. Thank God no one noticed, because so often I was told how much my patience was admired. I was pleased with this praise, but I was also ashamed, because I didn't deserve it. They cannot see into my innermost being. We all had so much to do that every hour counted.*

*That little boy was my personal favorite. Next was a man with a full leg amputation. He later got a staph infection and died. He had been a medical intern. On the first day, while he was still in the Gymnasium, he was actually doing quite well, with the exception of a rather nasty fever. On the second day, he was already beginning to act a bit peculiar and started to say funny things. Then, from the third day on, he began fantasizing such dreadful things. Each day thereafter, it got worse. When it came time to change his bandages and give him new bedding, he talked to us as though he were in a sanatorium.*

*"Schwester, when will breakfast be served? Are the men also coming to see me? Am I lying correctly here in the sun?" Then he hallucinated such strange ideas, like "Did the car already take off? We must test the tires before it does. There's not a minute of time to be lost. We must leave quickly now! . . . But I must see my mother first . . . But, Schwester, you mustn't leave me here, because I'm a cripple. I can't do anything on my own, and they've stolen my crutches." This, then, was his continual conversation.*

*It may have been on the evening before he died. I had given him one last shot of morphine. I still sat with him, trying to convince him that he should sleep. Meanwhile, "The chauffeur is preparing the car. Tomorrow I shall leave. It's beneath the dignity of the Herr Doktor to begin a trip in the night, you know. So I must sleep until morning." And on and on it went.*

*He wanted us all to sleep with him and to not leave him alone. Slowly he became calmer, and I finally left his bedside. During the night he hallucinated again, and it was even worse the next day. His fever rose, his pulse was at 190, then down to 130 but weak and difficult to find.*

*The next morning his bed was empty by the time I came to work. The Sanis had already removed his corpse. I still ran out after him to bring him a flower as a sign that we will never consider any of our patients an "ex." Sadly, he had already been buried in the mass grave in the yard.*

*Why does Death disfigure the faces of His victims so? Why does He torture them so, allowing them to struggle so long between living and dying? He is always the victorious one in the end anyway.*

*Either in the night or early the next morning, there was a young boy, a Hitler Youth, who finally died from a bullet wound to his bladder. He had been suffering for such a long time. That afternoon another patient came to us, another Hitler Youth, in paraplegic condition. I was to give him morphine immediately, but soon that order was negated, as it was no longer necessary. I sat with him for another twenty minutes, occasionally feeling his pulse, until it was no longer detectable. Thank God, the boy was unconscious, because to die with such pain is horrible. His breathing came in fits and starts.*

*It made me think about Dieter. Did he too simply fall asleep like this?*

*"Young boy, sleep. You may be the luckiest of us all. You were very brave. Now you have a wicked wound that will never have a chance to heal. Sleep. It's much nicer over there on the other side. Let me close your eyes for you, and I'll cover you with your blanket."*

*The tears ran from my eyes. When the little one had died, and after I covered him with his blanket and wanted to get up from my chair, I noticed the Landser around me, standing quietly, deeply moved to see him, this small offer of a child. Every one of them surely was thinking of home—about life and about joy—about death and war, sorrow and wounds, and about this terrible war.*

*Good night.*

*Your Grete*

*31 May 1945*

*My very dearest Peter,*

*You won't be mad at me, will you? I probably won't be able to show you all that I've written. I feel reluctant . . .*

*The next day I was in the Gymnasium. That's where those who were most ill were lying, and those who were most recently operated on. They lay there so pitiably: wooden double beds with straw sacks—no mattresses, no sheets, no bedcovers. Others were on the ground, back on their gurneys.*

*The Gymnasium was divided into three stations. There were roughly one hundred patients and three nurses. The first thing we did each morning was change the beds, after which everyone was given a bath. We could really only bathe a few, as there was always a scarcity of water—and a shortage of time. We went row by row and, first of all, washed everyone's face. Then, with the same water, everyone's hands. Of course there were no towels. Even things like an old rag or a pillowcase would have been useful, but if ever something like that was found, it was immediately stolen.*

*Doctor's hours were around ten, when all bandages were opened. Just this job alone went until almost three or even four in the afternoon. And boy, that could smell foul! The stench of pus can be so putrid that you cannot stand to breathe anymore. Often we become nauseous. Once a doctor treated us all to a bit of schnapps after changing a bandage of rather "highest quality." When pus smells this foul—so sweet-sour foul—it can take your breath right out of you. And to have to breathe this all morning long! Thank God, today only two of our patients smelled this putrid.*

*I dread having to change those bandages of our amputees. Often we give them something as an intoxicant first, because it's so painful.*

*The rail embankment held up against the Russians. Reinforcements arrived in the morning and the Russians were forced back. I'm not sure what exactly was happening out there.*

*We were, in fact, a bit exasperated that here we were, right in the middle of a battle zone, yet we knew nothing of what was going on.*

*Once, a few of our Sanis went out just to get an idea of our situation. Apparently, on this side of the Heerstrasse, our troops were able to defend us, and yet just on the other side of the street, the Russians were shooting from inside the houses there.*

*All in all, though, things seem to be calming down. Certainly we hear artillery fire, and come evening and even during the day, there is noticeable enemy air activity. But we now feel safe enough to venture into the upper stories of our building from time to time. The Gymnasium was badly damaged. And even my station, Station II on the third floor, is in ruins. As we had surmised earlier, the aim of the enemy fire did seem to avoid hitting us by firing on either side of the Lazarett, and for the most part they were successful. However, there were a few direct hits.*

*At night we sleep on gurneys wherever we can find space. It's a real bohemian lifestyle. In our dresses, shoes, and stockings, we just lie down, not knowing what will transpire while we sleep. We're very afraid of the Russians. Some of the nurses are sleeping in the boiler room, others in the bunker. I decided on the place that has the freshest air: the bathroom. There are relatively few who want to sleep there. Often I bring one of the young patients into the bathroom with me, because to be alone is too sinister for me. Even though he couldn't help me if anything did happen, we could at least hold on to one another. The image is much like a drowning person clinging to a drinking straw—useless.*

*Occasionally the bathroom is used at night to "booze." There are a few of us nurses and doctors who meet here after the day's work is done. These are actually our most healing moments of the day.*

*Doesn't this sound like some exquisitely romantic poem? By candlelight in the bathroom, a stool with a blanket holding a vase with a few lovely flowers, sipping red wine, or something similar that someone saved or was otherwise contraband. We have plenty of cigarettes.*

*The Partei came to visit once more to bring us donations. So, in this time of such great danger, thank God, these supplies are still being distributed to those who need them before they can be robbed or confiscated by the enemy.*

*My God! What a time it is! Dirty, unwashed, edgy, troubled, scared, overtired—it is utterly impossible to describe this situation within the context of a cultivated and civilized existence.*

*On the 30th of April—I still remember it exactly—I heard the voices of a couple of BDM girls in the kitchen, singing folk songs. They happened to be singing "Listen, What Is That I Hear Coming Through My Window?" And then afterwards "The Evening's Stillness Is Everywhere." It was evening. It brought tears to my eyes. Such a sweet song during such difficult times! Like a little bell that you might hear, distantly, in the midst of a snowstorm.*

*The next day was the first of May. These young girls sang a little May Day song. Oh my, how that made the Landser happy! Several had tears of joy in their eyes, and they were visibly moved with emotion. Will this be the last time these beautiful German folksongs will be sung from the mouths of our German girls? Or was this singing now coming to us as the incoming spring bringing courage and joy for the next battles—both internal and external—when Germany will have definitively lost the war?*

*Around noon, a wounded Russian arrived as a patient. We treated him like a prince. For most of us, it was quite difficult to do, but of course it was our duty to treat him. A Russian civil servant who could speak German was needed to translate.*

*I happened to have been in conversation with my boss. This Russian said that no harm should come to the Red Cross. They will allow the nurses and the doctors to perform their work. In one Lazarett there were wounded Russian men, wounded German men, Russian doctors, and German doctors. The Russians treated the Russian soldiers, the Germans treated the German soldiers. The nurses were not harmed. One is to pass another without ever doing the other harm.*

*Oh, I was so ecstatic! Next to the hallway where this conversation took place were the beds of two very amiable patients, two older, refined gentlemen. I've had numerous very pleasant conversations with them already. I now went over to them; I could hardly speak for joy. If I could have, I would have thrown my arms around their necks. I only said, "The Russians are going to leave us alone!" And I wept like a little girl. I couldn't help myself. It was that final release after all those days of such tremendous fear.*

*Those two patients were too kind! I was embarrassed; I laughed and then wiped away my tears. I was crying even though I wasn't sad at all. Every time I visited them after that, both gentlemen would say, "And Schwester, once you came to us and cried, but you cried for joy. Do you remember that?" If ever I had any sorrow or worry, I was to come to them. They both wanted to take me with them and marry me—the one in particular. But for a number of reasons, that was out of the question . . .*

*On the evening of May 1, we were all sitting in a comfortable circle in our bathroom. It must have been one o'clock already when the Uffz arrived from the police station to announce the news of Hitler's death.[47] So now the last of this senseless struggle shall be finished. "Born April 20th, 1889, killed in action on May 1st, 1945." Where are Himmler, Goebbels, Göring, and the others?*

*What will become of the German people, for whom they still prophesied a historic turnaround, and even a final victory? Now everything has been destroyed. Like voiceless orphans, we all lie here in the streets, everything we've ever had or have known has been surrendered. Husbands, sons, brothers, and fathers—all in prison camps. The enemy has overrun our country. Everything is broken, burnt, destroyed, dead. We are in poverty and have nothing to eat. Industry is dead. Unemployment, ruins, and nothing but rags to wear. Dönitz took command and announced our future over the radio.*[48]

*All those who were in the Zoo Bunker—this is where Command Headquarters held out—surrendered without a fight. They had too many wounded people whom they could no longer keep safe. Those from Command Headquarters retreated through the U–Bahn tunnels to the Reichssportfeld, where they hoped to find shelter. There they were to join the rest of the Berliner fighting army and try to break through the Russian-occupied beltway. I think this may have happened already during the night of April 30th through the first of May.*

*The Russian who was here yesterday came to notify us that they would take possession of our Lazarett tomorrow. I just now verified the dates once more: On May 1st at one in the early morning came the announcement of Hitler's death. On the same day, the Russians broke through at several locations, surrounded us, and came at us from behind.*

*We owe our gratitude to our Dr. von Lutzky, who spoke fluent Russian, and who was well received by the Russians. He negotiated everything with them. We have him to thank that the Russians treated us so decently and never caused any of us any harm. He had never been a member of the PG. Thank God.*

*In a final military order, an emergency inspection was made of all Lazarett occupants, searching for hidden weapons and ammunition, and everything was destroyed. But the Russians didn't search our hospital at all—perhaps because they were so well received by us that they did not see the need to suspect anything here. But we didn't flirt with danger either. Our doctors have far too much pride for that. They were, as you know, officers once.*

*On the first of May, around noon, Schwester Luise came to me and whispered, "The Russians are here!" And just then, some of the first* of them entered our doors. Some were drunk. They came to see about their comrades. Then an officer arrived and greeted us with, "Guten Morgen." Dr. von Lutzky showed him around. This officer spoke to us. Dr. von Lutzky translated and informed us that the Russians had nothing against us. We should continue to care for the sick. The war is now over. "Hurrah!" was the chorus of all our soldiers who were so sick of war. They wanted only to return to their families and to their homes.

The orders came that all those patients who were ambulatory should go out into the garden. Here the Russian officers told them very similar things to what was later told to us. A colonel, as our translator told us, said that it had come to the end that Hitler and Goebbels had intended for us all along. And we have them to thank for these terrible consequences. We should now care for the wounded and heal the sick. When they are well, they should go home. And we can eventually go home as well. Germany will become a democracy. They do not intend to do us any harm.

Our soldiers all cried "Bravo!" when the word was out that they could go home. We walked off, speechless. We sat somewhere in a corner and wept. "What is to become of us? Will we really see our homes again? How will the soldiers get home? Where are they still fighting? What will become of our lives and all the hopes that all of us young people still have?" We women are so much more helpless than men. Our soldiers always acknowledged that fact to us.

On the 2nd of May, Berlin capitulated.

Over and over again, women came to us who had been mistreated by a Russian while a pistol or gun was pointed at them. The Russians plundered houses and apartments, everywhere, and raped women and young girls. Age made no difference. Some neighborhoods were maliciously destroyed, all the belongings taken away. We are very likely the only Lazarett or hospital in which no nurse has been mistreated by a Russian, and from which none of us has been taken away as prisoner. In many, all the Schwestern were mistreated in evil ways. In the Martin Luther Hospital, they raped all the nurses, and the head nurse, who tried to protect them, was beaten and then thrown down a flight of stairs. In Tempelhof, patients and hospital employees, along with the nurses and doctors, were transported off, probably to Herzberg, Lichtenberg, Frankfurt an der Oder, Vienna? Where to?

Here, all they did was come one day to gather up all the patients who were between the ages of 16 and 45. The older ones, those unable to travel, and the amputees were left behind. They were to be transported to Herzberg near Berlin. That afternoon, one of them who had "bolted" returned to us. He told us that all the soldiers, other than the officers, had their heads shaved. They were told that they were now prisoners of war and they now had five years of work on the land ahead of them. There were German doctors and nurses among them.

In the meantime we have become a civilian hospital. There is no longer a threat of being taken prisoner. Anyway, the Russians are only taking fully licensed nurses to Russia or to the Eastern Zone.

So, for today, I wish you a good night.

Your Grete

1 June 1945

My dearest Peter,

I am very sick and still at home, so I have time to write.

Thank God, all the horror is over. It was so awful back then when the Stalin Organs were being fired! It must have been around the 27th or 28th of April. I was in the Gymnasium. It was about 5:00 in the afternoon. There was a tremendously loud explosion outside. The entire building shook. Everything went dark from the dust and all that debris that fell from the walls and the windows.

*Everyone ran every which way, looking for shelter anywhere they could. The entire roof of the larger wing of the building was suddenly gone. In our bandage room everything was completely covered in debris. Everyone in the Gymnasium who could jumped from their beds and ran for cover.*

*The panic is, of course, always the worst part—that initial heart-skip. We ran immediately to the most wounded soldiers, to see if they had been injured. But, thank God, no one was harmed. We ripped all their pillows from beneath their heads and covered their faces so at least they felt somewhat protected. And then, suddenly, there was calm again.*

*Daily now, it's becoming quieter out there. The Russian soldiers really behaved in uncouth ways during those first days. But our soldiers said that often—and nobody corrected them—our SS were much worse. So there you have it! What did we know of all this? We always spoke of humanity. We stressed it over and over again: we would be treated as our soldiers had treated others. But our own SS were no better than highway robbers.*

*I never liked those "Brothers" anyway. I was always afraid they would force me to become a "German mother," and if I resisted, I'd only have been thrown into the concentration camp.*

*In the streets, the Russians often grabbed women and young girls and threw them into vacant hallways and raped them. Many of those innocent young girls were so weak or so ill, they couldn't defend themselves. But I suppose this sort of character lives everywhere. Many were even robbed of their very last possessions. But then, even our dear fellow Berliners, to some extent, committed these very same crimes against our own people. One will rob the next of something he himself has lost, and the next will do the same, and so it goes.*

*On the Windscheidstrasse, they ransacked our bomb shelter and broke open the suitcases, plundering what they could. But somehow we are able to find luck in the midst of misfortune. Not long ago, it was mandated that all this plundering was illegal, as were their shameful advances toward the women.*

*If one addresses them with "Commander" or "Kommisar," they actually do show some respect, and at this point it has, for the most part, stopped altogether. Many of the Russians have even returned home. At most, they broke into homes and have taken the few items that could be used to furnish the officers' mess rooms. Then I heard from one of our nurses, who lives in the Grunewald-Villen district, that she was forced to have a Russian live with her. This Russian wanted a carpet and an easy chair, and a few other things, so all these items were taken from a neighbor's apartment and given to him.*

*It's imperative to watch out for yourself when the Russians are drunk. On Sundays, or in the evenings after a celebration or a parade, as a woman, you must never allow yourself to be seen outside.*

*The Russian is really a peculiar sort of person. As inhumane and brutal as he can be, he can also be quite good-natured. It's not infrequent that he will give away all his bread and sausage.*

*The other day there was a car in front of our house. It was full of Russians. One, in particular, was beside himself with joy over the children's delight when he handed them handfuls of sugar that he had pulled out of a bag. Like innocent children is how they often appear to me. The Russian commandant who came to us seemed to be just such a good-natured person. I heard this from many who had talked with him or asked him for certain things. Russians look to us to be strange and rather alien. I'm not attracted to them—I have to be honest. But then, we probably don't appeal to them either.*

*The PGs are being hunted down. From the Gauleiter down,[49] everyone has been shot. Even those who worked for them are being dealt with as if they were PGs themselves, regardless of whether they were members of the Partei or not. They are thrown out of the homes they've been living in, and the space is cleared out for the Jews to reinhabit. All PGs who were members of the Partei before 1933 will no longer receive food ration cards. Instead, they now spend the entire day shoveling rubble and then are fed only once a day and only from the Goulaschkanone. But this is what they did to the Jews.*

*I think they're only this strict in Charlottenburg because the Werewolf is still very active here.*[50] *For a while, food warehouses were set on fire during the night—those same warehouses that, earlier in the day, the Russians had stocked full of supplies intended to go to the German people. What madness in these young boys! Who is it they are trying to help by doing this? They are taking the very food meant for their own people. This is complete sabotage because we already surrendered unconditionally as of May 7th!*

*As punishment for the Werewolf activities, they shot 100 Hitler boys. Isn't this sad? So much unnecessary bloodshed for the sake of a few scoundrels. They were mere children who had not been raised properly, and had been influenced by circumstances of war.*

*And now all of Charlottenburg is being punished for their crimes. In other districts the people are much better provided for. Here we only began receiving lard and barely a few potatoes as of the first of May. Other sectors of the city have received much more to eat. We were even refused the "Stalin donation."*

*Who shall receive provisions has been divided into several groups: the ordinary users; workers (of which I happen to be one) who receive 500 grams of bread each day; and the heavy-duty workers (I believe doctors and clergymen belong to this group). They receive significantly more to eat.*

*Stalin should feel obligated to at least feed us all.*

*Oh, my dear man, surely you're sighing with the greatest relief that this wretched war is over. Such a dreadful end is something none of us had wished for. It is also so distressing that no one knows what's to become of us, and that we have been so helplessly handed over to, and are at the mercy of, our enemy.*

*All women, ages 15 to 50, need to register as labor reservists. Should, for example, Mutti suddenly try to find work? Which work? Should she just wait and see what is to be? Is it also possible that all those able to work will be hauled off to the east? Where is one sure to find work? There's no money anyway.*

*We need to stay in the Lazarett until the very end. At the hospital where one of my colleagues and a former classmate of mine, Renate Wisselmann, works, several of the helpers were replaced by fully registered nurses as of May 31st. In a sense, it's good, in a time of such massive unemployment, to have a source for bread. But I am beginning to realize how very stressed I have been. Even though, during the day, I don't seem to have a fever, every night my temperature rises again. The doctor recommends rest. Very often everything goes black in front of my eyes when I try to stand. Today I sat out on our balcony for the first time. I feel like an old woman. As if I were really quite ill. I know I cannot go back to work just yet. I would love to be able to just get around, but my strength is only coming back very slowly. I am very unhappy with all this.*

*A doctor let me know, through a conversation he had with Mutti, that Sauerbruch is still taking interns for the next three weeks.*[51] *Should I try for an interview? I would love to do that. Besides, I would love to find a position as doctor's assistant somewhere.*

*Oh, Franzel, if only you would just come! Then everything would make me so much happier. I would have to work anyway, as we need to be able to eat. But you will be with me. Today Mutti told me that if you came, and if you asked me to marry you, she would give her permission. My father also gave his permission. Even before he took off, he called from the train station. I happened to answer the telephone. I asked him just once more, that if we were to get engaged, and if by chance he were not to return before we wanted to marry, would he be against our marriage. He said that if I wanted it so badly and it was my absolute resolve to do so, and if we simply could not wait any longer, then it would be all right!! That was his very last word! It's kind, don't you think? Soon, certainly, you shall be with me.*

*Will you be upset with me then, that even though we made all these promises to one another, I will continue to study? How long we will be able to study, and how long we will have money, is anyone's guess anyway. Perhaps I could earn the money for the lecture fees on the side. I have to try now to earn money for my daily bread and for my future. But then, as soon as you return, I will conclude my studies.*

*Dear one, please return soon! Soon we should have mail service again. That would certainly be good. But what an appalling idea— to never to see you again. Would my intuitions deceive me? Intuition never lies. I knew this even a year ago—that the friendship with you was not over and that certainly we would see each other again. I felt it but never wanted to believe it. I was always so happy when I thought of you. I often compare other men to you: I even tell them so. It's as if I'm being "thought," I'm being "experienced," my tasks are being "done" by something other than me. Sometimes I think, too, that someone like you will never come my way again. There is no one for whom I feel as much as I do for you.*

*And then, when I think about my present circumstances and I think about you, I get angry with you, and am not ready to reconcile with you yet. So many days have passed during which we've been apart, I have completely new and different ideas in my head about you. My studies are much more important and more interesting to me than you.*

*But, my love, I think of you so often. People are already beginning to laugh at me for still believing you'll be with me again one day, and that we'll still begin a life together after the war.*

*I have become friends with a colleague here in Berlin who took the civil service exam. At first he used to tell me that a man should fight for his woman, and he would, if you were to return, not give up that fight over me. But now I have convinced him that that is a useless effort, that it's just pointless. The other day he asked me if he could be the godfather for my first child. This was said half jokingly and half in all seriousness. I laughed so hard, and I told him that not long after we married I would have a little son. That is already written in the books! (I even already know what he looks like. In fact, he looks a lot like his Papa!)*

*Out here on the balcony, next to me and the lounge chair on which I am lying, is a picture of you, and next to that is your little stuffed animal. Mutti brought it from Calau a while back. I just want to be well again, and be able to go outside. Outside somewhere, where it is beautiful. If only the upcoming demarcation of our country were not going to happen! Very soon the peace negotiations are to be finalized so that we will finally know how things will be.*

*My dear Peter, we'll never live in the city, will we? We'll live where nature, tranquility, and love prevail. We will live somewhere quietly and alone, even if it's only a little hut. A small house offers so much peace. Then we'll engage in art, science, literature, philosophy—as much as we please. We'll be far away from all outside influences. We'll sink ourselves into the aesthetics of literature. That will be so wonderful!*

*I so longed to live back in that contemplative Biedermeier era and wished away the war, technology and machines, inventions and weapons. I have never been a friend of Physics, Mathematics, and certain strains of Chemistry. You can, of course, see this in how often I attended the Physics lecture: five times, of which two had bomb alarms go off and we needed to flee the hall. And the first visit I made was only so that I could get my lecture certification. That makes it three times. In one lecture we ate radishes, and then at other times I overslept and missed the whole thing.*

*Oh, dear one, to be as happy and free as I was as a student in Jena! The whole world seemed to open its arms during this gloriously romantic student's life. Science, literature, art . . . one loved it and gained its knowledge, all in university fashion: "universitas." One listened to lectures one wanted to hear, one did what one wanted to do. Nothing was anyone else's business. "The world belongs to us students!" was our motto. How often we just lay in the sun with all our books and then returned home in the evenings without ever having opened a single one of them. That lovely old student town of Jena. All those beautiful traditions have now been destroyed. Only the memory lives on.*

*My dear man, all this will exist again! We just need to have patience. So, for today, my dear Peter, everything is well. I have reported everything in long and elaborate detail. I'm so curious to know what you have to report. The majority of it, though, is news one cannot ever speak about accurately.*

*So for now, take from me my most loving caresses, and in the quiet of your dreams, know that I send you a kiss,*

*Your Grete*

*1 June 1945*

*My Dear One!*

*How did it go for you on the 25th of May? One of the nurses has her birthday on that day. When she told me once that her birthday is in May, and I asked her on which day in May, it was almost as if an oracle had spoken: I was thinking of May 25th, and then immediately thought, yes, Schwester Luise's birthday must be on the 25th, because it's such a holy day. When she said it in that very instant, "on the 25th," I was frightened by my thoughts and that this oracle was actually speaking.*

*The night before, Schwester Ruth, the head nurse on my station, and I went out to pick a few flowers. It was already quite late at night, and because of that stupid Russian time we have now, it was actually two hours later in the day than what the sun's position said. We walked along the avenue and saw, to our right, something hidden deep within an enclosure.*

*We continued deeper into the woods and into this enclosure, and discovered, way down beneath everything, something hidden and wild—it was a little creek or pond, but so romantically overgrown. As always, and everywhere, I thought of you. An overgrown boulder towered about ten to twenty meters up ahead, at the other end of our little stream. Grass, gnarled tree roots, and thicket were everywhere. In my memory, it looked to be quite large and craggy. But maybe it was simply a small hill. Nevertheless, it appeared like an enchanted castle that had been asleep for a hundred years. No human hand had ever brought this to order; everything grew just as it wanted. Just this gave it its romanticism. It was misty and cool. Suddenly the song "The Two Royal Children" came into my head, and I said to Schwester Ruth, "It's just like in the song. Over there, on the other side, are the Americans, in the middle is the River Elbe—the Line of Demarcation—and over here are the Russians. We are so close to our loved ones, and still cannot get to them.*

*There were two royal children,*
*They loved each other dearly,*
*But they could not come to one another*
*Because the water was much too deep.*

*Yes, so that's how it is now. But even these chains can be broken, and we'll be together again! This is what I concluded, without saying so out loud.*

*That night we arranged the flowers we had picked in some vases and prepared her birthday table. The next morning, her birthday proper, we woke up quite early just to get the rest ready for her. We had an early breakfast together and everything was in a festive mood in our station tea kitchen. I placed two little flower bouquets on my nightstand, with such sweet little forget-me-nots. Then in front of them I placed your picture. Over and over again, I thought so deeply about you, and had no fear whatsoever, as I thought I might at first. I was so happy that that decisive May 25th was going to be over, a day on which you would surely be safe and well.*

*On the 25th of May, if possible, we were going to give the birthday girl an afternoon off. I did her afternoon chores. There was much to do, as everything was in chaos. I always seem to have the good luck that when it's my turn to oversee the station, all hell breaks loose. The men suddenly have hemorrhages, or new patients are admitted, or newly operated patients arrive who need to be injected on an hourly basis, or someone dies, or a wound needs to be rebandaged, or someone messes on himself and his bedding needs changing, or someone suddenly has a spike in his fever or has an attack of some kind or another, and the necessary medication is nowhere to be found, and then even the keys for the narcotics cabinet are missing. Usually much of it, or all of it, happens all at once. This is how it was today. At six I finally finished taking everyone's temperature and changing all the wet bandages. Schwester Ruth then took over and worked alone. Luise returned at around seven and helped with the injections.*

*That evening, Schwester Ruth invited the two of us, Luise and me, to be with her. We had a cozy dinner, drank a little liqueur that we had saved from our last rationings, smoked a few cigarettes, and gossiped a bit. Schwester Ruth read some rather sweet but funny soldiers' stories to us. Tears of laughter rolled down our cheeks. And then that night as I was falling asleep, I thought again of you, my dear Peter. Every night I fall asleep with thoughts of you, and then awake again with thoughts of you. If I see clouds or look at the sky, I think of you, and I think, how beautiful the sky is now in the summertime, and how free and lovely the world is now, and that*

*God surely always wants what is beautiful to be, and that surely He too would want to see us two united.*

*All we want is to learn to have gratitude for God's kindness and love, and to be able to see it and be allowed to enjoy it.*

*So, please, just fulfill this one wish, dear Father in Heaven. It would be so sweet and we would be so grateful. I beg You so deeply and with such earnestness.*

*Good night my dearest Peter.*

*Always,*
*Your Grete*


*2 June 1945*

*My dearest Peter,*

*Poetry from Goethe and Mörike are what I would like to read today. That is precisely what would befit today's mood. I would love to lie in the grass, to dream, to let the summer's sun bathe me.*

*My dear, you shall soon be here! In one month it will already be the 10th of July.*[52] *I wonder if I will have received a letter from you by then? Oh, would that be a lovely birthday present! Four years ago, I also waited for a birthday wish from you, but I did not hear from you for a long, long time. I was very sad about that. Back then the Tanzschule had just finished. At that time I still had a few other admirers that were hard to shake off. One gave me a beautiful large bouquet of roses, deep dark red ones, as a gift. I wasn't even grateful for them and did not thank him even once. I feel like a bird in a cage. I am imprisoned and have just to wait to see what will become of me.*

*Everyone in the hospital is overworked and everyone is sick. Does one have to allow oneself to be so used up? As soon as I feel a bit better, I will try to contact Professor Sauerbruch, so that I can begin my studies again. I will look around too to see if I can get a position as an assistant lecturer. It's nearly equivalent to the medical lab work necessary for a* medical student to experience. Besides that, I know how to use medical instruments and can teach myself much more while doing so.

We ought to be taking a walk in the lovely summer breeze right now. Or we should be in Jena, or at the seashore, or near your home at the beautiful Rhine. You know I am such a water rat. I love all water sports, and at the end I'll jump into any body of water to swim and dive under. But I'm sure you swim much faster than I, because you're so much bigger and stronger.

Do you know what I did once? I was with a friend from the Tanzschule at a swimming pool. I really didn't like the fellow all that much anyway. When he couldn't even dive, not once headfirst into the water the way I can, and instead he timidly climbed down the ladder, my feelings for him sank low, until, when I challenged him to a swim race, and I was nearly halfway around the pool ahead of him, they hit rock bottom. That's when I lost all respect for him.

Dear Peter, right now we should be in our little boat and either rowing or paddling. Do you know what my greatest dream is? To one day ride the waves behind a motorboat. When one day we have the money for this, we should buy a beautiful boat with which we'll take many long tours.

I remember once in Swinemünde, there were such beautiful large yachts in the harbor. But I think they are too showy for me, really. I prefer small and sporty ones because the so-called gentleman's sports are not my particular passion.

Oh, dear one. I love you so much, and am so happy, thinking about you and about this lovely summer. If I had my way, I would put on a rucksack and make the trek to see you.

Off into the wilds
With a butter sandwich and some bacon.

I send you sweet greeting and kiss you with love,
Your Grete

*3 June 1945*

*Dearest Peter,*

*Today I was in a deep depression. I believe that you don't love me anymore, and that you found a replacement companion long ago. Yes, I would be very sad over this. Because I was always faithful to you, and only because of my trust in you did I manage to live through all the frightful horrors of the last two months. But you know my stubbornness. And you know I always find my way out, rise above it, and know exactly where I am headed in life.*

*So now, with both hands and both feet, I will attempt to study again. I have discovered that this service is my life's calling, and I can see I have an inclination and a talent for it as well. Even colleagues who know me, and who themselves have been declined for these positions, believe that I, in particular, will be able to, and should, continue my studies. They also believe I'll never finish, because I will surely marry first. I should see to it that I complete my studies anyway. You see, this is my opinion—that I must advance in my career, as I need to be able to earn a living.*

*And I don't want to run around in a nurse's cap anymore! I want to further my studies. I'm beginning to work my way through the Tuchel textbooks in Organic Chemistry and then will work my way through the Physiology book of Landois-Rosemann. If, then, I could also go to a lecture or two, or find a doctor who is willing to take me under his wing . . . ! Tomorrow I'll attempt to find a position as an assistant lecturer.*

*Today we discovered that our government gave us counterfeit money at the end: The paper money does not have the watermark in it anymore. In fact the 100 Deutschmark and the 50 Deutschmark bills—these out of all of them—are counterfeit. We, and many others like us, went to the bank so that we would have some cash—all of it was counterfeit! Such an insult!*

*It's Sunday today, a lovely, beautiful summer day. Yesterday I even went for a little walk. It did not go well, but it was at least something. Slowly everyone is crawling out of his hole. It was all a bit much for me, as this morning I felt wretchedly ill again. But I intend to take another walk today. Summer seems to pull us like a magnet out of the house.*

*5 June 1945*

*Dearest Peter,*

*The program has been changed! The Lazarett has let me go. As a civilian hospital it will now only employ fully registered nurses. The whole thing came about quite suddenly, much faster than I had thought. So today, first of all, I went to the magistrate to register myself at the Health Department.*

*I heard that the universities will reopen in October. I will try to find out from a colleague if the medical faculty will be teaching. Tomorrow I will go directly to the university to find out what they anticipate will happen. Besides that, I'm still looking for a position as an assistant lecturer. May my lucky star be with me so that I find something!*

*Yesterday I ran into my old boss, the director of the emergency services from the DRK.[53] The Red Cross is organizing crisis centers for which they will be hiring women who have proved themselves as nurses. Such luck. They want to recommend me for the position! They even want to arrange for me to attend lectures on the side. At least this is something in the right direction.*

*For several days now, it has been impossible to let this feeling go, that you are making a little side trip. Hopefully you will not forget me completely as you go about your business. You know how sensitive I am. And of course you know about my stubbornness. Can you tell I am having one of these pig-headed moments? It makes me happy to be concentrating on my studies again, which is something you never really liked. But surely you can see that I am able to master my own life, and that I'm happy doing so. I'm not the sort of person who will simply fall into your arms with my own outstretched. And I really don't need to wait for you forever with such uncertainty!!! You know that!*

*Oh well, I'm very upset with you today. Unfortunately you are sitting here passively by my side. But perhaps, too, my feelings are not deceiving me. It's difficult, I know, to begin such a fruitless effort, to search for a girlfriend who is somewhere within the Russian-occupied territory where the last of the battles took place. A girl who, for all you know, could be dead or has been carted off to a prison somewhere. There's no mail service, the trains aren't running. It's impossible to contact one another. Oh, why so many difficult circumstances because of one stupid cause? Let things roll as they do. She'll get over it eventually. No one really is to blame.*

*So, with that, everything is finished. I really wonder now if you even still think of me. Men are always so different about these things than women are. Women are much more faithful. But then, maybe today you're thinking the exact same thoughts about me as I am about you. Yes, my dear, I'm not a silly young virgin either, whose "love has only this one thought—to be true to her impatient yearnings until the very end." But nonetheless I have always been true to you. Even when one may fall in love a little here and there, it was never done in any sort of serious way, and we're still so young. I just couldn't handle it if there were another woman you loved more than me. Then just stay with her!*

*Oh, I'm in such a mess of a mood today. Do you still wear my ring? I'll bet it doesn't want to fit you right today! It should hurt you a bit and stick to your finger so it can't move. Your subconscious should torture you today and make a martyr of you. It's your good luck that you're not here today, or that my letters can't reach you today, because it would have been another stupid fight with me. Do you remember what it was like three months ago? It's that same sort of mood I'm in today. I was very angry with you, and thought, "Wait a minute! I can have it be otherwise! I can get along without him just as well. That is what he should know today. He should not feel all that sure about himself, because that security is not written in stone—not just yet!"*

*Best wishes to you, then, dear Peter, for today,*
*Your Grete*

*7 June 1945*

My dearest Peter,

*How many more books laden with letters to you shall I write, before we see each other again? Where, oh where, can you be? How are you? Oh, my dear Peter, I can hardly imagine that we will really see each other again. Keep my ring close to you. It was to bring you luck and be your talisman.*

*A friend of the family's, a pensioned admiral, came to visit today. I asked him if he had any news about the troops in Denmark, and he said that some of you have already been sent to Schleswig-Holstein to be held in a reentry camp. When will you be released? I wonder. How much longer must the cleanup work continue? Will you soldiers be able to write soon? Oh, my dearest, if I could only have some news from you. Hopefully you are at least well enough to do so. I love you so very much. You probably don't even know how much I have loved you. I would be so sad if you were never to return. That would be such an unspeakable sorrow that then I would only want to go to where you have gone. In my deepest beliefs, there is a reunion on that other side. Can you fathom what I mean by all this? Franzel, if I could show you, just once, that there is no one else in the world I love as much as you. Oh, how horrible it would be to know that you love someone else more than me.*

*Oh, my dearest love, I pray to God every night that He keep you safe, and that you are well, and that He will reunite us soon. It was so incredibly beautiful that we ran into each other that winter night just before the "locking of the gates."*[54] *And that 14th of December came, and everything was so lovely. I'm so very thankful for that moment, and I take it as an omen that our future is protected.*

*Would that you could be with me now, and I could lie against your chest and just cry till there were no more tears left. Then we would both take up our walking sticks and march into our new lives together. I know that you, too, are sitting somewhere today, having these same thoughts about me. Yes, dear one, we're both still alive and we do still have our sights on our new life together.*

*14 June 1945*

Auf Wiedersehen, *my dear Franzel. I will return to you, if you'll let me know where you are. I think only of you, and love no one as dearly as I do you. This is true, and I'll stay with you forever.*

All my love,
Your Grete

# Epilogue

After the official end of the Second World War, May 8, 1945, 2.6 million German people, most of whom were women and children, died from starvation or lack of medical care. Of the 1.2 million German prisoners of war who died, over one million died in Soviet camps. In all, twenty-two million people of all nationalities continued to die in eastern European and Russian prison camps during the first years after the war.

❧

What is written here in Margarete's letters is all that is known of Peter's whereabouts. Margarete makes one reference to a Frau Steffens and hints that he lived on the Rhine River, and we know he was a German soldier in Denmark, but those are the only clues we have. Trying to track down a man named Peter, or Franzel, who had been a German soldier in Denmark, who lived on the Rhine and who was known by a Frau Steffens, brought me few answers. I contacted as many school friends and relatives of Margarete's as I knew. Many had died. One, I was told by her daughter, had Alzheimer's disease to such an extent she would not even remember Margarete. The answer to my questions "Did you ever know a man named Peter? Or Franzel?" was in all but one case negative.

It was an e-mail I wrote to the daughter of a school friend, who kindly responded, saying yes, indeed her mother remembered Margarete and a man named Peter. "His name was Peter. I do remember that. They met in the S-Bahn one day. He was a soldier, that's all I know. I believe they knew each other for several years. But that's all I remember."

Alas, Peter, or Franzel, remains to this day a mystery man whom my mother loved and never reconnected with. As I read and reread the letters—as I have so many times over the years since I found them—I can only conclude that they, and her undying love for this man, gave her the will to go on living through those most unforgiving months of war.

～

In November of 1944, Karl Spaeth fled Albania after its liberation from German control. Through the bitter winter months of 1944–45, he and two comrades crept through forests and over the rugged mountain passes of the Balkans, running at night and hiding in chicken coops and barns during the day. All three arrived in Germany safely sometime just before the war's end in the spring of 1945.

Bound by duty, Karl Spaeth traveled on to Berlin, came home briefly to tell Helga not to worry—he'd be home in a few weeks—and left for Flensburg, where he was in attendance as the capitulation negotiations took place between Grand Admiral Dönitz and the Allied commanders. Afterwards he was held in American detention for several months, where, in his words, he was treated very well.

Upon his return to Berlin, Margarete and Helga had already left for Sweden on the infamous "Raoul Wallenberg" train. By the time he learned of their departure, it was clear they never made it to Sweden—he had contacted relatives there who said they had never arrived—and the Russians were unwilling to give any word about prisoners. Although Margarete and Helga were told so often upon their reentry to Germany, "We thought you were dead," there must have always been some hope that they had been taken prisoner. After all, fourteen million Germans and East Europeans, and countless others from countries as far away as Japan and Greece, were released from Russian Gulags in the decade to follow.

Alone, with everything in ruin and his military career dead, Karl Spaeth, at the age of fifty-six, decided to study medicine. He moved to Göttingen in northern Germany, where he spent the next several years studying. Eventually he and Helga reunited and for a brief period immigrated to the United States. After a year, they returned to Germany and took up residence in Hamburg, where Karl practiced medicine as a private physician until his death in the late 1960s. Helga lived to be seventy-two and died in a convalescent home in 1973.

⁓

Jürgen Möller followed Margarete to Sweden several months after she arrived, and there he concluded his medical studies. They were married on April 16, 1952, at the *Tyska kyrkan,* or German Church, sometimes called St. Gertrude's in Gamla stan, the old town in central Stockholm.

I was their first child, born to them eight months later, to the day, in Stockholm. Within a year, they received their residency papers for the United States, immigrated to St. Paul, Minnesota, and eventually became U.S. citizens.

Here Margarete took a job as a nurse's assistant while Jürgen finished his medical residency. She never did realize her dream of becoming a doctor. Rather, she spent the remainder of her life as a mother and homemaker, conforming to the norms of a wife in the 1950s.

After raising three daughters and a son of Jürgen's from a previous relationship, Margarete and Jürgen eventually divorced in 1978. Jürgen moved back to northern Germany, where he lived with his second wife until his death in 1983.

On July 12, 2005, two days after her eighty-first birthday, Margarete died in Boulder, Colorado. The cause of death was heart failure.

⁓

Dieter was killed on February 15, 1945, on the outskirts of a village then named Wildforth, now Prostyna, in Poland. One evening many years after his death, Dieter's commanding officer came to Mutti's door with an official letter, explaining what he believed had happened.

According to this officer, Dieter was with his platoon in an area near Stettin, which is now in Poland. They were in a forest with a clearing, a meadow of sorts, just in front of them. On the other side of the meadow were several farmhouses, and they knew there were women and children in those houses because they could hear them screaming. Dieter, as did all the men, understood very well the probable cause of their screaming with the Russians so nearby. They would surely be raped, and then murdered.

Dieter and a friend, another soldier, ran across that field to save them. Neither he nor any of the men he was with had weapons; they had been sent into the field without them, as there were no weapons left to give the soldiers at the end of the war. Dieter and his comrade crept through the field and reached the farmhouse. Quickly they snatched two children and a woman, and, showing them how to stay low to the ground, they ran back across the same field in hopes of reaching the safety of the forest. It was in this field that a hand grenade exploded and killed all of them at once.

The officer told Helga that he was very sorry to report that they were not able to identify Dieter's body, and what they were able to find of the bodies was placed in a shallow grave. They had to do it quickly, and left no marker. But the officer had felt personally obligated to share the story of Dieter's death with his family, "to let you know who this son of yours was."

That was the last news anyone would ever hear of Dieter.

His remains have, to this day, not been identified, and the field that was described by his officer has been overgrown with forest. A stele, however, was erected in Stare Czarnowo, Poland, near the site of his death, on July 15, 2006. Upon it, the names of thirty German soldiers have been engraved. Dieter Dos is one of them.

⤫

Hilde and her family lived out the war in Berlin. Neither her Jewish mother nor any of the rest of her family was ever sent away during the pogrom. Berlin, in fact, had the greatest number of Jews of any city in Germany still living at large by the end of the war. Those who survived either looked "Aryan" enough to pass, or were simply protected by neighbors and friends.

Kerstin Jurke, Susanne Erichsen, Ilse, and Brigitte Martins all remained close friends with Margarete throughout the remainder of their lives.

⤫

"What became of the six paintings?" I asked my mother.

"The Dürer, yes. That one was valuable. All the others weren't so. We had, you remember, stored all the valuable art in a bunker outside the city. Of course, when the Allies came through, all those things were plundered and we never saw a bit of it again."

"But what happened to the paintings?" I asked again. She didn't know. I only know of one—I have it in my possession. It is an oil painting, about eighteen inches by twenty-four, and hangs in my bedroom. It is signed by an artist unknown to me, and dated 1926. It is a melancholic scene—a Russian, or perhaps a Polish, farmhouse in the snow. The scene is reflected in the water of a flowing river, and there are bare trees in the foreground, maybe birch. The back of the painting has a note from my mother: "To my daughter, Kerstin. This picture has been hit by grenade slivers in Berlin during the war, 1945. It has accompanied us through Russia's Gulag camps, 1945–1947. The damage shall be remembered forever!"

# Acknowledgments

My immeasurable gratitude goes to my uncle Axel, my mother's cousin, who was eight years old when the war ended, and who lived through the terrible famine during the early postwar years in Germany. When I asked for his help with this book, he was delighted and graciously went to work. There were many things that I, as an American, did not understand from a German perspective—the German politics of the time, the prewar state of that country, or how it affected its civilians—and on these points Axel was of tremendous help. He spent countless hours correcting my history when I wasn't sure of it, correcting my German when I misspelled it, and in all cases he helped to verify events Margarete talked about.

My mother's handwriting has always been difficult for me to read. Many, if not most, of her handwritten words look to be a series of *w*s, *m*s, *n*s, and *u*s. I have learned since, it is because she went to grammar school at a time when handwriting was still taught in the Sütterlin script. My uncle Axel once again came to my rescue. He happened to have grown up in an era when students were taught handwriting in both Sütterlin and Latin. He was all too happy to transcribe her letters to typewritten form, so that I could translate from them. I am deeply indebted to him for all his studious help. Without Axel, this story would not have nearly as much German character, and the historical and geographical detail would have been much more vague, drab even.

To express my deep thanks to those who saw this book's potential, and who encouraged me to move forward and "keep writing," is a near impossibility. It begins with Peter Thompson, my amazing translation professor, who read some of my mother's letters and exclaimed, "These need to be published!" It was through his selfless persistence that I eventually met Judith Weber, my agent, whose incredible patience and encouragement caused this book to come to be. Thank you, Judith, for all your helpful work! Tom Kennedy, as my professor and mentor, I cannot thank enough for his kind prodding and insights in helping with my manuscript, and for encouraging me when I wanted to give up. Victor Rangel is a dear man I've never met other than through e-mail, yet his online comments and insights were invaluable. And then dear Anna Bliss, my editor, my patient editor—I believe my mother, from her side of the grave, has fallen in love with her! Because of her, each sentence and every scene was meticulously groomed. I owe her my heartfelt gratitude and compliments for an eye that would not leave a single word unnoticed, or an event not researched. I would be remiss if I did not mention my writer buddies who spent two years with me on this project, reading chapters, analyzing and critiquing, nursing this manuscript to bring it to what it has become. Paige, Scott, Margaret, and Phil, you know who you are: This book would not be if it weren't for you! To the many friends and family members who've stood by me throughout this process—the names so many, they'd fill another page and I'd be afraid to forget one of you— thank you for putting up with me.

Finally, my mother must not be forgotten in these acknowledgments. It was she whose courage it took to live through those dreadful years and then to talk about them fifty years later. Her eternal optimism and strength in the face of extreme hardships has been an inspiration throughout my life. I hope the passion she had for living is recognized in the pages of this memoir.

# Endnotes

1   Swinemünde, a city in an area of Germany once called Pomerania, is now in Poland and has been renamed Świnoujście.

2   Margarete's father probably oversaw the operations of a lignite mine.

3   The Enabling Act, passed by the parliament on March 23, 1933, gave Hitler's dictatorship the right to exist.

4   At the Nazi rally in Nuremberg on September 15, 1935, Hitler announced the ratification of the Nuremberg Laws, which, among a number of other points, revoked German citizenship for Jews and forbade marriage, or even extramarital relationships, between Jews and Aryans.

5   Margarete was mistaken. The Nazis did allow officers to join the Nazi Party, unlike the former Weimar Republic, which kept their party affiliation on hold while in service. However, even during the Nazi era, most officers chose not to join the *Partei* anyway and, as had been the custom prior to the rise of Hitler's regime, stayed "party-neutral."

6   The *Wehrmacht* was the term for the German armed forces between 1935 and 1945.

7   As a half Jew, Hilde was allowed to attend the Tanzschule. Only official organizations, such as the Hitler Youth and the BDM, withheld memberships from Jews. Although various sources state vague or conflicting standards as to who was deemed Jewish and who was deemed Aryan, Margarete said the "Jewish laws" related to

anyone with more than one-eighth Jewish blood. If she was right, her Annenpass would support that, as it certified her genealogy ten generations back.

8   This law was actually not enacted until after July 20, 1944.

9   Margarete was somehow mistaken. The war was declared on September 1, 1939, but that date fell on a Friday. They were either at the beach on a Friday, which seems unlikely as the children would have been at school, or the announcement said that food was going to be rationed.

10  Although Margarete remembers being hungry right from the beginning of the war, when food was rationed, real food shortages did not occur in Germany until the years just after the war. Her memories may well have been influenced by the *change* in food supplies, such as the *Gulaschkanonen* she describes and the new bread made with ever more creative "ersatz" ingredients.

11  To be clear, Germans were not starving during the war years. Food, although rationed, was available. The true hunger remembered by the Germans from that time occurred during the first years after the war during the Allied Occupation.

12  I.G. Farbenindustrie is infamously known for having provided the stabilizer to produce Zyklon B, the cyanide-based pesticide used to kill humans in the gas chambers during the Holocaust.

13  The *Völkischer Beobachter* (Observer of the German Folk) was the official Nazi newspaper from 1920 to 1945. *Volk* means people, nation, tribe, race; in Nazi parlance, *völkisch* meant "pure German" and by extension "anti-Semitic."

14  I have not been able to verify this. I do not know if this "first bomb" happened during the first RAF bombing raids of Berlin, or during the much more serious raids two years later.

15  The RAF bombed Berlin in 1940 on August 26, August 28, September 23, and September 25, and then nearly every day from then through December 21. Then suddenly the bombings over Berlin stopped until March 1, 1943, at which time the bombs were much more sophisticated and devastating. From the descriptions Margarete gives of these nights in the bunkers, it is possible that they occurred after March 1, 1943.

16  Margarete was incorrect in calling this wind a true firestorm, as such firestorms did not, of record, occur in Berlin. It is also possible that this scene occurred after 1943, when much heavier and more destructive bombardments fell on Berlin.

17  Margarete is referring to Operation Gomorrah, a bombing campaign on Hamburg that began July 24, 1943. The bombing, which lasted eight days, has been called "the Hiroshima of Germany."

18  Brest-Litovsk is now Brest, Poland.

19  Large gas-filled *Fesselballons*—captive or tethered balloons—would release a thick haze when enemy aircraft were sighted, in hopes of camouflaging important public works and factories.

20  Buchenwald concentration camp was just twenty kilometers from Jena.

21  Although my mother wanted me to know that even Americans bombed innocent civilian ships, the most famous sinking of a refugee ship in the Baltic was the sinking of the *Wilhelm Gustloff,* which was hit by a Russian torpedo.

22  Margarete is referring to General Patton.

23  From the description, he may have been a field marshal, not a general.

24  Raoul Wallenberg was a member of the Swedish royalty, known primarily for issuing Swedish passports to the Jewish population

of Budapest, Hungary, saving tens of thousands from potential capture by the Nazis.

25 No Swedish church could be found to have been near the Invaliden U-Bahn station. However, there were, and still are, two Swedish churches in Wilmersdorf, a borough very near her home in Charlottenburg. Margarete may have forgotten that she and Helga took several forms of transportation to the U-Bahn station on that memorable night.

26 Margarete incorrectly called it Camp One. In fact, it was a prison camp, well known for its detention of German officers, but named Camp 27, and they were in Zone One.

27 It is now known that Raoul Wallenberg entered the Lubyanka Prison in Moscow on February 6, 1945, half a year before Margarete's train left Berlin, making it impossible that he could have organized such an endeavor.

28 Anna Iwanowna must have made a great impression on Margarete, because she always called her by both her given name and her patronymic. She was also mentioned in Margarete's diary, this time with a surname: Anna Iwanowna Ladowitsch. Susanne Erichsen, in her autobiography, *Ein Nerz und eine Krone,* mentions her as well. The spelling, however, is different: Anna Ivanowna.

29 After her release from the Gulag, Susanne Erichsen was crowned Miss Germany 1950 and Miss Europe 1950 and later became one of Germany's most beloved high-fashion models. After working in New York, she was nicknamed *das Fräuleinwunder,* the girl wonder of Germany. Shortly before her death in 2002, she published her autobiography, *Ein Nerz und eine Krone* (A Mink and a Crown).

30 Margarete's birth father, Werner, was a mining engineer who told her many stories about his work. Thus an English word like "lignite" would not have been unusual for her, a woman foreign to that language, to know.

31 Although Margarete never told what happened with the babies, Anne Applebaum, in her Pulitzer Prize–winning book *Gulag: A History*, describes some of the women's ordeals with regard to this issue.

32 Although she says they were "the poor ones," the kulaks were those peasants who refused to give up their lands for the collective farms. Many of them were actually quite well off before they were either imprisoned or exiled to Siberia.

33 It is possible that the train stopped in Brest, where the Russian broad-gauge tracks meet the European standard gauge. However, Margarete mentions Brest later in her dialogue. She may have forgotten or, in her memory, collapsed two train stations into one. The story remains as she told it: "somewhere in the wide-open nothingness of Russia."

34 When Gronenfelde was closed for good in 1950, more than one million German prisoners returning from Russian Gulags had passed through its gates.

35 The Schlesischer Bahnhof is today's Ostbahnhof.

36 After 1945 the Allied occupying governments required all German citizens to carry identification documents to travel from one sector to another. In the city of Berlin, citizens needed travel documents to cross even between the sectors in their own city. With the issuance of these passports, officials hoped to mitigate the huge influx of refugees fleeing the east, and it was also an effort to find former Nazis.

37 Königsberg is now Kaliningrad in the Kaliningrad Oblast of Russia.

38 HVP: *Hauptverbandplatz*, the "main bandaging station" or "main first aid station."

39 Ivan was the nickname for the Russians, Tomy (or Tommy in English) for the British.

40 Himmler was, up until that time, the appointed *Reichsführer* of the SS.

41 Possibly this date was his birthday or their anniversary.

42 PGs: *Parteigenosse,* the official members of the NSDAP, the Nazi Party.

43 Sankas: *Sanitärskraftwagen,* ambulances used during the war.

44 Frau Steffens may have been a housemate in Franzel's home, or perhaps a housekeeper. Her identity is not known.

45 OP: Operating room.

46 *Urrä-urrä:* The Russian war cry often heard as they began an assault.

47 *Uffz: Unteroffizier,* a noncommissioned officer.

48 Grand Admiral Dönitz, of the German navy, was named by Hitler as his successor.

49 *Gauleiter:* District commander.

50 "Werewolf" was a vernacular term for the Hitler Youth who fought against the Russians in the final battle for Berlin.

51 Professor Sauerbruch was a well-known surgeon and professor at the Charité Institute, the university for medicine in Berlin.

52 July 10: Margarete's birthday.

53 DRK: Deutsches rote Kreutz, the German Red Cross.

54 *Torresschluss* is literally translated as "the locking of the gates." It stems from the Middle Ages, when the city gates were locked just before sundown. Those who did not make it back into the city before Torresschluss had to sleep outside the gates.

# Selected Bibliography

## Books

Anonymous. *A Woman in Berlin: Eight Weeks in the Conquered City.* Translated by Philip Boehm. New York: Henry Holt, 2005.

Applebaum, Anne. *Gulag: A History.* New York: Doubleday, 2003.

Bonhoeffer, Dietrich. *The Cost of Discipleship.* Rev. ed. Translated by R. H. Fuller and Irmgard Booth. London: SCM, 1959.

Brecht, Bertolt. *Mother Courage and Her Children.* Translated by David Hare. New York: Arcade, 1996.

Dönhoff, Marion, Countess. *Before the Storm: Memories of My Youth in Old Prussia.* Translated by Jean Steinberg. New York: Alfred A. Knopf, 1990.

Erichsen, Susanne. *Ein Nerz und eine Krone* [A Mink and a Crown]. With Dorothée Hansen. Munich: Econ, 2003.

Frazier, Ian. "On the Prison Highway: The Gulag's Silent Remains." *New Yorker,* August 30, 2010, 28–34.

Goethe, Johann Wolfgang von. *Faust: A Tragedy.* Translated by Walter Arndt. New York: W. W. Norton, 1976.

Grass, Günther. *Peeling the Onion.* Translated by Michael Henry Heim. Orlando: Harcourt, 2007.

Hautzig, Esther. *The Endless Steppe: Growing Up in Siberia.* New York: T. Y. Crowell, 1968.

Kobak, Annette. *Joe's War: My Father Decoded.* New York: Alfred A. Knopf, 2004.

Lonely Planet. *Germany.* London: Lonely Planet, 2004.

———. *Russia.* 5th ed. London: Lonely Planet, 2009.

Moorhouse, Roger. *Berlin at War.* New York: Basic Books, 2010.

Rilke, Rainer Maria. *The Selected Poetry of Rainer Maria Rilke.* Translated by Stephen Mitchell. New York: Random House, 1982.

Ryan, Cornelius. *The Last Battle.* New York: Simon & Schuster, 1966.

Sandulescu, Jacques. *Donbas: A True Story of an Escape Across Russia.* New York: David McKay, 1968.

Sebald, W. G. *Austerlitz.* Translated by Anthea Bell. New York: Random House, 2001.

———. *The Emigrants.* Translated by Michael Hulse. New York: New Directions, 1996.

———. *On the Natural History of Destruction.* Translated by Anthea Bell. New York: Random House, 2003.

Shirer, William L. *The Rise and Fall of the Third Reich: A History of Nazi Germany.* New York: Simon & Schuster, 1960.

Solzhenitsyn, Aleksandr I. *The Gulag Archipelago.* Vols. 1–3. Translated by Thomas P. Whitney. New York: Harper and Row, 1974–78.

Speer, Albert. *Inside the Third Reich.* Translated by Richard and Clara Winston. New York: Macmillan, 1970.

*Treibgut des Krieges: Zeugnisse von Flucht und Vertreibung der Deutschen* [Flotsam of the war: Germans' testimonies of escape and expulsion]. Kassel: Volksbund Deutsche Kriegsgräberfürsorge, 2008.

## FILMS

Flitton, Dave. *Occult History of the Third Reich.* Montreal: Castle Lamancha Co. (UK), 1992. Documentary, 155 min.

Grede, Kjell. *Good Evening, Mr. Wallenberg.* Budapest: FilmTeknik, 1990. Drama, 118 min.

Hachmeister, Lutz, and Michael Kloft. *The Goebbels Experiment.* New York: First Run Features, 2005. Documentary, 155 min.

Isbouts, Jean-Pierre, and William A. Schwartz. *Operation Valkyrie: The Stauffenberg Plot to Kill Hitler*. Santa Monica, CA: Pantheon Studios, 2008. Documentary, 108 min.

Müller, Ray. *The Wonderful, Horrible Life of Leni Riefenstahl*. Strasbourg: Arte, 1993. Documentary, 180 min.

Rees, Laurence. *The Nazis: A Warning From History*. New York: A&E Television Networks, 1998. 6-part documentary miniseries.

———. *Scorched Earth*. London: BBC, 1999. Documentary, 200 min.

Staudte, Wolfgang. *Die Mörder sind unter uns*. Babelsberg and Johannisthal, Germany: Deutsche Film, 1946. Drama, 91 min. Released in the United States as *Murderers Among Us*, 1948.

Many heartfelt thanks go to the Volksbund Deutsche Kriegsgräberfürsorge e.V. for their kind help in providing statistics regarding human casualties resulting from the Second World War.